Intelligence and Motivation

Intelligence and Motivation

Editor

V. C. Pandey

ISHA BOOKS

DELHI-110 033

Intelligence and Motivation

ISBN: 9788182051577

Reprinted in 2012 in India by
Isha Publications
B-69, New Gupta Colony
Near DDA Market
Delhi-110009

Printed at: G. Print Process, Delhi

Preface

Intelligence and motivation are the core factors which influence the learning process more than anything else. The term 'intelligence' is defined as the ability to comprehend; to understand and profit from experience. While the term 'motivation' is the driving force (desire) behind all actions of an organism. Motivation is based on emotions, specifically, on the search for positive emotional experiences and the avoidance of negative ones, where positive and negative are defined by the individual brain state, not by social norms. The expression emotional intelligence or EI indicates the mental ability we are born with which gives us our emotional sensitivity and our potential for emotional learning management skills which can help us maximize our long term health, happiness and survival.

The present volume comprehensively covers all basic aspects and significance of intelligence and motivation in the learning process. It contains solid description of topics including the Nature of Motivation; Characteristics of Motivation; Types of Motivation; Techniques of Increasing Learner Motivation; Maslow's Hierarchy of Needs; Intelligence: Meaning and Nature; Theories of Intelligence; Measurement of Intelligence and Types of Intelligence Tests. Besides teachers, educationists, parents and students, the content of the book will be of highly valuable to a wide range of audience from various fields.

Editor

CONTENTS

1

NATURE OF MOTIVATION

A vision that motivates is the standard constant for success across all social classes and/or lifestyles. It does not matter how many years a person spent in classrooms, a motivating vision is the common denominator for achievement. Abraham Lincoln never went to school; he became President of America, because he had a vision that motivated him. In addition, his vision was so powerful that it motivated everyone around him and that energy motivated the country.

ELEMENTS OF MOTIVATION

Motivation starts with the desire to be free, to be free from dependency on others, freedom to live the lifestyle we dream of, freedom to explore our ideas. Total freedom is not possible or desirable, but the struggle to achieve that ideal is the basis for motivation. Motivation is built on three basic elements:

1. Motivation starts with a need, vision, dream

or desire to achieve the seemingly impossible. Creativity is associated with ideas, projects, and goals, which can be considered a path to freedom.

2. Developing and maintaining a love-to-learn lifestyle become involved with risky ventures, and/or continually seek new opportunities learn what works and does not work.
3. Developing and maintaining a desire to overcome barriers and to bounce back from discouragement or failure. individuals learn to tolerate the agony failure brings. In any endeavor, that is worthwhile, barriers and failure will be there. Bouncing back requires creative thinking as it is a learning process. In addition, bouncing back requires starting again at number one.

A loss of any one part and motivation is on the rocks. For example;

1. If you like to be creative and love to learn but cannot face up to failure, you will not go back and try again. Persistent motivation is associated with bouncing back from failure.
2. If you have a unique idea but don't like taking risks, ideas' is all you will ever have.
3. There must be something in your life that turns you on. Some people work harder at finding it than others. You can start by analyzing the lifestyle you wish you could live. Remember, money is not a goal; it is a reward for achieving a goal.

Changing A Lifestyles

We have the opinion that money can buy a desired lifestyle. Money cannot buy a lifestyle! A desired lifestyle is the result of a vision with a burning desire to reach a goal. Achievement is the result of planned action to bust through barriers to make desired events happen. Success, money and resulting lifestyle are rewards only, not goals.

What is success, money or a desired lifestyle? Our society measures success with money. A lifestyle of personal achievement is real success - money is a reward or byproduct.

Seven Rules of Motivation

1 *Set a major goal, but follow a path.* The path has mini goals that go in many directions. When you learn to succeed at mini goals, you will be motivated to challenge grand goals.

2 *Finish what you start.* A half finished project is of no use to anyone. Quitting is a habit. Develop the habit of finishing self-motivated projects.

3 *Socialize with others of similar interest.* Mutual support is motivating.

4 *Learn how to learn.* Dependency on others for knowledge is a slow time consuming processes. Man has the ability to learn without instructors. In fact, when we learn the art of self-education we will find, if not create, opportunity to find success beyond our wildest dreams.

5 *Harmonize natural talent with interest that motivates.* Natural talent creates motivation, motivation creates persistence and persistence gets the job done.

6 *Increase knowledge of subjects that inspires.* The more we know about a subject, the more we want to learn about it. A self-propelled upward spiral develops.

7 *Take risk.* Failure and bouncing back are elements of motivation. Failure is a learning tool. No one has ever succeeded at anything worthwhile without a string of failures.

Develop a Dream

There are three types of dreams

1. Socially acceptable dreams are based on professional skills that are looked upon, by society, with high esteem. Every

parent wants their child to be an equivalent of an engineer, doctor, or lawyer. There are many high paying skills such as welder or machinist; that do not require a high school education. Society views these with low esteem; therefore, they are considered low ambition. Society encourages youth to avoid these skills, yet, many blue-collar skills pay more than those needing a degree.

2. Wishful thinking is the start of all dreams. It is the starter to get the motor running. For many, wishful thinking is used for all the wrong reasons, because their dreams are based on greed, to get something for nothing in return. There is no way to learn how to buy a winning lottery ticket and opportunity does not fall into people's lap without giving something in return such as a skill. Many professionals seem to think their learning days are over when they mastered the basics and revert to wishful thinking.
3. Socially unacceptable dreams cannot be comprehended by the public. Original ideas attract criticism; and are considered unrealistic until proven valid. Many people cannot face criticism; therefore, they avoid innovative ideas. This is where innovators find opportunity.

Dreams First, Education Second

With a dream, information is easy to process into knowledge. Money to reach our dream also becomes easier to acquire. People with a dream act differently, they seem to have meaning and purpose to their life. Bosses and customers favor positive attitudes and offered opportunity, which means higher income, usually. An upward spiral of high intensity motivation and opportunity continue to follow. In the formal education world, most technical colleges require students to have a GED certificate or better before they can learn welding or machine shop skills. This system requires all people to be an intellectual before they are allowed to develop dreams.

As a result, most would-be welders or machinists, who are technical, never have a chance. What if windjammer-training programs required all students to have a GED certificate and, required all students to read a compass and plot a course before they could come aboard? There would be empty ships, never developed dreams and lost opportunity. Experience builds dreams and a dream motivates people to learn. Technical colleges are intended for technical people who learn differently than intellectuals. Instead of heavy academic requirements, build dreams first, and then insert academics as students discover the need for them. The concept "opportunity first then knowledge" motivates people to learn. It works aboard windjammers, why not in school?

Society Attacks Dreamers

All children dream and play make-believe. For some reason, as they grow older, they are instructed to stop dreaming and face reality. Reality seems to be important, whether it be friends, parents, or teachers. Academic education has top priority while dreams have low priority. Yet, there has never been an achievement that did not begin with a dream. There has never been success without many failures. Why is it that society wants everyone to succeed without failure? Why does society have a need to kill dreams, especially with teenagers? During the dreaming stage, one is alone with his seemly impossible ideas. When talking about ideas, the first reaction is... "Where did he get that nutty idea?" All great inventors and achievers go through this phase, especially during the failure days. After a few successes, people say nothing about wild ideas. Add a few more successes; everyone will support any idea you have.

It takes persistence to find what works. Only you realize your ideas have possibilities, the public will not realize possibilities until you prove them to be of value. After the Wright Brothers invented the airplane and proved man can fly, it took two years before anyone thought flying was a practical idea.

The U.S. Army rejected consideration of the invention outright. All through the development years, people considered The Wright Brothers nuts. To shield themselves from criticism, they only informed people who could help them and took criticism, if necessary, for their help.

Employers want motivated people. The problem is, they want employees' motivation to be built around the company's interest. The fact is, people with ambitions are dedicated to anyone who will help them reach their goals. People who don't have dreams or ambitions are not motivated and are not dedicated to anything except the paycheck.

Many people yield to dream killers. In their thoughts, "my friends are right, my ideas are all nutty" and give up. This belief may be true when first exploring an idea. There is no such thing as success on the first try, except in the classroom. Giving up is losing ambition, opportunity, higher income, and eventual success. A downward spiral of self-esteem follows.

Perseverance

The common argument for failure is "I lost interest or I didn't have enough money." While true, neither one is valid. Motivation depends on many factors with the primary factor being the power of your dreams. Money is one of the barriers that can be overcome. Achievement requires developing attitudes/habits that keep you on track. Example, develop a habit of getting jobs done with resources available. With this skill, creativity will eliminate many money problems.

Persistence is a combination of factors such as a burning desire and pride, that programs the comfort zone to pressure us to keep bouncing back. We try again, but in a different direction. It is important to implement many motivational tools so the project will keep moving when we don't feel like it. In time, motivation will drive us even when the going becomes strenuous and we wish the project would go away. We all have times of weakness. Persistence may seem steady in others, but in reality, it flows like the ocean tide.

Fantasizing

Fantasizing is a startup tool to precondition the mind to believe it must achieve a clearly defined goal. Fantasizing is creating pictures in our mind on how we would react to events if our dream were real. Fantasizing has several important elements.

— Fantasizing creates a burning desire.

— Fantasizing prepares our mind to accept opportunity when it arrives. Without this preparation we would not recognizes opportunity or if we did, fear would set in and we would reject it.

— Fantasizing is a type of business plan written in our head. Questions are being asked, what will it take to make this idea work and how will problems be handled?

Burning Desire

A burning desire is the result of active fantasizing. It puts powerful motivating forces into action. It can overcome all self-imposed limits. Natural skills and learning methods may be barriers, but they are temporary. It has more potential than any education system can offer, because, to succeed, knowledge is needed to be the best we can be. If there is a destiny, this is where it starts.

Sometimes a dramatic personal impact, known or unknown causes a burning desire. This experience reveals a need for more information or services to help deal with it. Trying to understand, leads to knowledge, action, and/or opportunity. Sometimes it is necessary or advantages to take action before knowledge is acquired. In any case, a dramatic experience is highly motivating and all stops should be removed to benefit from it.

We all have a basic desire to be lazy. This is a powerful motivating force because we dream of being lazy and we work hard to fulfill that dream. It doesn't sound right, but it's true. People work hard to be lazy. Then there are people who don't dream about being lazy, they are.

There are two types of laziness:

— Constructive laziness increases creative skills because we don't like to do more work than necessary. People search for the easiest way to get jobs done. They also work hard for opportunity, to enjoy what life has to offer. The desire to be lazy is a motivating force.

— Destructive laziness is associated with people who are not motivated, the desire to do less takes over. They feel robbed of opportunity and the world passes them by.

Overcoming Failure

Failure Can Be Positive or Negative

Failure is a learning tool. Thomas Edison failed a thousand times before he invented the light bulb. Failure is trying to do things others have not considered. It is a temporary byproduct of creativity. It is challenging the learning process. It is experiential education at work. The real winners in life tolerate failure and the agony it produces. Success is achieved by those who are willing to take risk and lose.

Many people choose to engage in occupations and activities that are safe and conventional. They do not deliver satisfaction, fulfillment or joy in living. Their real failure is failing to move in the directions of their dreams.

Bouncing Back From Failure

Do you see the possibilities of an idea, project or goal? Are you experiencing barriers that prevents fulfillment? With every idea, there are barriers, hundreds of them, if not more.

If you vision something that is different from everyone else, there are two reasons, you have an idea that few have considered or it is not practical. How do you tell good ideas from bad one's, research and listening to people's reasons why it won't work? As a rule, no one will support an original idea until there is sufficient evidence that it is practical. Even when proving it is practical, people may reject it. Fifty years after the light bulb was invented, some people still rejected it. You have to do all the legwork to find evidence.

If you find evidence, skills and resources must be acquired at the same time everyone is telling you the idea is dumb. This is a very difficult barrier to overcome. You see the possibilities and potential of a project while everyone else sees the risk and barriers. Also note, there is no success where research, facing up to pros and cons, is not extensive. Evaluate negative opinions to stay on the right track. Without negative opinions, it is easy to stray off course. The original concept of the light bulb was a dumb idea.

Negative opinions can discourage one to give up. For this reason, it becomes necessary to limit exposure of the project to people who can help, even if they disapprove. Even a select group will not see the potential until you succeed. When you do succeed, others will no longer see the barriers, they are gone, they will want to know how you did it. What if the idea turns into a total failure? You learned a lot and next time you may get it right and succeed. No achiever has arrived without failure.

Most franchise, copying ideas and get-rich-quick schemes can be deadly traps. They come with high approval rating and no negative opinions. Their success is praised while the facts may be distorted. People believe what they want to, and easy success is what we want to hear. For this reason, there is little independent research. Lack of proper research leads to disaster. What if the fantastic project turns into total failure? What does it feel like to be a sucker? Buying into a promotion is like playing the lottery, there is no way to learn how to buy a winning lottery ticket.

Failure is a learning tool. Our first reaction to failure is to blame anyone/anything but ourselves. If we perceive others are to blame, then there is nothing we can do to correct the problem. We cannot change people's personalities, neither can they change ours. If we assume responsibility, then we can analyze what went wrong and take corrective action. This is the art of bouncing back from failure.

Failure is discouraging, it drains energy and resources, but it forces us to do things right. Failure separates those who think they want success from those who are determined to win. Failure narrows the playing field. The first people out are those that blame others, next out are those who lost interest. The weak go first. The strong learn to hang in there and keep bouncing back until they win.

Sometimes failure is telling us we are going in the wrong direction. Here's the dilemma. If we give up, is it because we were going in the wrong direction or because we gave up? The only way to tell is to abandon the project or put it to rest for a time. Very often, this is forced on us because we are out of money or resources. When the mind is free of pressures, realistic planning emerges. This lull was not wasted, it had great benefit, it is the art of redirection. When you try again, chances are you will get it right. New outlook's is the result of bouncing back from failure.

The Desire to Fail

For some reason, man has a natural desire to fail. This desire is difficult to identify because it is fulfilled in subtle ways. For example: People will max-out credit cards on trivia, creating debts that makes it impossible to fulfill their deepest dreams. They gamble when they know the odds are against them.

A habit of success requires the ability to recognize elements that destroy. The man that makes $30,000 fears risk. The man who makes $1,000,000 accepts risk. In the early stages, everyone in subtle ways fears risk and failure. Fears, whatever they are, must be faced up too and dealt with. Fantasizing can help accomplish this by creating a burning desire that is more powerful than fear.

Leaders, who demand control over others, are teaching them to fail and ultimately themselves. It is easy to control people who accept the belief that they are failures. In this situation, the motivation tool is reward and punishment. The intent may be to motivate people to cooperate, but very often the results remind people they are failures and many accept this as fact. Disciplinary action means internal motivation has not worked and external motivation is reverted to. In business, the long-term results could be deadly.

Comfort Zone

The Comfort Zone is our living, work, and social environments that we have grown accustom too. It determines the type of friends we make or people we associate with. It determines a life style we accept or reject.

Young people are very adaptable, they can adjust to changing comfort zones with ease. They can socialize with homeless people in the morning and be equally at east at a formal banquet in the evening. As we age, the ability to adapt to wide-ranging comfort zones, becomes more difficult. Social prejudice narrows the comfort zone range. Our present comfort zone is in one of the following conditions.

1. We want to maintain our current comfort zone.
2. We are dissatisfied with current conditions and want to move to another comfort zone.
3. We were suddenly thrust from our comfort zone and want back in.

4. We need to make decisions without supporting facts. The comfort zone can be a decision making tool.

Comfort zones are directly related to our dreams or goals, which is associated with self-fulfilling prophecy. In order to grow and change, we must first be discontent with our current comfort zone. To change to different life style, establishing a business, or succeeding at a challenging project, we must realize that all meaningful and lasting changes occur first in daydreaming (fantasizing) and then they work their way into reality. If we clearly and vividly imagine ourselves being and having the things we truly want, we will create a new picture of ourselves. The old comfort zone, in time, will be unacceptable and we will find ways to acquire the new.

For example, if we want to sail the South Pacific in our own sailboat, we must clearly and vividly, image ourselves sitting in the cockpit of our boat and think about the challenge this environment would bring. This includes accepting the dangers along with the pleasures. The key to upgrading our comfort zone is to raise our self-image and level of what we expect or want first, then we will find opportunity to make the goal reality.

The more clearly and vividly we fantasize our dream, with frequent repetitions and emotional impact, the stronger and more real the pictures on the subconscious level will become. Once our subconscious accepts this image and its expectation, the subconscious will go to work, searching for a way to bring it into reality. If we feel that these things are too good for us, we will find ways to fail. If, however, we intentionally use our imagination to:

— Imagine the change we want.

— Build an expectation of the change.

— Mentally and emotionally, prepare ourselves for the change by anticipating what it will be like.

We will find ways to acquire dream and, when mentally ready, it will arrive faster than we ever thought possible. In effect, what we are doing is deliberately preparing for self-fulfilling prophecy. As has been repeated many times, "Whatever the mind can conceive and believe, it can achieve."

For some people, problems, suffering, poverty, bad breaks are their comfort zone. Try to take away these problems and they will fight back. They find comfort in finding fault and complaining about their misfortune. The same is true for businesses. Daily crisis, employees making bad decisions, accidents, trivial problems, confrontation between management and workers is a workforce comfort zone. Management and workers have grown accustom to seeing things go wrong and expect them too. Management finds comfort in finding fault with workers and workers find comfort in finding fault with management.

Negative comfort zones can be overcome by setting and thinking about positive goals. What we think about all day and what we expect, be it positive or negative, is our comfort zone.

A Goal Is a Journey of Decisions

A goal is a desire that sends us on a journey using decisions to transport us to an unknown destination. Very often, this destination is vague because we encounter opportunities/ experiences that change our thinking which changes our direction. One thing is certain; the destination will be exhilarating or discouraging. On this journey, we set priorities and make decisions, which will prevent or create problems.

Journeys of unknown destinations require experiments. Every reasonable idea must be tried and tested. Testing ideas, results in gaining experience, which increases our knowledge. Very often, decisions give us an uncomfortable gut feeling long before we know the results. Gut feelings are intuitive forces that are signaling us to consider other options. If our lives were not filled with so many emotions, gut feeling would be a reliable alert-flag that would prevent problems or lead us to opportunity.

Some decisions may help for a short while, and then they become wrong. A needed service or information was acquired that will be needed in the future. It is discouraging that something seems right, and then turns wrong, but this is normal. As we gain experience, quality choices become obvious.

In reality, every decision is a success. The results may not be what we had in mind, but we gain valuable experience, that will influence future decision-making. Anyhow, we know what works and does not work. In our imaginary journey the path winds around an imaginary lake named Lake Success. On the other side, we see potential customers waving money around and we want to get over there fast. The path around Lake Success requires that we acquire many skills. The only way we can safely arrive is to stay on the path and learn what it takes to make every step right. At the end, we will have quality information to make quality decisions. With this information, we can control the results.

But there is a distraction. On the other side of the lake, we see customers waving money. Easy money is extremely tempting. We are tempted to take a short cut, swim over and grab it. We may be dragging a heavy debt load and new money would relieve this burden. There are a hundred valid reasons to take shortcuts so we will try. While swimming across the lake we focus on the money and off the service that first motivated us. We make costly unwise decisions that created many costly problems. If the debt load does not drown us into total failure, we will be forced back to shore and on the path, poorer but wiser.

There are no rewards until we learn to complete tasks right. We must stay focused on what we want to accomplish, not the money. Money, power, and influence are rewards only, not goals. Only winners reap the rewards, because winners focus on doing jobs right. Some people will succeed in crossing the lake, taking shortcuts, but they never learn how to do jobs' right. People who had some success with shortcuts will always use shortcuts. If it worked once, it will work again, so they reason. For them, rewards will be limited and growth will not be possible because a shortcut is a loser.

Learning to Make Quality Decisions

We need to find the correct path. With each step, we will learn how to complete small projects. At the end, we will collect all the small accomplishments and combine them into a successful achievement.

Knowing what path we are on, we can make quality decisions that will guide us to our goal. Others can help if they know what our goal is.

We need to learn how to prevent problems. Problems are caused by a lack of knowledge, not bad luck. Problems destroy dreams, not money.

As leaders, we need to know how to bring the best out of people. No one knows what their true potential until opportunity presents itself.

The rewards of success are money, power, and influence.

MOTIVATIONAL SPEAKERS, EMOTIONAL REACTION AND RHETORIC HYPE

A good motivational speaker is a pleasure to listen to and can inspire us to keep pushing when nothing seems to be happening. Emotional hype can become a trap. We all want to feel we're on top of the world and motivational speakers can make us feel we are there. After our first experience, we want to hear others, and each seems to have the ability to send us to a new high. With a steady flow of motivational material, addiction is sure to follow. At this time, the passive follower becomes hooked; and has changed his primary goal.

The new goal, "seek and maintain an emotional high." By maintaining an emotional high, he feels his goals are just around the corner. All he has to do is maintain a vision, have positive attitudes and maintain that good feeling. His new goal is emotional highs with his former goal as a tool to get there. An addict becomes dependent on motivational material to maintain this illusion and, in time, can't live without them.

When Thomas Edison invented the light bulb, it is reported that he tried a thousand times before he found a way to burn a steel wire white hot that did not burn up. A thousand failures is not motivating and does not make one feel good. Back in his day, there was no such thing as a motivational speaker. So what kept him bouncing back from repeated failure?

A desire to explore and discover the world he lived in, a desire to learn, and a desire to do the impossible. He loved the challenge and accepted the disappointments. His belief that something could burn white hot and not burn up was the laughing stock of the scientific world. This is a depressing feeling, not a feel-good feeling. The fact is, success is the result of bouncing back during times of discouragement without dependency on others. Thomas Edison used discouragement as a stepping-stone to achievement. Each failure was a challenge to try harder.

If discouragement is the stepping-stone to success, then motivational speakers should support depressing feelings. But then, who wants to hear about discouragement, something we experience frequently without outside help? The fact is, emotional hype sells. A steady diet of feeling-good does not produce winners, but it produces wealth for the promoters. A steady flow of emotional hype is a cover-up that leads us into a false sense of progresses. There is no creativity in emotional hype other than ideas sound good. People don't remember ideas, they remember feeling good. Many people spend money and time getting an emotional high rather than trying ideas and taking risk. They lose sight of their primary goal.

— Motivation is a complex subject and it is easy to go in the wrong direction. Some dead-end paths to consider:

— Everyone has a goal of more money, but few are willing to develop a plan, provide a service, or take risk to make it happen. Money is not a goal; money is a reward for achieving a goal that provides a service to others.

— Goals of money (greed) become self-destructive. Money by itself is not motivating; we always want more which leaves no sense of accomplishment.

— Most people turn off their desire to learn after they acquire a professional skill that meets basic needs. At that time, motivation is replaced with wishful thinking. They dream but don't act with a hundred reasons why they can't act. Many replace action with emotional hype.

We have all been in organizations where they tried to increase membership or increase income above the normal with little results. They use emotional rhetoric, contest or games to motivate members into action. There is no analysis of current policy, which may be the source of their problems. They want to achieve more with the same policy. People as a group, does not want change and will fight change if someone tried to do things differently. At the same time, people are greedy; they want more of something without making any policy changes.

What is true for organizations is true for individuals. The older we get, the stronger our resistance to change becomes and the stronger our desire for greed becomes. We do not want to learn new skills that could bring the desired lifestyle, so we embrace methods that give the allusion of achieving results. Greed is in control, not self-development. This is not the way winners are made. Winners continually analyze what they are doing right and wrong and learn how to correct the wrong. They acquire knowledge by taking risk, tying different ways to achieve the desired results. They learn to bounce back from discouragement and failure without outside help. If you love what you are doing, you are not dependent on others for motivation. BUT, an occasional motivational seminar can be extremely inspiring. Coupling this with a learning process that's related to your goal, you will be a winner.

Some self-motivating goals are follows:

— Advancing in an organization. Each step is clear and is recognized by others. Recognition is a powerful motivating force.

— Developing ideas. Creativity is a natural self motivator. We want to prove to ourselves that we can do it.

— Adventure. Exploring is learning more about the world we live in.

— Exploring is a high-powered learning environment.

— Providing a service that others want and are willing to pay for. Seeking continual change and adapting to it. Very often, this is related to achieving a goal, then going after another. This requires the desire to maintain a continual learning environment. The result is bragging rights.

2

CHARACTERISTICS OF MOTIVATION

Motivation include 3 common characteristics:

1. It concerns with what activates human behavior.
2. It involves what directs this behavior toward a particular goal.
3. Motivation concerns how this behavior is sustained.

BASIC NEEDS OF HUMAN MOTIVATION

The 'physiological' needs.

The needs that are usually taken as the starting point for motivation theory are the so-called physiological drives. Two recent lines of research make it necessary to revise our customary notions about these needs, first, the development of the concept of homeostasis, and second, the finding that appetites (preferential choices among foods) are a fairly efficient indication of actual needs or lacks in the body.

Homeostasis refers to the body's automatic efforts to maintain a constant, normal state of the blood stream, Cannon has described this process for (1) the water content of the blood, (2) salt content, (3) sugar content, (4) protein content, (5) fat content, (6) calcium content, (7) oxygen content, (8) constant hydrogen-ion level (acid-base balance) and (9) constant temperature of the blood. Obviously this list can be extended to include other minerals, the hormones, vitamins, etc.

Young in a recent article has summarized the work on appetite in its relation to body needs. If the body lacks some chemical, the individual will tend to develop a specific appetite or partial hunger for that food element. Thus it seems impossible as well as useless to make any list of fundamental physiological needs for they can come to almost any number one might wish, depending on the degree of specificity of description. We can not identify all physiological needs as homeostatic. That sexual desire, sleepiness, sheer activity and maternal behaviour in animals, are homeostatic, has not yet been demonstrated. Furthermore, this list would not include the various sensory pleasures (tastes, smells, tickling, stroking) which are probably physiological and which may become the goals of motivated behaviour.

These physiological drives or needs are to be considered unusual rather than typical because they are isolable, and because they are localizable somatically. That is to say, they are relatively independent of each other, of other motivations and of the organism as a whole, and secondly, in many cases, it is possible to demonstrate a localized, underlying somatic base for the drive. This is true less generally than has been thought (exceptions are fatigue, sleepiness, maternal responses) but it is still true in the classic instances of hunger, sex, and thirst.

It should be pointed out again that any of the physiological needs and the consummatory behaviour involved with them serve as channels for all sorts of other needs as well. That is to say, the person who thinks he is hungry may actually be seeking more for comfort, or dependence, than for vitamins or proteins. Conversely, it is possible to satisfy the hunger need in part by other activities such as drinking water or smoking cigarettes. In other words, relatively isolable as these physiological needs are, they are not completely so.

Undoubtedly these physiological needs are the most prepotent of all needs. What this means specifically is, that in the human being who is missing everything in life in an extreme fashion, it is most likely that the major motivation would be the physiological needs rather than any others. A person who is lacking food, safety, love, and esteem would most probably hunger for food more strongly than for anything else.

If all the needs are unsatisfied, and the organism is then dominated by the physiological needs, all other needs may become simply non-existent or be pushed into the background. It is then fair to characterize the whole organism by saying simply that it is hungry, for consciousness is almost completely preempted by hunger. All capacities are put into the service of hunger-satisfaction, and the organization of these capacities is almost entirely determined by the one purpose of satisfying hunger. The receptors and effectors, the intelligence, memory, habits, all may now be defined simply as hunger-gratifying tools. Capacities that are not useful for this purpose lie dormant, or are pushed into the background.

The urge to write poetry, the desire to acquire an automobile, the interest in American history, the desire for a new pair of shoes are, in the extreme case, forgotten or become of secondary importance. For the man who is extremely and dangerously hungry, no other interests exist but food. He dreams food, he remembers food, he thinks about food, he emotes only about food, he perceives only food and he wants only food. The more subtle determinants that ordinarily fuse with the physiological drives in organizing even feeding, drinking or sexual behaviour, may now be so completely overwhelmed as to allow us to speak at this time (but only at this time) of pure hunger drive and behaviour, with the one unqualified aim of relief.

Another peculiar characteristic of the human organism when it is dominated by a certain need is that the whole philosophy of the future tends also to change. For our chronically and extremely hungry man, Utopia can be defined very simply as a place where there is plenty of food. He tends to think that, if only he is guaranteed food for the rest of his life, he will be perfectly happy and will never want anything more. Life itself tends to be defined in terms of eating. Anything else will be defined as unimportant. Freedom, love, community feeling, respect, philosophy, may all be waved aside as fripperies which are useless since they fail to fill the stomach. Such a man may fairly be said to live by bread alone.

It cannot possibly be denied that such things are true but their *generality* can be denied. Emergency conditions are, almost by definition, rare in the normally functioning peaceful society. That this truism can be forgotten is due mainly to two reasons. First, rats have few motivations other than physiological ones, and since so much of the research upon motivation has been made with these animals, it is easy to carry the rat-picture over to the human being.

Secondly, it is too often not realized that culture itself is an adaptive tool, one of whose main functions is to make the physiological emergencies come less and less often. In most of the known societies, chronic extreme hunger of the emergency type is rare, rather than common. In any case, this is still true in the United States. The average American citizen is experiencing appetite rather than hunger when he says "I am hungry." He is apt to experience sheer life-and-death hunger only by accident and then only a few times through his entire life.

Obviously a good way to obscure the 'higher' motivations, and to get a lopsided view of human capacities and human nature, is to make the organism extremely and chronically hungry or thirsty. Anyone who attempts to make an emergency picture into a typical one, and who will measure all of man's goals and desires by his behaviour during extreme physiological deprivation is certainly being blind to many things. It is quite true that man lives by bread alone — when there is no bread. But what happens to man's desires when there is plenty of bread and when his belly is chronically filled?

At once other (and 'higher') needs emerge and these, rather than physiological hungers, dominate the organism. And when these in turn are satisfied, again new (and still 'higher') needs emerge and so on. This is what we mean by saying that the basic human needs are organized into a hierarchy of relative prepotency.

One main implication of this phrasing is that gratification becomes as important a concept as deprivation in motivation theory, for it releases the organism from the domination of a relatively more physiological need, permitting thereby the emergence of other more social goals. The physiological needs, along with their partial goals, when chronically gratified cease to exist as active determinants or organizers of behaviour. They now exist only in a potential fashion in the sense that they may emerge again to dominate the organism if they are thwarted. But a want that is satisfied is no longer a want. The organism is dominated and its behaviour organized only by unsatisfied needs. If hunger is satisfied, it becomes unimportant in the current dynamics of the individual.

The Safety needs

If the physiological needs are relatively well gratified, there then emerges a new set of needs, which we may categorize roughly as the safety needs. All that has been said of the physiological needs is equally true, although in lesser degree, of these desires. The organism may equally well be wholly dominated by them. They may serve as the almost exclusive organizers of behaviour, recruiting all the capacities of the organism in their service, and we may then fairly describe the whole organism as a safety-seeking mechanism. Again we may say of the receptors, the effectors, of the intellect and the other capacities that they are primarily safety-seeking tools.

Again, as in the hungry man, we find that the dominating goal is a strong determinant not only of his current world-outlook and philosophy but also of his philosophy of the future.

Practically everything looks less important than safety, (even sometimes the physiological needs which being satisfied, are now underestimated). A man, in this state, if it is extreme enough and chronic enough, may be characterized as living almost for safety alone.

In infants we can see a much more direct reaction to bodily illnesses of various kinds. Sometimes these illnesses seem to be immediately and *per se* threatening and seem to make the child feel unsafe. For instance, vomiting, colic or other sharp pains seem to make the child look at the whole world in a different way. At such a moment of pain, it may be postulated that, for the child, the appearance of the whole world suddenly changes from sunniness to darkness, so to speak, and becomes a place in which anything at all might happen, in which previously stable things have suddenly become unstable. Thus a child who because of some bad food is taken ill may, for a day or two, develop fear, nightmares, and a need for protection and reassurance never seen in him before his illness.

Another indication of the child's need for safety is his preference for some kind of undisrupted routine or rhythm. He seems to want a predictable, orderly world. For instance, injustice, unfairness, or inconsistency in the parents seems to make a child feel anxious and unsafe. This attitude may be not so much because of the injustice *per se* or any particular pains involved, but rather because this treatment threatens to make the world look unreliable, or unsafe, or unpredictable. Young children seem to thrive better under a system which has at least a skeletal outline of rigidity, In which there is a schedule of a kind, some sort of routine, something that can be counted upon, not only for the present but also far into the future. Perhaps one could express this more accurately by saying that the child needs an organized world rather than an unorganized or unstructured one.

The central role of the parents and the normal family setup are indisputable. Quarreling, physical assault, separation, divorce or death within the family may be particularly terrifying. Also parental outbursts of rage or threats of punishment directed to the child, calling him names, speaking to him harshly, shaking him, handling him roughly, or actual physical punishment sometimes elicit such total panic and terror in the child that we must assume more is involved than the physical pain alone. While it is true that in some children this terror may represent also a fear of loss of parental love, it can also occur in completely rejected children, who seem to cling to the hating parents more for sheer safety and protection than because of hope of love.

Confronting the average child with new, unfamiliar, strange, unmanageable stimuli or situations will too frequently elicit the danger or terror reaction, as for example, getting lost or even being separated from the parents for a short time, being confronted with new faces, new situations or new tasks, the sight of strange, unfamiliar or uncontrollable objects, illness or death. Particularly at such times, the child's frantic clinging to his parents is eloquent testimony to their role as protectors (quite apart from their roles as food-givers and love-givers).

From these and similar observations, we may generalize and say that the average child in our society generally prefers a safe, orderly, predictable, organized world, which he can count, on, and in which unexpected, unmanageable or other dangerous things do not happen, and in which, in any case, he has all-powerful parents who protect and shield him from harm.

That these reactions may so easily be observed in children is in a way a proof of the fact that children in our society, feel too unsafe (or, in a word, are badly brought up). Children who are reared in an unthreatening, loving family do not ordinarily react as we have described above. In such children the danger reactions are apt to come mostly to objects or situations that adults too would consider dangerous.

The healthy, normal, fortunate adult in our culture is largely satisfied in his safety needs. The peaceful, smoothly running, 'good' society ordinarily makes its members feel safe enough from wild animals, extremes of temperature, criminals, assault and murder, tyranny, etc. Therefore, in a very real sense, he no longer has any safety needs as active motivators. Just as a sated man no longer feels hungry, a safe man no longer feels endangered. If we wish to see these needs directly and clearly we must turn to neurotic or near-neurotic individuals, and to the economic and social underdogs. In between these extremes, we can perceive the expressions of safety needs only in such phenomena as, for instance, the common preference for a job with tenure and protection, the desire for a savings account, and for insurance of various kinds (medical, dental, unemployment, disability, old age).

Other broader aspects of the attempt to seek safety and stability in the world are seen in the very common preference for familiar rather than unfamiliar things, or for the known rather than the unknown. The tendency to have some religion or world-philosophy that organizes the universe and the men in it into some sort of satisfactorily coherent, meaningful whole is also in part motivated by safety-seeking. Here too we may list science and philosophy in general as partially motivated by the safety needs. Otherwise the need for safety is seen as an active and dominant mobilizer of the organism's resources only in emergencies, *e. g.*, war, disease, natural catastrophes, crime waves, societal disorganization, neurosis, brain injury, chronically bad situation.

Some neurotic adults in our society are, in many ways, like the unsafe child in their desire for safety, although in the former it takes on a somewhat special appearance. Their reaction is often to unknown, psychological dangers in a world that is perceived to be hostile, overwhelming and threatening. Such a person behaves as if a great catastrophe were almost always impending, i.e., he is usually responding as if to an emergency. His safety needs often find specific expression in a search for a protector, or a stronger person on whom he may depend, or perhaps, a Fuehrer.

The neurotic individual may be described in a slightly different way with some usefulness as a grown-up person who retains his childish attitudes toward the world. That is to say, a neurotic adult may be said to behave 'as if' he were actually afraid of a spanking, or of his mother's disapproval, or of being abandoned by his parents, or having his food taken away from him. It is as if his childish attitudes of fear and threat reaction to a dangerous world had gone underground, and untouched by the growing up and learning processes, were now ready to be called out by any stimulus that would make a child feel endangered and threatened.

The neurosis in which the search for safety takes its dearest form is in the compulsive-obsessive neurosis. Compulsive-obsessives try frantically to order and stabilize the world so that no unmanageable, unexpected or unfamiliar dangers will ever appear; They hedge themselves about with all sorts of ceremonials, rules and formulas so that every possible contingency may be provided for and so that no new contingencies may appear.

They are much like the brain injured cases, described by Goldstein, who manage to maintain their equilibrium by avoiding everything unfamiliar and strange and by ordering their restricted world in such a neat, disciplined, orderly fashion that everything in the world can be counted upon. They try to arrange the world so that anything unexpected (dangers) cannot possibly occur. If, through no fault of their own, something unexpected does occur, they go into a panic reaction as if this unexpected occurrence constituted a grave danger. What we can see only as a none-too-strong preference in the healthy person, *e. g.*, preference for the familiar, becomes a life-and-death. necessity in abnormal cases.

The love needs

If both the physiological and the safety needs are fairly well gratified, then there will emerge the love and affection and belongingness needs, and the whole cycle already described will repeat itself with this new center. Now the person will feel keenly, as never before, the absence of friends, or a sweetheart, or a wife, or children. He will hunger for affectionate relations with people in general, namely, for a place in his group, and he will strive with great intensity to achieve this goal. He will want to attain such a place more than anything else in the world and may even forget that once, when he was hungry, he sneered at love.

In our society the thwarting of these needs is the most commonly found core in cases of maladjustment and more severe psychopathology. Love and affection, as well as their possible expression in sexuality, are generally looked upon with ambivalence and are customarily hedged about with many restrictions and inhibitions. Practically all theorisis of psychopathology have stressed thwarting of the love needs as basic in the picture of maladjustment. Many clinical studies have therefore been made of this need and we know more about it perhaps than any of the other needs except the physiological ones.

One thing that must be stressed at this point is that love is not synonymous with sex. Sex may be studied as a purely physiological need. Ordinarily sexual behaviour is multi-determined, that is to say, determined not only by sexual but also by other needs, chief among which are the love and affection needs. Also not to be overlooked is the fact that the love needs involve both giving *and* receiving love.

The esteem needs

All people in our society have a need or desire for a stable, firmly based, (usually) high evaluation of themselves, for self-respect, or self-esteem, and for the esteem of others. By firmly based self-esteem, we mean that which is soundly based upon real capacity, achievement and respect from others. These needs may be classified into two subsidiary sets. These are, first, the desire for strength, for achievement, for adequacy, for confidence in the face of the world, and for independence and freedom.

Secondly, we have what we may call the desire for reputation or prestige (defining it as respect or esteem from other people), recognition, attention, importance or appreciation. These needs have been relatively stressed by Alfred Adler and his followers, and have been relatively neglected by Freud and the psychoanalysts. More and more today however there is appearing widespread appreciation of their central importance.

Satisfaction of the self-esteem need leads to feelings of self-confidence, worth, strength, capability and adequacy of being useful and necessary in the world. But thwarting of these needs produces feelings of inferiority, of weakness and of helplessness. These feelings in turn give rise to either basic discouragement or else compensatory or neurotic trends. An appreciation of the necessity of basic self-confidence and an understanding of how helpless people are without it, can be easily gained from a study of severe traumatic neurosis.

The need for self-actualization

Even if all these needs are satisfied, we may still often (if not always) expect that a new discontent and restlessness will soon develop, unless the individual is doing what he is fitted for. A musician must make music, an artist must paint, a poet must write, if he is to be ultimately happy. What a man *can* be, he *must* be. This need we may call self-actualization.

Kurt Goldstein, used a much more specific and limited fashion. It refers to the desire for self-fulfillment, namely, to the tendency for him to become actualized in what he is potentially. This tendency might be phrased as the desire to become more and more what one is, to become everything that one is capable of becoming. The specific form that these needs will take will of course vary greatly from person to person. In one individual it may take the form of the desire to be an ideal mother, in another it may be expressed athletically, and in still another it may be expressed in painting pictures or in inventions. It is not necessarily a creative urge although in people who have any capacities for creation it will take this form.

The clear emergence of these needs rests upon prior satisfaction of the physiological, safety, love and esteem needs. We shall call people who are satisfied in these needs, basically satisfied people, and it is from these that we may expect the fullest (and healthiest) creativeness. Since, in our society, basically satisfied people are the exception, we do not know much about self-actualization, either experimentally or clinically. It remains a challenging problem for research.

The preconditions for the basic need satisfactions

There are certain conditions which are immediate prerequisites for the basic need satisfactions. Danger to these is reacted to almost as if it were a direct danger to the basic needs themselves. Such conditions as freedom to speak, freedom to do what one wishes so long as no harm is done to others, freedom to express one's self, freedom to investigate and seek for information, freedom to defend one's self, justice, fairness, honesty, orderliness in the group are examples of such preconditions for basic need satisfactions.

Thwarting in these freedoms will be reacted to with a threat or emergency response. These conditions are not ends in themselves but they are *almost* so since they are so closely related to the basic needs, which are apparently the only ends in themselves. These conditions are defended because without them the basic satisfactions are quite impossible, or at least, very severely endangered.

If we remember that the cognitive capacities (perceptual, intellectual, learning) are a set of adjustive tools, which have, among other functions, that of satisfaction of our basic needs, then it is clear that any danger to them, any deprivation or blocking of their free use, must also be indirectly threatening to the basic needs themselves. Such a statement is a partial solution of the general problems of curiosity, the search for knowledge, truth and wisdom, and the ever-persistent urge to solve the cosmic mysteries.

We must therefore introduce another hypothesis and speak of degrees of closeness to the basic needs, for we have already pointed out that *any* conscious desires (partial goals) are more or less important as they are more or less close to the basic needs. The same statement may be made for various behaviour acts. An act is psychologically important if it contributes directly to satisfaction of basic needs. The less directly it so contributes, or the weaker this contribution is, the less important this act must be conceived to be from the point of view of dynamic psychology.

A similar statement may be made for the various defence or coping mechanisms. Some are very directly related to the protection or attainment of the basic needs, others are only weakly and distantly related. Indeed if we wished, we could speak of more basic and less basic defence mechanisms, and then affirm that danger to the more basic defenses is more threatening than danger to less basic defenses (always remembering that this is so only because of their relationship to the basic needs).

The desires to know and to understand

So far, we have mentioned the cognitive needs only in passing. Acquiring knowledge and systematizing the universe have been considered as, in part, techniques for the achievement of basic safety in the world, or, for the intelligent man, expressions of self-actualization. Also freedom of inquiry and expression have been discussed as preconditions of satisfactions of the basic needs. True though these formulations may be, they do not constitute definitive answers to the question as to the motivation role of curiosity, learning, philosophizing, experimenting, etc. They are, at best, no more than partial answers.

Curiosity, exploration, desire for the facts, desire to know may certainly be observed easily enough. The fact that they often are pursued even at great cost to the individual's safety is an earnest of the partial character of our previous discussion. In addition, the writer must admit that, though he has sufficient clinical evidence to postulate the desire to know as a very strong drive in intelligent people, no data are available for unintelligent people. It may then be largely a function of relatively high intelligence. Rather tentatively, then, and largely in the hope of stimulating discussion and research, we shall postulate a basic desire to know, to be aware of reality, to get the facts, to satisfy curiosity, or as Wertheimer phrases it, to see rather than to be blind.

This postulation, however, is not enough. Even after we know, we are impelled to know more and more minutely and microscopically on the one hand, and on the other, more and more extensively in the direction of a world philosophy, religion, etc. The facts that we acquire, if they are isolated or atomistic, inevitably get theorized about, and either analyzed or organized or both. This process has been phrased by some as the search for 'meaning.' We shall then postulate a desire to understand, to systematize, to organize, to analyze, to look for relations and meanings.

CHARACTERISTICS OF THE BASIC NEEDS

The degree of fixity of the hierarchy of basic needs

We have spoken so far as if this hierarchy were a fixed order but actually it is not nearly as rigid as we may have implied. It is true that most of the people with whom we have worked have seemed to have these basic needs in about the order that has been indicated. However, there have been a number of exceptions.

(1) There are some people in whom, for instance, self-esteem seems to be more important than love. This most common reversal in the hierarchy is usually due to the development of the notion that the person who is most likely to be loved is a strong or powerful person, one who inspires respect or fear, and who is self confident or aggressive. Therefore such people who lack love and seek it, may try hard to put on a front of aggressive, confident behaviour. But essentially they seek high self-esteem and its behaviour expressions more as a means-to-an-end than for its own sake; they seek self-assertion for the sake of love rather than for self-esteem itself.

(2) There are other, apparently innately creative people in whom the drive to creativeness seems to be more important than any other counter-determinant. Their creativeness might appear not as self-actualization released by basic satisfaction, but in spite of lack of basic satisfaction.

(3) In certain people the level of aspiration may be permanently deadened or lowered. That is to say, the less pre-potent goals may simply be lost, and may disappear forever, so that the person who has experienced life at a very low level, *i. e.*, chronic unemployment, may continue to be satisfied for the rest of his life if only he can get enough food.

(4) The so-called 'psychopathic personality' is another example of permanent loss of the love needs. These are people who, according to the best data available, have been starved for love in the earliest months of their lives and have simply lost forever the desire and the ability to give and to receive affection (as animals lose sucking or pecking reflexes that are not exercised soon enough after birth).

(5) Another cause of reversal of the hierarchy is that when a need has been satisfied for a long time, this need may be underevaluated. People who have never experienced chronic hunger are apt to underestimate its effects and to look upon food as a rather unimportant thing. If they are dominated by a higher need, this higher need will seem

to be the most important of all. It then becomes possible, and indeed does actually happen, that they may, for the sake of this higher need, put themselves into the position of being deprived in a more basic need. We may expect that after a long-time deprivation of the more basic need there will be a tendency to reevaluate both needs so that the more pre-potent need will actually become consciously prepotent for the individual who may have given it up very lightly. Thus, a man who has given up his job rather than lose his self-respect, and who then starves for six months or so, may be willing to take his job back even at the price of losing his a self-respect.

(6) Another partial explanation of *apparent* reversals is seen in the fact that we have been talking about the hierarchy of prepotency in terms of consciously felt wants or desires rather than of behaviour. Looking at behaviour itself may give us the wrong impression. What we have claimed is that the person will want the more basic of two needs when deprived in both. There is no necessary implication here that he will act upon his desires. Let us say again that there are many determinants of behaviour other than the needs and desires.

(7) Perhaps more important than all these exceptions are the ones that involve ideals, high social standards, high values and the like. With such values people become martyrs; they give up everything for the sake of a particular ideal, or value. These people may be understood, at least in part, by reference to one basic concept (or hypothesis) which may be called 'increased frustration-tolerance through early gratification'. People who have been satisfied in their basic needs throughout their lives, particularly in their earlier years, seem to develop exceptional power to withstand present or future thwarting of these needs simply because they have strong, healthy character structure as a result of basic satisfaction. They are the 'strong' people who can easily weather disagreement or opposition, who can swim against the stream of public opinion and who can stand up for the truth at great personal cost. It is just the ones

who have loved and been well loved, and who have had many deep friendships who can hold out against hatred, rejection or persecution.

Unconscious character of needs

These needs are neither necessarily conscious nor unconscious. On the whole, however, in the average person, they are more often unconscious rather than conscious. It is not necessary at this point to overhaul the tremendous mass of evidence which indicates the crucial importance of unconscious motivation. It would by now be expected, on a priori grounds alone, that unconscious motivations would on the whole be rather more important than the conscious motivations. What we have called the basic needs are very often largely unconscious although they may, with suitable techniques, and with sophisticated people become conscious.

Cultural specificity and generality of needs

This classification of basic needs makes some attempt to take account of the relative unity behind the superficial differences in specific desires from one culture to another. Certainly in any particular culture an individual's conscious motivational content will usually be extremely different from the conscious motivational content of an individual in another society. However, it is the common experience of anthropologists that people, even in different societies, are much more alike than we would think from our first contact with them, and that as we know them better we seem to find more and more of this commonness, We then recognize the most startling differences to be superficial rather than basic, *e. g.*, differences in style of hair-dress, clothes, tastes in food, etc.

Our classification of basic needs is in part an attempt to account for this unity behind the apparent diversity from culture to culture. No claim is made that it is ultimate or universal for all cultures. The claim is made only that it is relatively *more* ultimate, more universal, more basic, than the superficial conscious desires from culture to culture, and makes a somewhat closer approach to common-human characteristics, Basic needs are *more* common-human than superficial desires or behaviours.

Multiple motivations of behaviour

These needs must be understood not to be *exclusive* or single determiners of certain kinds of behaviour. An example may be found in any behaviour that seems to be physiologically motivated, such as eating, or sexual play or the like. The clinical psychologists have long since found that any behaviour may be a channel through which flow various determinants. Or to say it in another way, most behaviour is multi-motivated. Within the sphere of motivational determinants any behaviour tends to be determined by several or *all* of the basic needs simultaneously rather than by only one of them. The latter would be more an exception than the former. Eating may be partially for the sake of filling the stomach, and partially for the sake of comfort and amelioration of other needs. One may make love not only for pure sexual release, but also to convince one's self of one's masculinity, or to make a conquest, to feel powerful, or to win more basic affection.

Multiple determinants of behaviour

Not all behaviour is determined by the basic needs. We might even say that not all behaviour is motivated. There are many determinants of behaviour other than motives. For instance, one other important class of determinants is the so-called 'field' determinants. Theoretically, at least, behaviour may be determined completely by the field, or even by specific isolated external stimuli, as in association of ideas, or certain conditioned reflexes.

Secondly, we may call attention again to the concept of 'degree of closeness to the basic needs' or 'degree of motivation.' Some behaviour is highly motivated, other behaviour is only weakly motivated. Some is not motivated at all (but all behaviour is determined).

Another important point is that there is a basic difference between expressive behaviour and coping behaviour. An expressive behaviour does not try to do anything; it is simply a reflection of the personality. A stupid man behaves stupidly, not because he wants to, or tries to, or is motivated to, but simply because he is what he is. The random movements of a healthy child, the smile on the face of a happy man even when he is alone, the springiness of the healthy man's walk, and the erectness of his carriage are other examples of expressive, non-functional behaviour. Also the *style* in which a man carries out almost all his behaviour, motivated as well as unmotivated, is often expressive.

We may then ask, is *all* behaviour expressive or reflective of the character structure? The answer is 'No.' Rote, habitual, automatized, or conventional behaviour may or may not be expressive. The same is true for most 'stimulus-bound' behaviours. It is finally necessary to stress that expressiveness of behaviour, and goal-directedness of behaviour are not mutually exclusive categories. Average behaviour is usually both.

Goals as centering principle in motivation theory

It will be observed that the basic principle in our classification has been neither the instigation nor the motivated behaviour but rather the functions, effects, purposes, or goals of the behaviour. It has been proven sufficiently by various people that this is the most suitable point for centering in any motivation theory.

Animal- and human-centering

This theory starts with the human being rather than any lower and presumably 'simpler' animal. Too many of the findings that have been made in animals have been proven to be true for animals but not for the human being. There is no reason whatsoever why we should start with animals in order to study human motivation. The logic or rather illogic behind this general fallacy of 'pseudo-simplicity' has been exposed often enough by philosophers and logicians as well as by scientists in each of the various fields. It is no more necessary to study animals before one can study man than it is to study mathematics before one can study geology or psychology or biology.

We may also reject the old, naive, behaviorism which assumed that it was somehow necessary, or at least more 'scientific' to judge human beings by animal standards. One consequence of this belief was that the whole notion of purpose and goal was excluded from motivational psychology simply because one could not ask a white rat about his purposes. Tolman has long since proven in animal studies themselves that this exclusion was not necessary.

Motivation and the theory of psychopathogenesis

The conscious motivational content of everyday life has, according to the foregoing, been conceived to be relatively important or unimportant accordingly as it is more or less closely related to the basic goals. A desire for an ice cream cone might actually be an indirect expression of a desire for love. If it is, then this desire for the ice cream cone becomes extremely important motivation. If however the ice cream is simply something to cool the mouth with, or a casual appetitive reaction, then the desire is relatively unimportant.

Everyday conscious desires are to be regarded as symptoms, as *surface indicators of more basic needs*. If we were to take these superficial desires at their face value me would find ourselves in a state of complete confusion which could never be resolved, since we would be dealing seriously with symptoms rather than with what lay behind the symptoms.

Thwarting of unimportant desires produces no psychopathological results; thwarting of a basically important need does produce such results. Any theory of psychopathogenesis must then be based on a sound theory of motivation. A conflict or a frustration is not necessarily pathogenic. It becomes so only when it threatens or thwarts the basic needs, or partial needs that are closely related to the basic needs.

The role of gratified needs

It has been pointed out above several times that our needs usually emerge only when more prepotent needs have been gratified. Thus gratification has an important role in motivation theory. Apart from this, however, needs cease to play an active determining or organizing role as soon as they are gratified. What this means is that, *e. g.*, a basically satisfied person no longer has the needs for esteem, love, safety, etc. The only sense in which he might be said to have them is in the almost metaphysical sense that a sated man has hunger, or a filled bottle has emptiness. If we are interested in what *actually* motivates us, and not in what has, will, or might motivate us, then a satisfied need is not a motivator. It must be considered for all practical purposes simply not to exist, to have disappeared.

The perfectly healthy, normal, fortunate man has no sex needs or hunger needs, or needs for safety, or for love, or for prestige, or self-esteem, except in stray moments of quickly passing threat. If we were to say otherwise, we should also have to aver that every man had all the pathological reflexes, *e. g.*, Babinski, etc., because if his nervous system were damaged, these would appear.

It is such considerations as these that suggest the bold postulation that a man who is thwarted in any of his basic needs may fairly be envisaged simply as a sick man. This is a fair parallel to our designation as 'sick' of the man who lacks vitamins or minerals. Who is to say that a lack of love is less important than a lack of vitamins?

A SELF CONCEPT- BASED MODEL OF WORK MOTIVATION

There is a growing realization that traditional models of motivation do not explain the diversity of behaviour found in organizational settings. While research and theory building in the areas of goal setting, reward systems, leadership, and job design have advanced our understanding of organizational behaviour.

In addition, some researchers have called attention to the role of dispositions and volitional processes in models of motivation. Others point out that we have a variety of motivation theories that have no unifying theme and are not supported well by the research. In an effort to address these issues, some researchers have turned to self theory as an alternative explanation for organizational behaviour. Specifically, social identity theory, self presentation theory, and self efficacy theory, are all fundamentally rooted in the concept of self.

There have been a number of attempts at developing models of self concept-based motivation, but none as yet have been integrated into the mainstream of organizational research and teaching. Most organizational behaviour textbooks provide only a cursory overview of self-based constructs. What is missing is a model of the self concept that clearly defines these constructs and explains how they can be integrated with traditional work motivation models. After reviewing the literature on motivation, we have determined that there are four major reasons why we need the addition of self concept-based constructs to more completely understand and predict organizational behaviour.

Specifically, these four reasons are: (1) the need to explain non-calculative-based work behaviour; (2) the need to better account for internal sources of motivation; (3) the need to integrate dispositional and situational explanations of behaviour; and (4) the need to integrate existing self-based theories in the literature.

Need to Explain Non-Calculative-Based Work Behaviour: Most of our currently popular theories of work motivation assume that individuals are "rational maximizer(s) of personal utility". For example, expectancy theory assumes that motivation is a result of calculatively determined probabilities associated with different levels or types of behaviour and the valences of the outcomes associated with these behaviours. Equity theory may be considered calculative insofar as it assumes that people cognitively assess their own attitudes and job performance by comparing their input/outcome ratio to that of a referent other. If this ratio indicates an imbalance between inputs and rewards as compared to the referent, then inequity is produced. This inequity causes cognitive dissonance that the individual is motivated to reduce. These cognitive choice or calculative models assume that behaviours are the result of hedonistic processes (i.e., people will behave in ways that maximize positive outcomes and minimize negative outcomes).

Although research over the past twenty years in decision-making, occupational choice, and achievement motivation has provided strong support for these calculative models, they cannot account for the full range of motivated behaviour. For example, these models do not explain changes in behaviour across situations when expectancies and valences remain constant. In addition, individuals may differ in the use of expectancy and instrumentality information. Self theory supplements calculative models by suggesting the concept of self as a basis for non-calculative explanations of behaviour.

Need to Account for Internal Sources of Motivation: There are a number of theories that attempt to capture types or sources of motivation affecting organizational members. For instance, in discussing internal and external causes of behaviour, deCharms suggested the dichotomy of intrinsic versus extrinsic motivation to characterize the different loci of causality.

Intrinsically motivated behaviours (i.e., those behaviours that occur in the absence of external controls) are said to represent internal causality, whereas behaviours that are induced by external forces are said to represent external causality. Deci explored the effects of extrinsic rewards on intrinsic motivation and in doing so, tried to shed some light on the meaning of intrinsic motivation. He suggested that intrinsically motivated behaviours fall into two categories. The first category includes behaviours that individuals engage in to seek out challenging situations. These challenges represent incongruities between stimuli and comparison standards. The second category includes behaviours aimed at reducing these incongruities (i.e., overcoming challenges). Thus, intrinsically motivated behaviour, according to Deci, is conceptualized as a continual process of seeking and overcoming challenges.

Another understanding of intrinsic motivation is offered by Katz and Kahn. They argue that the bases of motivation can be categorized in terms of legal compliance, external rewards (i.e., instrumental satisfaction), and internalized motivation. Internalized motivation is further broken down into self-expression, derived directly from role performance and internalized values, resulting when group or organizational goals become incorporated into the value system of the individual. Etzioni takes a similar view when arguing that organizations induce involvement from their members by one of three means: alienative, calculative, or moral. Alienative and calculative involvement are explained by exchange processes. Moral involvement is more complex.

According to Etzioni, there are two kinds of moral involvement, pure and social. Pure moral involvement is the result of internalization of norms, while social involvement results from sensitivity to pressures of primary groups and their members. Moral involvement is not based on expected satisfaction of needs and may even demand the denial of need satisfaction and the sacrifice of personal pleasure. For example, military personnel who serve in the armed forces demonstrate the value of serving one's country to the point of risking their lives, and the individual who works a double shift for a friend who needs the night off demonstrates the value of friendship. In these instances, the consequence of acting in line with one's internalized values is not a sense of pleasure or need fulfillment, but rather a sense of affirmation attained when the person abides by his or her moral commitments.

The above approaches are strikingly similar in that they allow for both an instrumental, or exchange basis of motivation, and an expressive basis of motivation, whether it is termed intrinsic motivation, intrinsically motivated behaviour, moral involvement, or internalized motivation.

Need to Integrate Dispositional and Situational Explanations of Behaviour: Psychologists have long postulated that individual dispositions or personalities are significant determinants of behaviour. The assumptions underlying this approach are that (1) there are individual differences in ways of behaving; (2) individual behaviour is somewhat stable over time; and (3) individual behaviour is somewhat consistent across situations.

At the other extreme is the view that behaviour is determined by situational factors and that similarity in behaviour results from similarity of situational circumstances. Supporting this latter view, Mischel argued that personality traits have accounted for little variance in behaviour across situations. Recently, some researchers have begun to provide new evidence for the dispositional view. For example, Staw and Ross found in a longitudinal study, that job attitudes were significantly stable over a five year period and that there was significant cross-situational consistency when individuals changed occupations and/or employers. Gerhardt replicated these findings using a younger sample of both men and women and a more sophisticated methodology that controlled for job complexity. Arvey, Bouchard, Segal, and Abraham have even provided evidence for a genetic disposition in the determination of job satisfaction.

Today, most researchers have taken an interactionist view that states that behaviour is a function of both environment and personality Specifically, these researchers are suggesting that a dynamic reciprocal interaction occurs between the person and the situation. Pervin challenges researchers to develop models that will explain how people are able to shift from situation to situation, often exhibiting different patterns of behaviour, while still retaining a recognizable personality structure.

Need to Integrate Existing Self-Based Theories: In recent years, a plethora of self-based theories have been proposed. All of these theories are based on the assumption that "human beings have a fundamental need to maintain or enhance the phenomenal self". Because of this fundamental need, individuals are motivated to behave in ways that are consistent with existing self-perceptions. Thus, these theories may be useful in expanding our notion of motivated behaviour in the workplace.

Unfortunately, because of the different streams of research in this area, our knowledge of self theory is piecemeal in nature and highly disorganized. Further, a proliferation of terms and concepts that often overlap in meaning has resulted. What is needed is an integrative model of the self-concept that will clarify the nature of self theory constructs and organize them in a nomological net that will guide empirical research.

If self theory is to be useful to organizational researchers, it must do a number of things. First, it must provide a detailed description of the structure and content of the self concept and an understanding of how it is developed. Second, it must address how the self concept influences behaviour in organizations. Third, it must explain how the self concept affects employee reactions to organizational systems that are in place to induce specific behaviours (e.g., reward systems, cultural systems, etc.).

Structure and Development of Self Concept

A study of Markus & Wurf state that the most dramatic advances in the last decade of research on the self concept can be found in work on its structure and content. Historically, one of the major stumbling blocks to linking the self concept to behaviour has been the view of the self concept as a stable, generalized, or average view of the self. More recent research in social psychology has resolved this problem by conceptualizing of the self concept as a multifaceted phenomenon composed of a set of images, schemas and prototypes. There has been a similar movement in sociology where the self is defined in terms of multiple identities.

Identities include personal characteristics, features and experiences, as well as roles and social statuses. In both streams of research, authors define the self concept in terms of various self-representations. Their work indicates that some self-representations are more important than others; some are representations of what the self is perceived to be, versus what the self would like to be; some are core conceptions or salient identities while others are more peripheral; and some are relatively stable while others are dynamic.

In the self concept-based model of motivation which we are proposing, one's concept of self is composed of four interrelated self-perceptions: the perceived self, the ideal self, one's self esteem, and a set of social identities. Each of these elements plays a crucial role in understanding how the self concept relates to energizing, directing and sustaining organizational behaviour. Each of these self-representations will be described and their interrelationships discussed.

The Perceived Self

Most models and descriptions of the self involve elements of self perceptions; however, most are unclear as to what aspects of the self the individual holds perceptions of. One of the earliest theorists writing on the nature of the self was William James. He saw the self as consisting of whatever the individual views as belonging to himself or herself, which includes a material, a social, and a spiritual self. The perceptions of the material self are those of one's own body, family, and possessions.

The social self includes the views others have of the individual, and the spiritual includes perceptions of one's emotions and desires. Kihlstrom, Cantor, and their associates suggest that individuals hold perceptions of themselves in terms of traits and values, their attributes, experiences, thoughts and actions, and their physical appearance, demographic attributes and dispositions of various sorts. Gecas asserts that the content of the self concept consists of perceptions of social and personal identities, traits, attributes, and possessions.

The model which we propose utilizes three general categories of self-perceptions which we believe incorporate most of those suggested in earlier research. These include traits, competencies and values.

Traits: Traits are labels for broad reaction tendencies and express relatively permanent patterns of behaviour. Fundamental to this definition is the assumption that people make internal attributions to individuals who demonstrate a particular behaviour pattern in different situations or at different times without apparent external reasons. The more cross-situational consistency one observes, and the more external causes of behaviour seem to be lacking, the more likely one would make an internal or dispositional attribution. It is not important at this point to understand what really motivates aggressive behaviour. What is important is that individuals hold a set of self perceptions regarding many different traits.

Competencies: A second element in the perceived self is competencies. Individuals hold perceptions of what skills, abilities, talents, and knowledge they possess. These can range from very specific skills, such as the ability to run a turret lathe, to more general competencies, such as the leadership skills to create and manage change.

Values: Values are defined as concepts and beliefs about desirable end states or behaviours that transcend specific situations, guide selection or evaluation of behaviour and events, and are ordered by relative importance. Individuals demonstrate certain values through their speech and actions. This element of the perceived self is concerned with the set of values that the individual believes guides his or her decisions and actions.

An individual's perception of his/her attributes (i.e., traits, competencies, and values), can be describe in terms of two separate dimensions, level and strength. Level of self perception refers to the degree to which the individual perceives he/she possesses this attribute. Does the individual see himself or herself as highly introverted (trait), or a very good tennis player (competency), or a hard worker (value)? This dimension deals with the issue of where individuals see themselves, relative to their ideal selves, and is directly related to the issue of high and low self esteem.

When determining the level of an attribute, individuals use two types of evaluative frames of reference. An ordinal standard or frame of reference is used when the individual rates or compares himself or herself to others (i.e., how good is he or she relative to others). To be first or the best is the ultimate criterion when using this type of standard. An individual may also use a fixed standard, whereby he/she rates or evaluates attributes against a goal or predetermined metric or criterion (i.e., to earn a bachelors' degree). This may take the form of reaching a set of internalized goals or timetables.

The second dimension of the perceived self is the *strength* of the perception, and refers to how strongly the individual holds the perception of attribute level. Individuals with strong perceived selves are relatively firm in their perceptions of an attribute level. These strong perceptions of self are a result of consistent and clear feedback regarding the attribute. A weak perceived self is reflected in individuals who are relatively unsure of an attribute level, often resulting from conflicting or ambiguous feedback regarding the attribute. How these self perceptions develop is explained next.

Development of Perceived Self: Self perceptions are determined through interaction with one's environment. Processes of attitude formation, attitude change, and self attribution all contribute to the development of a set of self perceptions. As indicated above, when feedback is unambiguous, plentiful, and consistent, a set of strongly held self perceptions is formed. Ambiguous, lacking, or inconsistent feedback results in weakly held self perceptions.

Two primary forms of information one receives about the self from the environment come in the form of task feedback and social feedback. Task feedback comes directly from observation of the results of one's efforts on different task activities. Completion of a project, accomplishment of a goal, and winning a competition are all forms of task feedback. Social feedback is probably the most prevalent type of feedback one receives regarding his or her traits, competencies, and values. It is the feedback one derives from the behaviour and communication, verbal and non-verbal, of others.

The link between social feedback and the perceived self is grounded in the process of attribution. As people seek to understand the behaviour of a particular individual, they make certain attributions as to the causes of patterns of behaviour they observe in that individual . Under certain conditions, observers make internal or dispositional attributions, mostly in the form of traits, competencies, or values, and these internal attributions become the basis for self perceptions. These attributions are communicated to the person in a number of ways, both directly and indirectly. Attributions may be communicated directly in the form of written or oral evaluation, praise, reprimand, or recognition. For example, direct feedback may be regarding a trait (you're too aggressive), a competency (you're an excellent teacher), or a value (you're an honest person).

In addition, attributions are communicated indirectly in a number of ways. An evaluative statement regarding a project or task for which the individual feels responsible is an example of indirect social feedback. Other types of indirect social feedback come in the form of inclusion or non-inclusion of the individual by group members in their activities, the bestowing of positions of status on the individual, and when others accept or fail to accept an individual's influence by acting or failing to act on his or her advice, recommendations, or orders. It is important to note that the feedback provider does not have to intend to provide feedback for the feedback receiver to interpret an action as social feedback.

The Ideal Self

While the perceived self describes the set of perceptions individuals hold of their actual traits, competencies, and values, the ideal self represents the set of traits, competencies and values an individual would like to possess. By possess we mean that the individual desires to believe that he/she actually has a particular trait, competency, or value, or wants others to believe that the individual has the trait, competency, or value. This view of ideal self is similar to Schlenker's "idealized image" (i.e., the ultimate person one would like to be).

Development of the Ideal Self: In the early stages of interaction with a reference group, whether the reference group is the primary group (i.e., the family for a young child) or a secondary group (i.e., one's peers or co-workers), choices and decisions are channeled through the existing social system. As an individual interacts with the reference group, he/she receives feedback from reference group members. If the feedback is positive and unconditional, the individual will internalize the traits, competencies and values which are important to that reference group.

In this case, the individual becomes inner-directed, using the internalized traits, competencies and values as a measure of his/her own successes/failures. Internalized competencies and values have been suggested as the basis of the ideal self and as an internal standard for behaviour. If the individual receives negative feedback or positive but conditional feedback, the individual may not internalize or only partially internalize the traits, competencies and values of the reference group. This type of individual becomes other-directed and will either withdraw from the group or seek constant feedback from group members.

Thus, the establishment of the ideal self is determined through a mix of external, or other-directed standards, and internal, or inner-directed standards, depending on one's orientation to the world. The ideal self of the other-directed individual is developed largely through the established norms and role expectations of reference group members. The audience for one's actions becomes the reference group, in that it is important that reference group members see the individual as possessing accepted attributes.

For the inner-directed individual, the ideal self is determined largely through the development of a set of internalized goals and standards, and the individual becomes his or her own audience. Gottfredson's perspective on individual and social achievement motivation is similar to this conceptualization. This latter author asserts that in individually-oriented achievement motivation, the individual strives to achieve some internalized standards of excellence. In contrast, socially-oriented achievement motivation reflects an individual's perseverance to fulfill the expectations of significant others.

Social Identities

According to Ashforth and Mael, social identification is a process by which individuals classify themselves and others into different social categories, such as "woman," "Catholic," and "nurse." This classification process serves the functions of segmenting and ordering the social environment and enabling the individual to locate or define him- or herself in that social environment. Thus, social identification provides a partial answer to the question, "Who am I?" Social identities are thus those aspects of an individual's self-concept that derive from the social categories to which he or she perceives him- or herself as belonging .

Development of Social Identities: Individuals establish social identities through involvement with reference groups in social situations. Reference groups provide three major functions with respect to social identities: (1) the determination of the profile of traits, competencies, and values for a particular social identity; (2) the establishment and communication of the relative value and status of various social roles or identities; and (3) are the basis of social feedback regarding one's level of these traits, competencies, and values.

Specifically, social identities link individuals to reference groups. These groups establish a set of role expectations and norms which guide the individual's behaviour within each of the social identities. For example, the identity of an accountant may be associated with reserve and self control (traits), analytical ability and good memory (competencies), and honesty and free enterprise (values). Individuals who desire to be identified with the reference group will attempt to demonstrate the traits, competencies, and values associated with that identity. These aspired-to traits, competencies, and values serve as the basis for the ideal self. Once established, the attributes then reinforce the identity. The determination of the relevant set of attributes that comprise the identity is not fixed, but rather is the result of an interaction process between individuals and subgroups and members of the relevant reference group. This definition and redefinition of the identity is a constant process.

Individual's establish at least two types of social identities: a *global identity* and *role-specific identities*. The global identity is the identity one wishes to portray across all situations, across various roles, and to various reference groups. The global identity exists independently of any specific social identity. The reference·group for the global identity includes those members of one's primary group, and the traits, competencies and values which are relevant to the individual are those which are reinforced by the individual's culture. The global identity is formed early in life, and one's family, functioning as a primary reference group, performs the three functions mentioned above.

The global identity provides a starting point for role-specific identities. As the individual matures, the control of the primary group lessens and the individual begins to establish certain role-specific social identities. Role-specific social identities are those identities established for a specific reference group or a specific social role. It is this process of selecting and "earning" the identity that acts to define one's self to various reference groups. By "earning" the identity, we are describing the process whereby the individual meets basic expectations of the reference group (either formal or informal credentialling) necessary to carry out the role.

As an individual begins to interact with reference group members in a role-specific identity, the global identity provides input to this specific identity. However, as an individual remains in a role-specific identity and receives positive feedback from group members, the role-specific identity begins to provide input to the global identity. The reference groups in these social situations (e.g., one's co-workers, friends, etc.) begin to perform the functions which were previously performed by the primary reference group. The individual is now exposed to the traits, competencies, and values which are valued by each new reference group. The identity-specific reference groups also provide the social feedback important in the development of the perceived self.

Thus, identities may be thought to exist in a hierarchy, starting with the global identity and working through role-specific identities. As reference groups become more specific, the identity becomes more specific, and thus the attributes associated with the identity become more specific. For example, an individual may identify him/herself as an academic at one level, a member of the business administration faculty at another, and a finance professor at yet another level of specificity. Roberts and Donahue provide empirical evidence that individuals do see themselves differently in each of their roles and, in particular, they rate the trait attributes of some roles more highly than the trait attributes of others. They also found that general self perceptions (i.e., global identity) are related to the role-specific self perceptions.

As participation in a social identity continues over time, the reference group itself becomes the basis of identification, and the success or failure of the reference group as a whole becomes a source of feedback for the individual. As defined by social identity theory, social identification is the perception of oneness with or belonging-ness to a reference group. When an individual identifies with a social referenced group, he/she perceives the fate of the group as his/her own. The more an individual identifies with a social identity, the more the individual vests his/her self concept in the identity.

Self Esteem

The self esteem is the evaluative component of the self concept. It is a function of the distance between the ideal self and the perceived self. When the perceived self matches the ideal self, self esteem is relatively high. Low self esteem occurs when the perceived self is significantly lower than the ideal self. Since the distance between the ideal and perceived self constantly varies depending on task and social feedback, self esteem is a dynamic component of the self concept and it is always in a state of change and development.

Korman suggests three types of self esteem: *chronic self esteem*, which is defined as a relatively persistent personality trait or dispositional state that occurs consistently across various situations; *task-specific self esteem*, which is one's self perception of his/her competence concerning a particular task or job; and *socially-influenced self esteem*, which is a function of the expectations of others. Chronic self esteem is the result of past experience and focuses on one's competencies. An individual's confidence in his/her competencies directs the individual into situations which will require the use of those competencies. Task-specific self esteem is the result of feedback which comes directly from observation of the results of one's efforts. Lastly, socially-influenced self esteem results from communication or feedback from reference group members or society as a whole, concerning the value of an identity and the individual's ability to meet the expectations of the reference group and/or society as a whole.

The structure of the self concept may be thought of as a relatively stable set of cognitions that provide the basis for the expectancies, instrumentalities, and valences in instrumental or calculative motivation. However, there is also an expressive component of the self concept, which refers to how an individual processes information (feedback, observations, etc.) and uses the structure of the self concept to filter incoming information and translate this information into action. Much of the work in motivation relies heavily on cognitive models of behaviour, and while many behaviours are the result of thought processes that are open to the individual's conscious inspection, other behaviours are the result of a process that is not entirely understood or conscious to the individual. We will refer to these *acognitive processes*, as the expressive component of the self concept. Both the expressive or acognitive processes, as well as the cognitive processes, are important in understanding the link between the self concept and behaviour.

It is proposed that self perceptions of one's traits, competencies and values exist as knowledge structures which serve to monitor and control current experience, thought and actions. Some knowledge structures are cognitive in nature and provide data for information processing in a given social situation. These knowledge structures lead to behavioural patterns that appear stable across situations. Other knowledge structures, under certain conditions, may be inaccessible to retrieval and conscious introspection.

Kihlstrom et al. call these aspects of the self, preconscious or subconscious. These acognitive knowledge structures account for individual behaviour which seems to counter individual goals, or behaviour which deviates from the individual's intentions and causes the individual to behave in ways that appear variable across situations. Expressive motivation is best explained by these acognitive knowledge structures.

Nisbitt and Wilson argue that people have access to (know) the products of cognitive processes but cannot access the actual workings of those processes. When applied to the self, this would suggest that people utilize the knowledge structures which are cognitive in nature to determine motivation at a calculative level, while motivation which results from acognitive knowledge structures must be inferred indirectly on the basis of behaviour. Both cognitive knowledge structures and acognitive structures are often termed schema, or schemata, and provide a framework that helps the individual organize his or her world and provide meaning and structure to incoming information.

Schlenker refers to these self-schemata as "identities" and defines an identity as a theory or schema of an individual that describes, interrelates, and explains his or her relevant features, characteristics, and experiences. Thus, an individual's identity specifies the contents of what he/she is like, and secondly, it guides and regulates his/her subsequent experience by affecting thoughts, feelings, behaviours, and outcomes.

The major purpose of developing a model of the self concept is to provide a unitary construct that is able to explain both cognitive and acognitive motivational processes. Before linking self concept-based ideas to such motivational processes, we must first discuss what we call the *sources of motivation*: instrumental, intrinsic process, goal internalization, and internal and external self concept-based motivation.

As indicated earlier, most motivation theorists have proposed that there are two major sources of motivation: extrinsic and intrinsic. Extrinsic motivation is that which derives from external forces and is represented in our model as instrumental sources of motivation. Intrinsic motivation as behaviours which occur in the absence of external controls. This expansion integrates Deci's classification of intrinsic motivation as behaviours that individuals engage in to seek out challenging situations or to overcome challenges, Katz and Kahn's definition of internalized motivation as self-expression or internalized values and Etzioni's conceptualization of pure moral involvement which results from internalized values, and social moral involvement which is results from feedback from reference group members. These types of motivation are represented in our model as intrinsic process, goal internalization, and both internal and external self concept-based processes. In this section, we will discuss each of the sources of motivation in more detail.

Instrumental Motivation: Instrumental rewards are a motivating source when individuals believe that the behaviours they engage in will lead to certain outcomes such as pay, praise, etc. Rooted in the work of Barnard and March and Simon, the basic assumption is that individuals and organizations constitute an exchange relationship. This is similar to Katz and Kahn's legal compliance and external rewards as bases of motivation and Etzioni's alienative and calculative involvement. Expectancy and equity theories are currently accepted models of motivation based on exchange relationships.

Intrinsic Process Motivation: Individuals are motivated by intrinsic process rewards when they perform a behaviour just because it is "fun". In other words, the motivation comes from the work itself. Individuals enjoy the work and feel rewarded simply by performing the task. There are no external controls regulating the behaviour and behaviour that is challenging may be considered enjoyable to some people. Hackman and Oldham's job characteristics model is representative of intrinsic process motivation.

Goal Internalization: Behaviour is motivated by goal internalization when the individual adopts attitudes and behaviours because their content is congruent with their value system. Katz and Kahn term this type of motivation, internalized values, and a similar concept is suggested by Etzioni's pure moral involvement. Some researchers have examined goal internalization as one dimension of organizational commitment.

Internal Self Concept-based Motivation: Self concept motivation will be internally based when the individual is primarily inner-directed. Internal self concept motivation takes the form of the individual setting internal standards that become the basis for the ideal self. The individual tends to use fixed rather than ordinal standards of self measurement as he/she attempts to first, reinforce perceptions of competency, and later achieve higher levels of competency. This need for achieving higher levels of competency is similar to what McClelland) refers to as a high need for achievement.

The motivating force for individuals who are inner-driven and motivated by their self concept is task feedback. It is important to these individual that their efforts are vital in achieving outcomes and that their ideas and actions are instrumental in performing a job well. It is not important that others provide reinforcing feedback as is true for other-directed individuals. This process is akin to Deci's idea of intrinsic motivation as representing one's attempt to seek out and overcome challenges, and Katz and Kahn's idea of internalized motivation as self-expression derived from role performance.

External Self Concept-based Motivation: Self concept motivation is externally based when the individual is primarily other-directed. In this case, the ideal self is derived by adopting the role expectations of reference groups. The individual attempts to meet the expectations of others by behaving in ways that will elicit social feedback consistent with self perceptions. When positive task feedback is obtained, the individual finds it necessary to communicate these results to members of the reference group. The individual behaves in ways which satisfy reference group members, first to gain acceptance, and after achieving that, to gain status. These two needs, for acceptance and status, are similar to McClelland's need for affiliation and need for power. The individual continually strives to earn the acceptance and status of reference group members. This status orientation usually leads to an ordinal standard of self evaluation. This type of motivation is also similar to Etzioni's social moral involvement.

Individuals experience both internally- and externally-based self concept motivation to varying degrees. Whether or not an individual will be motivated by his or her self concept and whether the source of that motivation is internal or external, are dependent on a number of things. As discussed above, an individual may have a high or low self concept, strong or weakly held self perceptions and utilize a fixed or ordinal standard of evaluation. These characteristics lead to individual self concept types and patterns of behaviour. In order to demonstrate how the proposed model of self concept-based motivation can increase our understanding of organizational behaviour, we will discuss two of these types as examples.

High and weakly held self concept, outer directed, using an ordinal standard. These individuals are highly competitive and self presentation is important. They have a need to put finger prints on success and to disassociate with failure. A prime concern for these individuals is establishing blame when failure occurs or establishing credits for group successes. These individuals are status and power oriented with a strong need for external or social affirmation.

High and weakly held self concept, inner directed, using a fixed standard. These individuals set high standards for themselves. Each project is a test of their competency. These individuals seek task feedback and involve themselves in projects that test competencies and allow for this type of feedback. They must have ownership (control) over project outcomes. While they have a high self concept, this is not strongly held and thus they need to continually seek feedback through task performance. If internal and external self concepts are valid bases of motivation distinct from the other sources, then they must be able to independently explain motivated behaviour.

SELF CONCEPT ON MOTIVATIONAL PROCESSES

The motivational processes of expectancy, attribution, cognitive dissonance, and reinforcement have all been used to explain motivation. The following section will describe how each of these motivational processes can be understood by using the self concept as a basis of motivation.

Expectancy

The concept of expectancy is the cornerstone of the cognitive school of motivation. Expectancy theory posits that individuals choose among a set of behavioural alternatives on the basis of the motivational force of each alternative. The motivational force is a multiplicative combination of expectancy (i.e., the perceived probability that effort will lead to a desired outcome), instrumentality (i.e., the probability that this outcome will lead to a desired reward), and valence (i.e., value of the reward).

In the self-concept framework, individuals cognitively assess the likelihood of given actions leading to levels and types of task and/or social feedback consistent with their self perceptions. The valence of this feedback is based on the value or values associated with the role-specific identity as determined by the reference group. In other words, individual behaviour is a choice process that is engaged in to obtain feedback on traits, competencies or values which are important in relation to the ideal self.

Attribution

The attribution process is concerned with the way in which individuals attempt to determine the causes of behaviour. External attributions are those that are made when the observer (self or other) of a behavioural pattern believes that the actor is responding to situational forces, such as the expectation of a bonus. Internal attributions are made when the observer believes that the behaviour is the result of some disposition of the actor such as a personality trait or internal value. Since the self concept is comprised of self perceptions of traits, competencies, and values, how the individual and others assess these attributes is important in the maintenance of these self perceptions.

In this process, the individual attempts to have others attribute certain traits, competencies and value to him/herself. The traits, competencies and values which the individual wishes to have attributed to him/her are those traits, competencies and values which are valued by the reference group to which the individual aspires. In order to achieve internal attribution, individuals must behave consistently across situations and across time. For example, with respect to competencies, individuals must establish control over task/project outcomes in order to generate the type of task/social feedback which is consistent with their self perceptions. In order for success to be attributed to the competencies of oneself, the other-directed individual seeks this control so that others attribute the outcomes of the task/project to him/herself. On the other hand, inner-directed individuals seek control of the task/project outcomes for their own satisfaction.

Cognitive Dissonance

According to the theory of cognitive dissonance, inconsistency between two cognitive elements, whether they represent beliefs, attitudes, or behaviour, gives rise to dissonance. Assumed to be unpleasant, the presence of dissonance is said to motivate the individual to change one or more cognitive elements in an attempt to eliminate the unpleasant state. With respect to the self concept, dissonance occurs when task or social feedback differs from self perception. When dissonance occurs, individuals attempt to resolve it by utilizing one or more of the following adaptive strategies.

Adaptive Strategies

Adaptive strategies are the primary mechanisms which

individuals use to deal with dissonance (i.e., conflict between their self perceptions and social or task feedback). The strategies may be cognitive, or they may take the form of acognitive scripts (i.e., patterns for behaviour) which people call upon regularly when faced with disconfirming feedback. These adaptive behaviours include:

- Motivation -Expending greater effort to improve the feedback in the future.
- Discounting Feedback - Seeking out confirming feedback to discount the disconfirming feedback, or discrediting the source of the disconfirming feedback.
- Changing Feedback - Presenting evidence, and/or arguing, that the individual's evaluation was incorrect.
- Disassociation - Disassociating oneself from the outcome of a project. Publicly showing that one was not really trying so that the link between task outcome and traits, competencies and values is not likely to be made.
- Association - Attempting to create a strong perceptual link between task outcome and traits, competencies and values. Linking oneself to successful or high status organizations or groups.
- Reaction Formation - Convincing the world, and oneself, that a particular trait, competency or value is of no importance.
- Feedback Avoidance - Avoiding the opportunity to receive feedback or to subject one's traits, competencies or values to confirmation.
- Reducing Status of Others - Attempting to show that others have lower traits, competencies or values than oneself.

Reinforcement

Reinforcement theory explains behaviour in terms of the reinforcing consequences of the behaviour. Individuals learn to repeat certain behaviours because they are rewarded and they discontinue behaviours that are either punished or not rewarded. Reinforcers are the stimuli that are presented to the individual upon engaging in a behaviour and serve to increase the probability of that behaviour in the future.

Task and social feedback which confirm self perceptions act as basic reinforcers. The strength of the self perception is a function of the relative amount of prior reinforcement. Perceptions that are consistently reinforced become strong and lead to a strong self concept. When feedback is lacking or inconsistent, the result is a relatively weak self concept. In other words, whether the self concept is perceived to be either high or low on any trait, competency or value, it is the consistency of the feedback which determines the strength of these perceptions. The weaker the self concept, the greater the need for either task or social feedback, and thus the stronger the self concept-based motivation.

Now that we have shown how motivation can be explained by utilizing the construct of the self concept, we need to discuss how organizational systems designed to induce motivation are related to such a construct.

MANAGERIAL IMPLICATIONS

Inducement systems are those design aspects of an organization which act to energize, direct, or sustain behaviour within the organization. The most commonly studied inducements systems are the reward, task, managerial, and social inducement systems. The reward system involves the design and implementation of formal reward systems in the organization, such as the compensation system and the promotional system. The task inducement system is involved with the motivational aspects of job and task design. The managerial inducement system derives its motivational properties from aspects of leadership style. Finally, the motivational impact of the work group or the organization as a social system defines the social inducement system.

The Reward Inducement System: The impact of reward systems on motivation has been analyzed mainly from a cognitive /instrumental perspective. The motivational properties of pay systems have thus been tied to the expectation that increased effort will lead to greater pay and the instrumental value of pay to the individual. Thus, instrumental motivation is the primary source of motivation that the reward system attempts to induce. From a self concept perspective, pay provides a very potent form of social feedback. It tends to reinforce one's perception of competencies and provides an important source of status. Therefore, maintenance of the external self concept is an alternative source of motivation induced by the reward system. For example, a pay raise may be a form of pure instrumental motivation, or it may provide the basis upon which the individual's self perceptions are reinforced or enhanced.

Task Inducement System: The task design literature points to autonomy, task significance, feedback, task identity, and skill variety as attributes of the task that impact motivation. These authors claim that work redesign provides a strategy for enhancing internal work motivation (i.e., the individual does the work because it interests or challenges him/her). In terms of the self concept, the degree of autonomy would affect an individual's opportunity to attribute outcomes to his/her traits, competencies and values. The significance of a task, and one's contribution to the success of the task, would determine how important the feedback (task for inner-directed and social for other-directed) is to traits, competencies and values that comprise a role-specific identity that may be crucial to an individual's self concept.

Task feedback is a necessary ingredient in reinforcement or affirmation of self perception, and one's ability to identify with a task would affect how important that feedback is to an individual's self concept. Skill variety would provide information regarding a number of traits, competencies and values that comprise different role specific identities. Goal internalization is the motivating source when the successful completion of a task helps fulfill important organizational goals that the individual has internalized into his/her own value system. Therefore, the task system induces motivation from all four of these sources (i.e., intrinsic process, internal and external self concept, and goal internalization) in significant ways.

The Managerial Inducement System: This inducement system also energizes, directs, and sustains behaviour through a number of sources. Transactional leadership style is based on exchange relationships and is best utilized with individuals who are primarily instrumentally motivated. Socio-emotional leadership style provides an important source of social feedback, and is especially effective with other-directed individuals. Task leadership style provides inner-directed individuals with important task feedback regarding traits, competencies, and values. Leadership style, in terms of conditional /unconditional feedback, impacts one's self perception as well as one's self esteem. It is affected by the employee's ability to attribute task results to him/herself, depending on whether the leader is autocratic or participative. Lastly, transformational leadership style motivates by appealing to values and interests of the organization that have been internalized by the employees.

Social Inducement System: Under this inducement system, instrumentally-motivated individuals respond to norms and sanctions enforced by the work group or organization. These norms and sanctions provide both rewards and punishments that direct and sustain behaviour. With regard to the self concept, individuals are motivated to demonstrate the traits, competencies, and values which are important to the work group. Thus, the social system provides the social feedback regarding one's level of these attributes.

3

TYPES OF MOTIVATION

In psychology, motivation is the driving force (desire) behind all actions of an organism. Motivation is based on emotions, specifically, on the search for positive emotional experiences and the avoidance of negative ones, where positive and negative are defined by the individual brain state, not by social norms: a person may be driven to self-injury or violence because their brain is conditioned to create a positive response to these actions. Following are the types of motivation

TISSUE NEEDS

The easiest kinds of motivation to analyse, at least superficially, are those based upon obvious physiological needs. These include hunger, thirst, and escape from pain. The analysis of the processes underlying such motivations can make use of research on animals, in ethology, comparative psychology, and physiological psychology, and the hormonal and brain processes involved in them seem to have much in common at least across all mammals and probably across all vertebrates.

However in humans even these basic motivations are modified and mediated through social and cultural influences of various kinds: for example no analysis of hunger in humans could ignore the issues of eating disorders such as anorexia nervosa and obesity, for which the parallels in other animals are unclear. Even in animals, it is clear that the earlier homeostatic "depletion-repletion" models of such motivations are no longer adequate, since many animals feed on a precautionary rather than a reactive basis, most obviously when preparing for hibernation.

OTHER BIOLOGICAL MOTIVATIONS

At the next level are motivations that have an obvious biological basis but are not required for the immediate survival of the organism. These include the powerful motivations for sex, parental care and aggression: again, the physiological bases of these are similar in humans and other animals, but the social complexities are greater in humans. In these areas insights from behavioural ecology and sociobiology have offered new analyses of both animal and human behaviour in the last decades of the twentieth century, though the extension of sociobiological analyses to humans remains highly controversial.

Perhaps similar, but perhaps at a rather different level, is the motivation for new stimulation - variously called exploration, curiosity, or arousal-seeking. A crucial issue in the analysis of such motivations is whether they have a homeostatic component, so that they build up over time if not discharged; this idea was a key component of early twentieth century analyses of sex and aggression by, for example, Freud and Konrad Lorenz, and is a feature of much popular psychology of motivation. The more informed biological analyses of recent decades, however, imply that such motivations are situational, arising when they are (or seem to be) needed to ensure an animal's fitness, and subsiding without consequences when the occasion for them passes.

SECONDARY GOALS

These important biological needs tend to generate more powerful emotions and thus more powerful motivation than secondary goals. This is described in models like Abraham

Maslow's hierarchy of needs. A distinction can also be made between direct and indirect motivation: In direct motivation, the action satisfies the need, in indirect motivation, the action satisfies an intermediate goal, which can in turn lead to the satisfaction of a need. In work environments, money is typically viewed as a powerful indirect motivation, whereas job satisfaction and a pleasant social environment are more direct motivations. However, this example highlights well that an indirect motivational factor (money) towards an important goal (having food, clothes etc.) may well be more powerful than the direct motivation provided by an enjoyable workplace.

COERCION

The most obvious form of motivation is coercion, where the avoidance of pain or other negative consequences has an immediate effect. When such coercion is permanent, it is considered slavery. While coercion is considered morally reprehensible in many philosophies, it is widely practiced on prisoners or in the form of conscription. Critics of modern capitalism charge that without social safety networks, wage slavery is inevitable. Successful coercion naturally takes priority over other types of motivation.

SELF CONTROL

The self-control of motivation is increasingly understood as a subset of emotional intelligence; a person may be highly intelligent according to a more conservative definition (as measured by many intelligence tests), yet unmotivated to dedicate this intelligence to certain tasks. Victor Vroom's "expectancy theory" provides an account of when people will decide whether to exert self control to pursue a particular goal. Self control is often contrasted with automatic processes of stimulus-response, as in the behaviorist's paradigm of B.F. Skinner.

CONTROLLING MOTIVATION

The control of motivation is only understood to a limited extent. There are many different approaches of motivation training, but many of these are considered pseudoscientific by critics. To understand how to control motivation it is first necessary to understand why many people lack motivation.

In recent years, non-work related activities like Internet surfing have become an increasing concern for employers in industrialized nations. Some companies have used prohibitive tactics to counter this perceived threat, others try to define certain limits, and many merely take action in extreme cases. Even for home users, Internet addiction is increasingly perceived as a risk. Similar concerns accompany the use of video games and television. It is true that for many people, these activities have reached the point of psychological addiction.

This can be explained with a positive feedback loop. The aforementioned activities can generate quick, positive emotional responses of different types — the humor of sitcoms, the ersatz family of soap operas, the endorphine release from action movies and video games, or the curiosity satisfied by visiting news sites. It is known that connections in the human brain's neural network are intensified by repeated activity, which means that it is often easier to continue to do what one is doing than to do something else. This is how a daily habit can, over time, turn into a psychological addiction that is hard to break.

The key question for motivation is then: Which activities generate a positive emotional response, and which ones do not? The answers to this question are increasingly explored by neuropsychology. It is known that, for most people, activities that involve powerful audiovisual input have a stronger emotional effect. Purely text-based information, on the other hand, is usually not very motivating. This seems intuitive given the fact that reading is a trained higher cortical skill, whereas large brain areals are congenitally devoted to processing audiovisual input. For this class of information, there are simply more connections from the processing areals of the brain's cortex to the lower emotional centers of the limbic system. It therefore seems logical to assume that motivation can be created easier through multimedia input.

Since humans are social animals, it also appears natural that social connections play a crucial role in motivation. Not much is known about the way the human brain deals with social relationships, but for the sake of the argument, it can be assumed that social connections are merely very powerful, emotionally encoded memories connected to others. An idea which is connected to these memories thus triggers the emotions. It follows logically, then, that negative social relationships are likely to decrease motivation, and that intrinsic desire to act has to be substituted within these relationships with coercion. For teachers and managers alike, it then seems desirable to maintain such positive relationships in order to provide a motivating atmosphere — however, personal reasons may stand in the way of this goal. This is why many motivation control programs try to teach managers to find outlets for their personal feelings other than their employees.

Organization

Besides the very direct approaches to motivation, beginning in early life, there are solutions which are more abstract but perhaps nevertheless more practical for self-motivation. It is usually suggested that it is critical to maintain a list of tasks, with a distinction between those which are completed and those which are not, thereby moving some of the required motivation for their completion from the tasks themselves into a "meta-task", namely the processing of the tasks in the task list, which can become a routine. The viewing of the list of completed tasks may also be considered motivating, as it can create a satisfying sense of accomplishment.

Most electronic to-do lists have this basic functionality, although the distinction between completed and non-completed tasks is not always clear (completed tasks are sometimes simply deleted, instead of kept in a separate list).

Other forms of information organization may also be motivational, such as the use of mindmaps to organize one's ideas, and thereby "train" the neural network that is the human brain to focus on the given task. More simpler forms of idea notation such as simple bullet-point style lists may also be sufficient, or even more useful to less visually oriented persons.

One interesting aspect that has been somewhat neglected by sociology is the addictive nature of role playing games, which work with a system of experience points and "levels" to motivate the player to keep going; when he has gained enough points, he can advance to the next level, thereby getting new abilities and a higher status in the community, if any. While many electronic motivation systems have a basic concept of priorities, few explore the possibility of using actual scores as a motivational factor. However, some online communities that have nothing to do with gaming use similar systems; notably, the Everything 2 collaborative writing community employs a complex voting/experience system. Perhaps such systems can also be used on a smaller scale.

Drugs

Some authors, especially in the transhumanist movement, have suggested the use of "smart drugs", also known as nootropics, as "motivation-enhancers". The effects of many of these drugs on the brain are not well understood, and their legal status often makes open experimentation difficult. It is a fact that some of history's most productive artists have also been drug users, although it is not clear whether this correlation is also of a causative nature.

MOTIVATION IN INSTRUCTIONAL DESIGN

Developing life-long learners who are intrinsically motivated, display intellectual curiosity, find learning enjoyable, and continue seeking knowledge after their formal instruction has ended has always been a major goal of education. Early motivational research was conducted primarily in the workplace, and centered on ways to motivate industrial workers to work harder, faster, and better.

More recent motivational research focuses on the identification of effective techniques for enhancing instructional design, improving classroom management, and meeting the needs of diverse student populations. Learning-motivation researchers are applying some of the same theories and concepts found to be effective in industry to the development of motivational models that enhance the teaching-learning environment. One such model is the ARCS Model of Motivational Design developed by John M. Keller of Florida State University. ARCS is a systematic model for designing motivating instruction.

The ARCS Model of Motivational Design

The ARCS Model of Motivational Design is a well-known and widely applied model of instructional design. Simple, yet powerful, the ARCS Model is rooted in a number of motivational theories and concepts, most notably expectancy-value theory.

In expectancy-value theory, "effort" is identified as the major measurable motivational outcome. For "effort" to occur, two necessary prerequisites are specified: (1) the person must value the task and (2) the person must believe he or she can succeed at the task. Therefore, in an instructional situation, the learning task needs to be presented in a way that is engaging and meaningful to the student, and in a way that promotes positive expectations for the successful achievement of learning objectives.

The ARCS Model identifies four essential strategy components for motivating instruction:

- [A]ttention strategies for arousing and sustaining curiosity and interest;
- [R]elevance strategies that link to learners' needs, interests, and motives;
- [C]onfidence strategies that help students develop a positive expectation for successful achievement; and
- [S]atisfaction strategies that provide extrinsic and intrinsic reinforcement for effort.

Keller breaks each of the four ARCS components down into three strategy sub-components. The strategy sub-components and instructionally relevant examples are shown below.

Attention

- *Perceptual Arousal*: provide novelty, surprise, incongruity or uncertainty. Ex. The teacher places a sealed box covered with question marks on a table in front of the class.
- *Inquiry Arousal*: stimulate curiosity by posing questions or problems to solve. Ex. The teacher presents a scenario of a problem situation and asks the class to brainstorm possible solutions based on what they have learned in the lesson.
- *Variability*: incorporate a range of methods and media to meet students' varying needs. Ex. After displaying and reviewing each step in the process on the overhead projector, the teacher divides the class into teams and assigns each team a set of practice problems.

Relevance

- *Goal Orientation*: present the objectives and useful purpose of the instruction and specific methods for successful achievement. Ex. The teacher explains the objectives of the lesson.
- *Motive Matching*: match objectives to student needs and motives. Ex. The teacher allows the students to present

their projects in writing or orally to accommodate different learning needs and styles.

— *Familiarity*: present content in ways that are understandable and that are related to the learners' experience and values. Ex. The teacher asks the students to provide examples from their own experiences for the concept presented in class.

Confidence

— *Learning Requirements*: inform students about learning and performance requirements and assessment criteria. Ex. The teacher provides students with a list of assessment criteria for their research projects and circulates examples of exemplary projects from past years.

— *Success Opportunities*: provide challenging and meaningful opportunities for successful learning. Ex. The teacher allows the students to practice extracting and summarizing information from various sources and then provides feedback before the students begin their research projects.

— *Personal Responsibility*: link learning success to students' personal effort and ability. Ex. The teacher provides written feedback on the quality of the students' performance and acknowledges the students' dedication and hard work.

Satisfaction

— *Intrinsic Reinforcement*: encourage and support intrinsic enjoyment of the learning experience. Ex. The teacher invites former students to provide testimonials on how learning these skills helped them with subsequent homework and class projects.

— *Extrinsic Rewards*: provide positive reinforcement and motivational feedback. Ex. The teacher awards certificates to students as they master the complete set of skills.

— *Equity*: maintain consistent standards and consequences for success. Ex. After the term project has been completed, the teacher provides evaluative feedback using the criteria described in class.

Motivation Assessment Instruments

Since the ARCS Model was introduced in the early 1980's, several instruments have been developed for assessing the motivational quality of instructional situations. The Instructional Materials Motivation Survey (IMMS) asks students to rate 36 ARCS-related statements in relation to the instructional materials they have just used. Some examples are:

— "These materials are eye-catching." (Attention)

— "It is clear to me how the content of this material is related to things I already know." (Relevance)

— "As I worked on this lesson, I was confident that I could learn the content." (Confidence)

— "Completing the exercises in this lesson gave me a satisfying feeling of accomplishment." (Satisfaction)

Keller and Keller developed the Motivational Delivery Checklist, a 47-item ARCS-based instrument for evaluating the motivational characteristics of an instructor's classroom delivery. Examples of items related to each ARCS component are:

— "Uses questions to pose problems or paradoxes." (Attention)

— "Uses language and terminology appropriate to learners and their context." (Relevance)

— "Provides feedback on performance promptly." (Confidence)

— "Makes statements giving recognition and credit to learners as appropriate." (Satisfaction)

The Website Motivational Analysis Checklist (WebMAC) is an instrument used for designing and assessing the motivational quality of World Wide Web sites. WebMAC builds on Keller's work, Taylor's Value-Added Model, and the research on relevance and information retrieval. Still in development and testing, WebMAC identifies 60 items that are categorized according to four general characteristics: Engaging, Meaningful, Organized, and Enjoyable.

The ARCS Model of Motivational Design is an easy-to-apply, heuristic approach to increasing the motivational appeal of instruction. ARCS provides a useful framework for both the design and improvement of the motivational quality of a range of informational entities—from classroom instruction to Internet resources—and increases the likelihood that these entities will be used and enjoyed.

SCHOOL LEADERSHIP AND STUDENT MOTIVATION

Much of the recent research on student motivation has rightly centered on the classroom, where the majority of learning takes place and where students are most likely to acquire a strong motivation to gain new knowledge. Making the classroom a place that naturally motivates students to learn is much easier when students and teachers function in an atmosphere where academic success and the motivation to learn are expected and rewarded. Such an atmosphere, especially when motivation to learn evolves into academic achievement, is a chief characteristic of an effective school.

How Can School Leaders Generate Student Motivation?

An environment that nurtures educational motivation can be cultivated in the home, in the classroom, or throughout an entire school. One of the most effective avenues for engendering student motivation is a school's culture. According to Deal, school culture can be embodied and transformed through channels such as shared values, heroes, rituals, ceremonies, stories, and cultural networks.

Davis suggests using a wide variety of activities and symbols to communicate motivational goals. "Visible symbols," he says, "illustrate and confirm what is considered to be important in the school." He suggests using "school newsletters, statements of goals, behaviour codes, rituals, symbols, and legends" to "convey messages of what the school really values." Staging academic awards assemblies, awarding trophies for academic success and displaying them in trophy cases, scheduling motivational speakers, and publicizing students' success can help them see that the desire to be successful academically is recognized and appreciated.

Klug notes that school leaders can influence levels of motivation by "shaping the school's instructional climate," which in turn shapes "the attitudes of teachers, students, parents, and the community at large toward education." By effectively managing this aspect of a school's culture, principals can "increase both student and teacher motivation and indirectly impact learning gains," Klug says.

Can School Restructuring Plans be used To increase student motivation?

School administrators can take advantage of times of educational change by including strategies for increasing student motivation. Acknowledging that school restructuring is inevitable, Maehr challenges school leaders to ensure that "motivation and the investment in learning of students will be enhanced" as a result of school reform. School leaders have seldom "considered motivation vis-a-vis the current restructuring movement," he says, "and few have considered that the school as an entity in its own right, may have effects that supersede those of individual classrooms and the acts of individual teachers."

A positive "psychological environment" strongly influences student motivation, says Maehr. School leaders can create this type of environment by establishing policies and programs that:

— stress goal setting and self-regulation/management

— offer students choices in instructional settings

— reward students for attaining "personal best" goals
— foster teamwork through group learning and problem-solving experiences
— replace social comparisons of achievement with self-assessment and evaluation techniques
— teach time management skills and offer self-paced instruction when possible

A School's organizational structure influence levels of Student Motivation

School structures sometimes perpetuate feelings of low self-worth and low levels of motivation among students. "Teachers and parents worry that [students] are unmotivated," Raffini says. "In reality, they are highly motivated to protect their sense of self-worth." He suggests using individual goal-setting structures, outcome-based instruction and evaluation, attribution retraining, and cooperative learning activities to remove motivational barriers and redirect student behaviour away from failure-avoiding activities in academic settings. Raffini describes how these four strategies can aid in promoting the rediscovery of an interest in learning:

— Individual goal-setting structures allow students to define their own criteria for success.
— Outcome-based instruction and evaluation make it possible for slower students to experience success without having to compete with faster students.
— Attribution retraining can help apathetic students view failure as a lack of effort rather than a lack of ability.
— Cooperative learning activities help students realize that personal effort can contribute to group as well as individual goals.

Several other researchers have criticized current instructional practices that sometimes hinder the development of motivation. Representative of these critics are Stipek and Eccles, Midgeley, and Adler. Stipek makes a strong case for strengthening the degree of intrinsic motivation students feel for learning. While she does not argue for the complete elimination of extrinsic reward systems, she believes that "there are many benefits to maximizing intrinsic motivation and many ways to foster it." Challenging but fair task assignments, the use of positive classroom language, mastery-based evaluation systems, and cooperative learning structures are among the methods she suggests.

Eccles, Midgeley, and Adler argue that motivation would increase if students were asked to assume "greater autonomy and control over their lives and learning" as they proceed through higher grade levels. They note that this process rarely takes place in most schools and recommend that school leaders create an "environment that would facilitate task involvement rather than ego involvement, particularly as children enter early adolescence."

Does A School Leader's Motivation To Succeed Influence student motivation?

The work of Leithwood and Montgomery is especially helpful in understanding the connections between a school administrator's motivation and the level of motivation that exists among students.

According to Leithwood and Montgomery, school administrators progress through a series of stages as they become more effective. At their highest level of effectiveness, they come to understand that "people are normally motivated to engage in behaviours which they believe will contribute to goal achievement. The strength of one's motivation to act depends on the importance attached to the goal in question and one's judgment about its achievability. Motivational strength also depends on one's judgment about how successful a particular behaviour will be in moving toward goal achievement."

Personal motivation on the part of the principal can translate into motivation among students and staff through the functioning of goals, according to Leithwood and Montgomery. "Personally valued goals," they say, "are a central element in the principal's motivational structure—a stimulus for action."

Establishing, communicating, and creating consensus around goals related to motivation and educational achievement can be a central feature of a school leader's own value system.

What Else Can School Leaders Do?

The complex array of problems that contribute to low levels of student motivation makes it impossible to devise a single, programmatic approach that will suddenly turn poorly motivated students into young people hungry for knowledge. Engendering student motivation is an ongoing process that requires creativity and energy. Grossnickle provides useful charts and inventories for monitoring motivation levels and lists many helpful ideas for promoting positive attitudes about motivation.

Here are a few other steps school leaders can take to improve student motivation at the school level:

— Analyze the ways that motivation operates in your own life and develop a clear way of communicating it to teachers and students.

— Seek ways to demonstrate how motivation plays an important role in noneducational settings, such as in sports and in the workplace.

— Show students that success is important. Recognize the variety of ways that students can succeed. Reward success in all its forms.

— Develop or participate in inservice programs that focus on motivation.

— Involve parents in discussing the issue of motivation and give them guidance in fostering it in their children.

— Demonstrate through your own actions that learning is a lifelong process that can be pleasurable for its own sake.

MOTIVATION AND TRANSFER IN LANGUAGE LEARNING

Transfer and motivation play important roles in learning. Transfer, the application of prior knowledge to new learning situations, is often seen as a learning goal, and thus the extent to which transfer occurs is a measure of learning success. Motivation, defined as the impetus to create and sustain intentions and goal-seeking acts, is important because it determines the extent of the learner's active involvement and attitude toward learning.

The Relationship Between transfer and motivation

Research suggests that transfer and motivation are mutually supportive in creating an optimal learning environment. If the learner perceives what he is learning to be relevant and transferable to other situations, he will find learning meaningful, and his motivation to acquire the skill or knowledge will increase. Similarly, for transfer to take place, the learner must be motivated to do two things. First, he must be able to recognize opportunities for transfer; second, he needs to possess the motivation to take advantage of these opportunities.

The challenge of teaching is thus to simultaneously enhance transfer and motivation so that they both support learning. To do this, teachers need to first understand the nature of transfer and the nature of motivation.

The Nature of Transfer

Teachers often ask themselves "What is in the learning situation that needs to be transferred?" The answer may be one or more of the following: content or conceptual knowledge, strategic or procedural knowledge, and appropriate dispositions for learning.

Proponents for the teaching of content knowledge over strategic knowledge argue that learners who have mastered the content knowledge of a particular domain are fully capable of displaying sophisticated use of effective strategies in new situations, including those strategies never explicitly taught. They claim that without requisite domain-specific knowledge, general strategies have a weak effect on enhancing performance in most tasks. At the same time, a common argument for emphasizing the teaching of strategic knowledge is that if one can identify and teach the general skills (e.g., metacognitive and problem-solving skills) that are applicable to a broad range of tasks, it is easier then to facilitate transfer of learning. Although proponents from the two camps disagree on the question of what exactly is transferred, they concur that positive dispositions toward learning are vital to learner success. These dispositions include traits like high motivation, risk-taking attitudes, mindfulness or attentiveness, and a sense of responsibility for learning.

Notions of Instrumental and Integrative Motivation

Gardner and Lambert introduced the notions of instrumental and integrative motivation. In the context of language learning, instrumental motivation refers to the learner's desire to learn a language for utilitarian purposes, whereas integrative motivation refers to the desire to learn a language to integrate successfully into the target language community. In later research studies, Crookes and Schmidt, and Gardner and Tremblay explored four other motivational orientations: (a) reason for learning, (b) desire to attain the learning goal, (c) positive attitude toward the learning situation, and (d) effortful behaviour.

Many theorists and researchers have found that it is important to recognize the construct of motivation not as a single entity but as a multi-factorial one. Oxford and Shearin analyzed a total of 12 motivational theories or models, including those from socio-psychology, cognitive development, and socio-cultural psychology, and identified six factors that impact motivation in language learning:

- attitudes (i.e., sentiments toward the learning community and the target language)
- beliefs about self (i.e., expectancies about one's attitudes to succeed, self-efficacy, and anxiety)
- goals (perceived clarity and relevance of learning goals as reasons for learning)
- involvement (i.e., extent to which the learner actively and consciously participates in the language learning process)
- environmental support (i.e., extent of teacher and peer support, and the integration of cultural and outside-of-class support into learning experience)
- personal attributes (i.e., aptitude, age, sex, and previous language learning experience).

Instructional Strategies To Enhance Student Motivation and Learning Transfer

Some research studies have shown that language acquisition is the result of an interplay between cognitive mechanism and environmental conditions. Understanding and creating optimal language learning environments thus becomes a primary concern of the language teacher. Teachers can observe circumstances under which learners acquire language and can make adjustments toward creating optimal learning conditions. In designing learning activities, the language teacher should remember that because language learning focuses on both the accuracy and appropriateness of application in various contexts of use, learners must be given opportunities to participate as language users in multiple contexts. These opportunities will result in learners' heightened motivation and awareness of the intricacies of language use.

Some teaching strategies that can be used to foster motivation and provide better transfer opportunities of language skills include the following:

— Encourage learners to take ownership in learning.

Have learners take ownership of the learning assignment by letting them identify and decide for themselves relevant learning goals. This will motivate them to apply what they have learned to attain these learning goals.

— Promote intentional cognition or mindfulness to learning in various contexts.

Learners must be able to practice language in multiple contexts in order to bridge domains and foster active abstraction of concepts learned. This will help learners recognize the relevance and transferability of different learning skills or knowledge.

— Increase authenticity of learning tasks and goals.

Learners should recognize a real need to accomplish learning goals that are relevant and holistic (rather than task-specific). This prepares them for the complexities of real-world tasks that require them to use language skills and knowledge that have to be continually transferred.

Learner anxiety and other negative feelings can be stumbling blocks to learners becoming cognizant of learning and transfer opportunities. Thus, providing our learners with the motivation to learn is one of the best steps we can take to facilitate learning success. This is best conveyed by Bruner: "The best way to create interest in a subject is to render it worth knowing, which means to make the knowledge gained usable in one's thinking beyond the situation in which learning has occurred."

STUDENT MOTIVATION TO LEARN

Infants and young children appear to be propelled by curiosity, driven by an intense need to explore, interact with, and make sense of their environment. As one author puts it, "Rarely does one hear parents complain that their pre-schooler is 'unmotivated' ".

Unfortunately, as children grow, their passion for learning frequently seems to shrink. Learning often becomes associated with drudgery instead of delight. A large number of students—more than one in four—leave school before graduating. Many more are physically present in the classroom but largely mentally absent; they fail to invest themselves fully in the experience of learning.

Awareness of how students' attitudes and beliefs about learning develop and what facilitates learning for its own sake can assist educators in reducing student apathy.

STUDENT MOTIVATION

Student motivation naturally has to do with students' desire to participate in the learning process. But it also concerns the reasons or goals that underlie their involvement or noninvolvement in academic activities. Although students may be equally motivated to perform a task, the sources of their motivation may differ.

A student who is INTRINSICALLY motivated undertakes an activity "for its own sake, for the enjoyment it provides, the learning it permits, or the feelings of accomplishment it evokes". An EXTRINSICALLY motivated student performs "IN ORDER TO obtain some reward or avoid some punishment external to the activity itself," such as grades, stickers, or teacher approval (Lepper).

The term motivation to learn has a slightly different meaning. It is defined by one author as "the meaningfulness, value, and benefits of academic tasks to the learner—regardless of whether or not they are intrinsically interesting". Another notes that motivation to learn is characterized by long-term, quality involvement in learning and commitment to the process of learning.

Factors for Decelopment of Student's Motivation

According to Jere Brophy, motivation to learn is a competence acquired "through general experience but stimulated most directly through modeling, communication of expectations, and direct instruction or socialization by significant others (especially parents and teachers)."

Children's home environment shapes the initial constellation of attitudes they develop toward learning. When parents nurture their children's natural curiosity about the world by welcoming their questions, encouraging exploration, and familiarizing them with resources that can enlarge their world, they are giving their children the message that learning is worthwhile and frequently fun and satisfying.

When children are raised in a home that nurtures a sense of self-worth, competence, autonomy, and self-efficacy, they will be more apt to accept the risks inherent in learning. Conversely, when children do not view themselves as basically competent and able, their freedom to engage in academically challenging pursuits and capacity to tolerate and cope with failure are greatly diminished.

Once children start school, they begin forming beliefs about their school-related successes and failures. The sources to which children attribute their successes (commonly effort, ability, luck, or level of task difficulty) and failures (often lack of ability or lack of effort) have important implications for how they approach and cope with learning situations.

The beliefs teachers themselves have about teaching and learning and the nature of the expectations they hold for students also exert a powerful influence (Raffini). As Deborah Stipek notes, "To a very large degree, students expect to learn if their teachers expect them to learn." Schoolwide goals, policies, and procedures also interact with classroom climate and practices to affirm or alter students' increasingly complex learning-related attitudes and beliefs.

And developmental changes comprise one more strand of the motivational web. For example, although young children tend to maintain high expectations for success even in the face of repeated failure, older students do not. And although younger children tend to see effort as uniformly positive, older children view it as a "double-edged sword" (Ames). To them, failure following high effort appears to carry more negative implications—especially for their self-concept of ability—than failure that results from minimal or no effort.

Advantages of Intrinsic Motivation

Does it really matter whether students are primarily intrinsically or extrinsically oriented toward learning? A growing body of evidence suggests that it does.

When intrinsically motivated, students tend to employ strategies that demand more effort and that enable them to process information more deeply (Lepper).

J. Condry and J. Chambers found that when students were confronted with complex intellectual tasks, those with an intrinsic orientation used more logical information-gathering and decision-making strategies than did students who were extrinsically oriented.

Students with an intrinsic orientation also tend to prefer tasks that are moderately challenging, whereas extrinsically oriented students gravitate toward tasks that are low in degree of difficulty. Extrinsically oriented students are inclined to put forth the minimal amount of effort necessary to get the maximal reward (Lepper).

Although every educational activity cannot, and perhaps should not, be intrinsically motivating, these findings suggest that when teachers can capitalize on existing intrinsic motivation, there are several potential benefits.

How can Motivation to Learn be Fostered on the School Setting?

Although students' motivational histories accompany them into each new classroom setting, it is essential for teachers to view themselves as "ACTIVE SOCIALIZATION AGENTS capable of stimulating...student motivation to learn".

Classroom climate is important. If students experience the classroom as a caring, supportive place where there is a sense of belonging and everyone is valued and respected, they will tend to participate more fully in the process of learning.

Various task dimensions can also foster motivation to learn. Ideally, tasks should be challenging but achievable. Relevance also promotes motivation, as does "contextualizing" learning, that is, helping students to see how skills can be applied in the real world (Lepper). Tasks that involve "a moderate amount of discrepancy or incongruity" are beneficial because they stimulate students' curiosity, an intrinsic motivator (Lepper).

In addition, defining tasks in terms of specific, short-term goals can assist students to associate effort with success (Stipek). Verbally noting the purposes of specific tasks when introducing them to students is also beneficial.

Extrinsic rewards, on the other hand, should be used with caution, for they have the potential for decreasing existing intrinsic motivation.

What takes place in the classroom is critical, but "the classroom is not an island". Depending on their degree of congruence with classroom goals and practices, schoolwide goals either dilute or enhance classroom efforts. To support motivation to learn, school-level policies and practices should stress "learning, task mastery, and effort" (Maehr and Midgley) rather than relative performance and competition.

What can be Done to Help Unmotivated Students?

A first step is for educators to recognize that even when students use strategies that are ultimately self-defeating (such as withholding effort, cheating, procrastination, and so forth), their goal is actually to protect their sense of self-worth (Raffini).

A process called ATTRIBUTION RETRAINING, which involves modeling, socialization, and practice exercises, is sometimes used with discouraged students. The goals of attribution retraining are to help students to (1) concentrate on the tasks rather than becoming distracted by fear of failure; (2) respond to frustration by retracing their steps to find mistakes or figuring out alternative ways of approaching a problem instead of giving up; and (3) attribute their failures to insufficient effort, lack of information, or reliance on ineffective strategies rather than to lack of ability.

Other potentially useful strategies include the following: portray effort as investment rather than risk, portray skill development as incremental and domain-specific, focus on mastery. Because the potential payoff—having students who value learning for its own sake—is priceless, it is crucial for parents, teachers, and school leaders to devote themselves fully to engendering, maintaining, and rekindling students' motivation to learn.

4

Techniques of Increasing Learner Motivation

High motivation and engagement in learning have consistently been linked to reduced dropout rates and increased levels of student success. Yet, keeping students interested in school and motivating them to succeed are challenges that present themselves year after year to even the most seasoned teachers. In fact, numerous studies have shown that student engagement in school drops considerably as students get older. By the time students reach middle school, lack of interest in schoolwork becomes increasingly apparent in more and more students, and by high school, as dropout rates attest, too many students are not sufficiently motivated to succeed in school.

There are many factors that contribute to students' interest and level of engagement in learning, and teachers have little control over many of those factors. However, research has shown that teachers can influence student motivation; that certain practices do work to increase time spent on task; and that there are ways to make assigned work more engaging and more effective for students at all levels.

There are myriad reasons that students become less engaged in learning as they grow older, including influences from both within and outside the school. As Lumsden notes, the earliest influences on children's motivation to learn are parents and others in the home. When students enter school, their level of interest and desire to engage in learning are also heavily influenced by teachers, administrators, the school environment, and their classmates. Although it may sometimes seem that teachers have no control over students' attitudes about learning, researchers confirm that they do. "To a very large degree, students expect to learn if their teachers expect them to learn, " notes Stipek.

Developmental factors and students' perceptions about their own abilities also play into their level of engagement in learning. The older students get, the less likely they are to take risks and engage themselves fully in activities at which they are not sure they will succeed. According to Lumsden, "although young children tend to maintain high expectations for success even in the face of repeated failure, older students do not". To older students, "failure following high effort appears to carry more negative implications — especially for their self-concept of ability — than failure that results from minimal or no effort".

Students' attitudes about their capabilities and their interpretation of success and failure further affect their willingness to engage themselves in learning. For example, students who understand poor performance as a lack of attainable skills, rather than as some innate personal deficiency, are more likely to re-engage themselves in a task and try again. Students whose self-concept is bound up in their history of failure, on the other hand, are less likely to be motivated to learn.

Mac Iver and Reuman add that middle school and high school-age students' level of engagement in school is also highly influenced by peers. As students grow older, their motivation to engage in learning may be influenced by their social group just as much as, if not more than it is by teachers, parents, and other adults. While peer influences can be either positive or negative, it is not uncommon for older students to discourage one another from actively participating in school.

Whether the decrease in student engagement is the result of unmotivated students or of school practices that fail to sufficiently interest and engage all learners, an ample body of research suggests that the situation can be changed.

In general terms, student motivation "refers to a student's willingness, need, desire and compulsion to participate in, and be successful in, the learning process". Skinner and Belmont develop the definition further, noting that students who are motivated to engage in school "select tasks at the border of their competencies, initiate action when given the opportunity, and exert intense effort and concentration in the implementation of learning tasks; they show generally positive emotions during ongoing action, including enthusiasm, optimism, curiosity, and interest". Less motivated or disengaged students, on the other hand, "are passive, do not try hard, and give up easily in the face of challenges".

STRATEGIES FOR INCREASING MOTIVATION

Ample research has demonstrated that school practices can and do affect a student's level of motivation. To be sure, efforts to promote student motivation need not be directed solely at students who have low levels of motivation. All students (and all schools, for that matter) would benefit from higher levels of engagement and motivation to succeed. Following are suggestions for both teachers and administrators seeking to increase students' motivation to learn:

At the classroom level:

— *Use extrinsic rewards sparingly*: If extrinsic motivators are to be used, they are most effective when rewards are closely related to the task accomplished. Also, rewards should only be given when they are clearly deserved. Giving a prize for minimally successful work sends the message that minimum effort is acceptable, and the reward then becomes meaningless.

— *Ensure that classroom expectations for performance and behavior are clear and consistent.* Help students understand the criteria for individual assignments by giving them examples of high-, average-, and low-level work and then providing an opportunity to discuss how each piece was evaluated.

— *Make students feel welcome and supported.* Elementary school students in particular need to feel that teachers are involved in their lives. Take time to get to know students, talk to them individually, and "express enjoyment in [your] interactions".

— Respond positively to student questions, and praise students verbally for work well done.

— Work to build quality relationships with students, especially those considered to be at-risk and without other positive adult interaction; this is a critical factor of student engagement that allows children to foster a sense of connection with school.

— *Break large tasks into a series of smaller goals*: Doing so prevents students from becoming overwhelmed and discouraged by lengthy projects.

— *Promote mastery learning.* "When a student completes an assignment that does not meet the expected criteria, give her or him one or more opportunities to tackle the task again, with guidelines on how to achieve the desired result".

— Evaluate student work as soon as possible after project completion, and be sure that feedback is clear and constructive.

— Evaluate students based on the task, not in comparison to other students.

At the school and district levels:

— Make increasing student motivation a priority in school reform and restructuring efforts.

— Create a school culture that emphasizes the importance of academic achievement. Design schoolwide symbols to show students that learning is valuable and that the entire staff is invested in students' success.

— Model and communicate the value of lifelong learning.

— Develop a school climate that recognizes individual differences, encourages creativity, and gives both teachers and students a sense of autonomy. Particularly important is allowing students and teachers to have some degree of control over teaching and learning.

— Support teachers' efforts to increase student motivation, encouraging student-centered learning and outcomes-based instruction. Additionally, recognize teachers' individual learning needs and be supportive of their continuing education and involvement in research.

— Provide and participate in professional development activities that deal with motivation, effective use of homework, and student engagement.

— Finally, develop ways to involve parents. Discuss the issue of motivation with parents, involve them in the school's efforts to increase student engagement, and "give them guidance in fostering [motivation] in their children".

MOTIVATING STUDENTS TO ENGAGE IN CLASS ACTIVITIES

It only makes sense that the more interesting an assignment is, the more likely students are to immerse themselves in the task and stick with it through completion. Even highly motivated students need schoolwork that actively engages them by building on their interests and prior knowledge. But what makes a task more interesting? What causes a student to be more engaged by one project than another? How can teachers design work that will keep students' attention at the same time it draws them more deeply into the process of learning?

Research tells that the teachers who are most successful in engaging students develop activities with students' basic psychological and intellectual needs in mind. In general, students need work that develops their sense of competency, allows them to develop connections with others, gives them some degree of autonomy, and provides opportunities for originality and self-expression. The challenge teachers face, then, is to create a learning environment that attends to all or most of these needs.

Following is a list of suggestions for designing more engaging in-class activities and increasing the amount of time students spend on task.

Ensure course materials relate to students' lives and highlight ways learning can be applied in real-life situations. Schoolwork should be meaningful to students outside the school building, as well as within. Students are more engaged in activities when they can build on prior knowledge and draw clear connections between what they are learning and the world they live in. They also need to feel that "school work is significant. valuable, and worthy of their efforts".

Allow students to have some degree of control over learning. This can be done in any number of ways, from giving students choices between different assignments, to minimizing adult supervision over group projects, to letting students monitor and evaluate their own progress. Anderman & Midgely note that this doesn't mean teachers must relinquish control of the classroom: "Even small opportunities for choice, such as whether to work with a partner or independently" give students a greater sense of autonomy.

Assign challenging but achievable tasks for all students, including at-risk, remedial, and learning disabled students. Tasks that seem impossible easily discourage learners, as do those tasks that are rote and repetitive. Remedial programs that limit students to repetitive basic skills activities actually "prompt students' lack of engagement in their schoolwork and frequently result in limited achievement". Students need to feel successful and that they've earned success.

Arouse students' curiosity about the topic being studied. Strong, Silver, and Robinson suggest using the "mystery" approach, in which students are presented with fragmentary or contradictory information about a subject and are then asked to examine available evidence to develop their own hypotheses. This kind of activity also builds on students' needs for competence and autonomy, giving students an opportunity to direct inquiry and "discover for themselves."

Design projects that allow students to share new knowledge with others. Strong, Silver & Robinson observe that when students do assignments that only the teacher will read, they are entering into a nonreciprocal relationship. More often than not, the teacher already knows and has no real need for the information the student is providing him or her. Projects are more engaging when students share what they are learning in reciprocal relationships, as in collaborative projects where each student's knowledge is needed by others in the group to complete an assignment.

It is also important to note that, in addition to instructional practice, certain elements of the classroom environment, such as seating arrangements and student behavior, will influence how long students remain on task and engaged in their work. Bonus and Riordan suggest teachers consider the goals of individual activities when determining how to arrange seats in the classroom. In their research into on-task behavior in second- and third-grade classrooms, they found that students remained engaged in learning longer when desks were arranged appropriately for the task at hand: U-shaped arrangements for class discussions, rows for test taking, etc.

Getting the Most Out of Homework

Much of what has been said about making in-class work more engaging can also be said of homework: out-of-class assignments should have a clear purpose, should be relevant to students' lives, and should be at the same time challenging and manageable. Homework carries with it some added complications, though. Not only does successfully engaging in homework depend a great deal on students' home environment, but homework experiences may also have a significant impact on students' long-term attitudes toward school.

In recent years there has been much debate about the value of homework. While some parents and educators firmly believe that assigning homework is an important part of school, others call the practice into question. Some critics of homework observe that not all students go home to a quiet and supportive study environment, and thus have little chance of being successful with out-of-school assignments. Still others point out that homework may contribute significantly to students' negative attitudes toward school, particularly if it is a source of conflict between students and parents, or is linked to punishment and other consequences at school.

Proponents of homework, on the other hand, argue that homework serves a number of purposes and can benefit students when used appropriately. The main purposes generally associated with homework are as follows:

— To give students a chance to "review and practice what they have learned"

— To prepare students for the next day's lesson

— To provide opportunities to identify and learn to use resources, such as the library, the Internet, reference books, and other community resources

— To allow for more in-depth exploration of topics than is possible during class time

— To help students develop time management, study, and organizational skills

As might be expected, the effectiveness of different types of homework varies according to students' age and ability level. Cooper's study found that homework raises achievement "substantially" for high school students, but only about half that for students in the middle grades. Cooper found no effect on academic achievement for students in grades 1-6. This is not to say that homework doesn't benefit younger students in different ways. Other studies have found that homework is most useful for elementary school students when it focuses on developing study habits and organizational skills.

Once you have established a reasonable length of time for students to spend on homework, consider the following list of "best practices" for making homework a more engaging and ultimately more positive learning experience for students.

Expectations. At the beginning of the school year, communicate your expectations for homework to both students and parents. Which days do you collect homework? What are the penalties for late or incomplete homework? How can parents and students reach you if there is a problem?

Consistency. Be as consistent as possible throughout the school year. Getting students accustomed to a regular homework pattern early in the year is helpful to all students, but may be especially important for students with learning disabilities.

Purpose. Make sure the purpose of homework assignments is clear to students. Students and parents alike are less likely to become frustrated when they understand the value and the objectives of an assignment.

Time. Don't underestimate the length of time it will take for students to complete assignments. Include time for gathering supplies and organizing materials in your calculation of how long your students will take to complete an assignment.

Explain. Take time to explain instructions to students, and give them an opportunity to ask questions before the end of class. When possible, give students time to get started on homework assignments in class, so you can be sure they understand what they are being asked to do.

Variety. Provide a variety of homework assignments throughout the school year to prevent homework from becoming boring or monotonous.

Coordinate. Make an effort to coordinate with other teachers, so students aren't overwhelmed with long assignments for several classes all on one night.

Evaluate. Finally, evaluate homework assignments and give students feedback on their work. When assignments are just checked off as completed, students perceive them as meaningless, which leads to frustration and low-quality work.

Developing a Homework Policy

If your school does not already have a homework policy in place, you might discuss this with other teachers and administrators. Homework policies, which function to define a standard set of expectations for and beliefs about homework, can be shared and reviewed with students, parents, and teachers at the beginning of each school year. At minimum, homework policies should define the role of homework in learning at each grade level, and the specific responsibilities of teachers, parents, and students.

While some educators caution that school and districtwide policies for homework can become restrictive, there are advantages to having a shared understanding of how homework is being used to support learning. Homework policies not only help define parents' role in homework, but also ensure that students and parents are informed about teachers' expectations.

Another benefit of homework policies is that they allow teachers to develop a consistent, schoolwide set of expectations for students, which is particularly helpful for students who have several different teachers throughout the day. Developing a homework policy is also a good way for educators to get together, review the research, and explore how homework can best be used to promote achievement and engagement in school.

Getting Parents Involved in Homework

Active parent involvement has been associated with numerous benefits for students, including increasing student motivation and engagement in school. When it comes to homework, though, parent involvement can take many different shapes, not all of which have a positive impact on learning. When working to increase student engagement and motivation, it is important to include parents and discuss ways they can support their children's learning both at school and at home.

First, it is important that parents understand what role teachers expect them to play, especially in terms of homework. What one parent views as helping out, a teacher might perceive as interference or cheating. And what a teacher might take for granted that parents can do-such as signing off on homework or checking spelling words-a parent may not have the skills or the time to follow through on. Clearly, it is important to communicate with parents about how to best help children learn. It is also necessary for educators to be sure their expectations are realistic, given parents' skills and schedules.

It is equally important to be clear with parents about what kinds of involvement are actually beneficial to students. Studies have shown that parents who offer rewards for grades, or who punish students for poor performance, may actually decrease students' motivation to do well. Fear of punishment, anxiety about meeting parents' expectations, and worrying about being compared to siblings not only cause stress for students, but can also detract from their intrinsic motivation and interest in learning. This is not to say that parents shouldn't be invested in how their children are doing in school. Rather, it suggests that there are more productive ways for them to be involved and show their interest in students' progress.

To help children be successful with work at home and at school, parents can:

— *Create a place at home that is conducive to studying*: Good study environments are well-lit and quiet. Although every child's learning style is different, most educators agree that students do best when the television is off and the student is free from distractions.

— *Set aside a specific time for homework each day*: This might involve limiting television-watching or phone calls until homework is finished. Parents should be careful, though, not to pit homework against activities students enjoy, or to create situations in which students rush through their work in order to get back to other activities. Paulu notes that family routines — which include set homework times — have been linked to higher student achievement.

— *Make sure students have all the supplies they need*: Parents should check in with students ahead of time about the kinds of projects they will be doing: It might be tough to find a calculator or a report cover at 9:00 the night before an assignment is due.

— *Be available if students have questions*: Parents can support their children by looking over homework and giving suggestions, but should not do the homework for them.

— *Make an effort to communicate regularly with teachers*: If necessary, parents should ask teachers to clarify their expectations. It is also a good idea to find out ahead of time what kinds of resources — such as tutors or services for second language students — are available to students if they need help.

— *Avoid linking rewards or punishment to school performance*: While it is important for parents to recognize students' achievements, they should avoid external motivators for performance. Instead, parents should emphasize the value of learning and show they appreciate their child's hard work.

ATTITUDE VERSUS APTITUDE

Efforts to evaluate the transition to higher-educational settings have been underway for some time, producing thousands of studies and yielding a considerable knowledge base in the fields of educational psychology and the sociology of education.

In developmental social psychology, there is a long-standing interest in person-context interactions, whereby various types of persons approach and experience the same context differently. Developmental contextualism is a relatively recent model that deals with person-context interactions, theorizing that different types of persons experience different "fits" in a given context. Lerner summarized the components of this model from the field of child and adolescent development as follows:

> Just as a child brings his or her characteristics of individuality to a particular social setting, there are demands placed on the child by virtue of the social and physical components of the setting. These demands may take the form of (a) attitudes, values, or stereotypes that are held by others in the context regarding the person's attributes ...; (b) the attributes (usually behavioural) of others in the context with whom the child must coordinate, or fit, his or her attributes ...for adaptive interactions to exist; or (c) the physical characteristics of a setting ...that require the child to possess certain attributes ...for the most efficient interaction within the setting to occur.

Lerner also noted that "those children whose characteristics match most of the settings within which they exist receive supportive or positive feedback from the contexts and show evidence of the most adaptive behavioural development".

The practical side of the Project on Education and Personal Development pertains to an institutional reconfiguration that has been taking place in Canada (and many other countries) as a result of two governmental policies. One is the policy of accessibility, and the other is fiscal restraint or educational retrenchment.

The policy of accessibility has been justified in part in terms of increasing human capital (educational output), and in part as an effort to democratize education, offering greater opportunity for the bulk of the population to obtain higher-educational credentials (in effect, increasing raw educational input). Two massive expansions of the Canadian system have raised the participation level so that it is second to the United States in terms of worldwide comparisons. In both countries, some 60% of high school graduates now go on to colleges and universities. Some observers are concerned that the unintended consequences of these social experiments in democratization include credentialism (i.e., education inflation in the process of job placement) and increasing rates of graduate underemployment.

Unfortunately, a policy of fiscal restraint has paralleled the accessibility policy. This educational retrenchment has been uneven, however, affecting some programs more than others. Since the mid-1990s, many administrators of undergraduate programs in the liberal arts and social sciences now simply assume a decreasing budget each year. This has meant smaller full-time faculty complements, larger part-time teaching staffs, and sometimes vastly increased class sizes. At the university studied here, it is not uncommon for even less popular courses to fill early, and for some students to be unable to fill their timetables. Even upper-year courses can have 80 students, with no teaching assistants, no essay requirements, and little direct contact with professors.

At other Canadian universities, it is not uncommon for classrooms to overflow with students when courses begin. Understandably, students who find themselves sitting in aisles are at risk for dropping out. At the very least, we should not be surprised to finds signs of disaffection among students attempting to learn under conditions of overcrowding and underfunding. We currently know little about the impact of these policies on individual students, on university learning environments, or on the actual amount of economic and personal return on educational investments. These policies are often evaluated in terms of the sheer quantity of credentials produced, but this is a fallacy if such credentials do not represent some quality that can be used later.

According to Statistics Canada, "almost two-thirds of new jobs between 1991 and 2000 will require at least 13 years of education or training and 45% will require more than 16 years". Yet, for many of these jobs, many of the skills taught in educational settings are not directly used, beyond certain levels of literacy and numeracy. In any event, evaluations of these government policies and labour force practices often use simple educational input-output logics, ignoring what takes place in between, particularly in classrooms and with student-faculty interactions.

A question that has not been addressed by the thousands of evaluation studies of higher education has to do with what becomes of educational input as a result of the accessibility-expansion of the public educational system. For instance, in the current expanded system do the keenest benefit most, or do the brightest? And, in this system, are the brightest also the keenest? Critics of current policies argue that the democratization of education by increasing the quantity of higher-educational participation simply lowers the quality of standards in favour of the admission of mediocre students, diluting net input talent and leaving the brighter students unchallenged. Consequently, less real human capital is being generated than the flood of degrees suggests, and the opportunity for achieving excellence in higher settings is diminished.

THE INTEGRATED PARADIGM OF STUDENT DEVELOPMENT

The integrated paradigm of student development that conceptualized the above issues in terms of educational input, throughput, and output. Figure 1 presents the basic factors constituting this paradigm, but because of its complexity, readers are directed to our previous report for specific details. This paradigm of student development is based on an integration of Lerner's human development theory with Astin's input-environment-output (I-E-O) model of educational development theory. Astin's theory was integrated with Lerner's developmental-contextualism model to specifically investigate the influence of educational settings in mediating inputs and outputs.

As Figure 1 shows, the paradigm is specific about the most general factors we believe are associated with optimal student input, optimal environmental-context throughput, and optimal skills output factors. Optimally, there is a student readiness to benefit and actively engage educational settings; optimally, there is a readiness of educational settings to engage students in bilateral relationships and in doing so to produce goodness of fits; and optimally, there are positive educational outcomes based on reciprocity between student and setting.

Inputs ---- → (T1)	– →Throughputs--→	----→Outputs (T2)
Optimal: Student readiness to benefit and actively engage educational settings	Optimal: Readiness of settings to engage students in bilateral relationships to produce goodness of fits	Optimal: Main and interaction effects showing positive outcomes based on reciprocation between student and setting
I. Student Motivations for Attending University (SMAU) (in empirical order of optimality) (Côté & Levine, 1997) a. Personal and intellectual development (PER) b. Careerism (CAR) c. Humanitarian (HUM) d. Expectation driven (EXP) e. Default (DEF) II. Academic achievement	I. Nurturant Learning Environment Scale (NLES)	I. Human Capital Skills Self-management (MAN) Self-motivation (MOT) Technical (TECH) II. Academic achievement Grades in final year (GPAT2)

and ability
High school grades (GPAHS)

Figure 1. The integrated model of student development.

Source: An integration of Astin's (1991) I-E-O model and Lerner's (1995) developmental contextualism.

With this integrated model, we specified possible bilateral relationships at the juncture of student motivational inputs and learning environment throughputs. We reasoned that if students are motivated to engage actively in the learning process when they enter university, they should be more likely to meet the university environment halfway in bilateral pedagogical relationships, and thereby experience a goodness of fit associated with positive outcomes. The integrated paradigm should thus help researchers understand why different types of students attend universities, what happens while they attend, and how these factors produce various outcomes. And, by examining the environment that mediates inputs and outputs, the paradigm addresses the black box problem that has plagued educational research.

With respect to input factors, we began with the assumption that students' readiness to benefit from what universities have to offer has been affected by prior experiences with their families, earlier educational settings, and the workplace (actual or anticipatory). Thus, the student body makes the transition to the educational marketplace with a variety of forms of preparation with which to make investments in themselves, such as acquiring human capital skills.

Learning environment throughput factors can be similarly conceptualized. Just as all students do not make the transition to universities with the same forms of motivational readiness, university environments (e.g., different faculties) do not all demonstrate the same degree of readiness to nurture student development by helping students cultivate their personal resources. Accordingly, some environments may be more successful than others in producing certain outcomes with throughput mechanisms that meet students halfway in bilateral pedagogical relationships.

In reference to outcomes, Astin noted that in addition to environmental main effects, interaction effects indicate that only certain types of students benefit in a given environment. With the integrated paradigm, we postulated that particular student characteristics may evoke certain responses from other individuals in a given environment. Under certain conditions, this should set up an ongoing reciprocal process with the student triggering an environmental response, which in turn affects his or her subsequent approach to that environment (positively or negatively), triggering further environmental responses.

A reciprocal process such as this is fundamental to the efficacy of the bilateral relationship between student and learning environment. Thus, two students in the same environment may have entirely different experiences of that environment because their attributes and behaviours evoke different environmental responses. For example, one student may have a keen desire to learn, whereas another may not. The former student is more likely to encounter a favourable university environment than is the latter (and rate it as such); so the former is more likely to experience and reap the benefits of a more positive, supportive learning environment-and to ultimately benefit as a result. Thus, the two persons differ in their goodness of fit with a context.

The integrated paradigm of student development constitutes a person-environment interaction model according to Pascarella and Terenzini's classification of theories of student change. In the field of human development, it constitutes a goodness-of-fit model of developmental contextualism as applied to higher-educational settings. In addition, it provides an approach to an issue that has plagued past research, namely, whether "the environment should be defined objectively, as a reality external to the individual, or perceptually, with reality being whatever the individual perceives it to be". The integrated model allows us to address this issue with the postulation that social settings are not neutral to persons within them, and persons are not neutral to the settings within which they interact.

In educational settings, there is a postulated implicit bilateral contract between teacher and student that affects both how a student approaches an environment (a push effect), and how he or she is treated in that environment (a pull effect). If this is true, the goodness-of-fit between a student and a context influences the objective nature of that environment for that person, thereby influencing experiences and perceptions of that environment. In other words, from this perspective there is no one objective structure; the objectivity of the structure varies for each student according to the role the student plays in it.

Accordingly, the perception of the environment is tied to the characteristics of the perceiver in relation to a given environment, and different types of students evoke different responses that shape their perceptions of that environment. Therefore, an important implication of this paradigm for researchers is that they should be looking for both interactions and reciprocal relationships between types of students and types of contexts. We have developed and assessed the following battery of empirical measures that help us assess student motivational input, contextual throughput, and human capital skills output factors.

Motivational Input

The Student Motivations for Attending University (SMAU) Scale has proven to be a reliable tool for measuring five input motivations. The careerist-materialist (CAR) motivation involves seeing the university as a means of gaining money, status, a career, success, and the finer things in life. With the personal-intellectual development (PER) motivation, the emphasis is on personal growth, studying and learning, and understanding the complexities of life and the world.

For the humanitarian (HUM) motivation, the concern is to help the less fortunate, improving the world, and changing the system. With the expectation-driven (EXP) motivation, the student is responding to expectations and pressures from family and friends to attend a university and get a degree. And, with the default (DEF) motivation, students report that they do not really know why they are attending university, except that they believe doing so is better than pursuing other available options.

Contextual Throughput

The Nurturant Learning Environment Scale (NLES) is a unidimensional scale that reliably measures the extent to which throughput learning environments provide a close academic, social, and personal tutelage of students in terms of concrete, day-to-day experiences with faculty members. It is based on Gamson's conceptualization of the normative dimension that can be found in educational settings. This dimension reflects how the role of teaching is approached by a particular department or faculty in terms of the degree to which its teaching philosophy or culture emphasizes a close academic, social, and personal tutelage of students.

Based on common-sense and past research, we reasoned that a nurturant environment should be more facilitative of positive learning outcomes, given its more direct approach to learning. In their extensive review of the literature, Pascarella and Terenzini concluded that students are more often positively affected by their learning environments when "faculty and students share common attitudes and values; where interpersonal exchanges are frequent, friendly, and not rigidly hierarchical; and where there is a departmental esprit de corps".

Skills Output

Finally, we have identified a set of items that reliably measure three facets of human capital skills: self-management, self-motivation, and technical skills. The PER motivation was most strongly and consistently associated with the NLES, suggesting that keener students perceived or received more support from their teachers, signifying a goodness of fit as part of a bilateral relationship with their teachers. The CAR motivation emerged as only moderately related to the NLES, which was surprising given the instrumental nature of this motivation in getting ahead by pursuing a career. We were not surprised to find that the DEF motivation was negatively associated with the NLES, suggesting a badness of fit for students high on the DEF motivation.

However, what truly surprised us in this research was the relative importance of ability and motivation in predicting educational outcomes. A striking finding of our study was that input grade attainment only predicted subsequent grade attainment, not skills acquisition. In fact, our study suggested that type of student motivation and type of environment were actually more important than high school grades in predicting university academic achievement in the settings we studied. The same nonsignificant relationships applied to skills acquisition and grades attained in university. When findings such as these are obtained for an educational setting, they strongly suggest that the most successful are not necessarily the most skilled at what is being certified.

The present research was undertaken to shed more light on the above possibilities, focusing on the role played by aptitude in relation to attitude. In the original PEPD sample, a subsample was willing to submit to more in-depth testing, including a measure of intelligence. In addition to the NLES, two more contextual throughput measures were added to the analysis with the hope of shedding more light on the aptitude/attitude issue. Specifically, the following three research questions were explored:

1. What is the weight of the evidence for which is more important in positive educational outcomes, intelligence or motivation to learn?
2. Are intelligence and the motivation to learn related?

3. Using the above input and throughput variables, can we gain a sense of why intelligence or motivation might be more important in predicting educational outcomes?

The Objective is to increase workplace efficiency by controlling elementary problems with workplace education tools. Workplace education finds efficient ways to get jobs done.

The Goal - The goal in any task is to get the job done. Leadership style controls efficiency, which controls competitive value of product or service, which determines the winner.

Leadership Innovation - Today, fast growing organizations are built on leadership innovation, that is, they are not built by product visionaries but by social visionaries - those who invent entirely new ways of organizing human effort. Southwest Airlines, Inc. is an example.

DEFINITION OF TERMS

Visionary Leadership increases efficiency by moving decision-making responsibility to the frontline. Efficiency is achieved with limited supervision. To make frontline responsibility effective, leadership must give workers opportunity to develop quality decision-making skills and learn to trust them. Wal-Mart stores use visionary leadership.

Standard leadership assumes employees to be robots and do as they are told. This is based on man's natural instinct that only leadership is capable of making quality decisions. This is known as command-and-control leadership. Low efficiency is caused by the disconnect between management and the frontline. Management is busy dealing with problems that affect them while ignoring problems that affect the frontline. Front line problems are only dealt with when they explode into a major problem. K-Mart stores use standard leadership.

Workplace education creates a workforce of quality decision makers. Employees at all levels have the opportunity to discover and develop their unique skills, thereby, inspiring them to become quality decision-makers. The key word is "opportunity." Not everyone will embrace this opportunity, but the few that do will inspire others with positive attitudes. This can only be achieved with visionary leadership.

PRIMARY ELEMENTS

Organization structure controls decision-making responsibility. Visionary leadership allows decision-making responsibility all the way down to the frontline. Standard leadership limits decision making to management.

Priorities - Organization priorities control leadership style.

— When priority is responsibility at the frontline, leadership will seek talent, people he can depend on to complete tasks with limited supervision. The policy will be "do it." The frontline develops quality decision-making skills that are also found in layers of management.

— When the priority is control, leadership will be organized in a way that all decisions must have approval. The policy will be "do not do anything until being told." Layers of management slow the final decision, while lowering efficiency.

Policies - Leadership style is controlled by workplace policies. Leaders will adapt their style to the organization priorities and its goals.

— High efficiency workplaces are based on visionary leadership, where workplace policies authorize decision-making responsibility at the frontline. Limited supervision is needed with worker responsibility.

— Standard leadership is based on man's instinctive desire for control, which is leadership by default. A leader's changing mood controls policy of the moment and no one knows what the priorities are - mood-changing priorities reduce efficiency. Standard leadership requires a high level of supervision.

Elementary problems - Leadership style controls the level of elementary problems, which controls workplace efficiency. Level of elementary problems is controlled, in part, by learning opportunities and leader's personal priority.

— Decision-making responsibility, at all levels, allows minor problems to be solved by those who are first aware of them. Management can stay focused on problems related to the organization goals. As a bonus, employee motivation is high when they feel what they are doing makes a difference.

— A leader's desire for control prevents minor problems from being solved, because no one can make a decision without approval. Leaders' priorities are based on high visibility events. As employees adjust work habits to minor problems, they become accepted as normal. The volume of these problems slowly grows and the workforce slowly becomes less efficient. Management blames workers for their lack of ability to get the job done. Assigning blame without responsibility solves nothing.

Learning opportunity - Quality of worker decisions is controlled by workplace learning opportunities.

— Learning to make quality decisions is the result of worker responsibility, resulting in the development of personal skills. An experienced workforce prevents elementary problems. Continuous learning opportunity is highly motivating-it controls employee inspiration, skill level and quality.

— People, who only follow orders, do not have learning opportunity, do not develop personal skills and do not learn quality decision making. A workforce that is indifferent to the needs of the organization increases elementary problems. Workers learn no more than necessary to their job.

— Achievers - Everyone wants to be an achiever in and out of the workplace. With workplace ambitions, leadership promotes or kills this desire.

— People, who have a burning drive to be an achiever, seek opportunity in organizations that have a reputation of supporting personal ambitions. Their presents inspire coworkers to do the same or simply be proud of their surroundings. Leadership welcomes subordinates more capable than themselves, because their first priority is to get the job done with limited supervision.

— Command-and-control leadership drives away visionary achievers. Should they become employed, they will soon quit or be fired. Leaders do not want their status threatened by ambitious subordinates or someone more capable than themselves, because their first priority is control. As a result, the workforce waits for official decisions and waits for things to happen. A high level of supervision in needed to keep things moving.

Natural talent - Leadership style controls the ability to recognize natural talent. No one knows what their true capabilities are until they are given opportunity and responsibility.

— Where workers have decision-making responsibility, unique skills and natural talent are soon recognized by coworkers and leadership. An employee may discover talent he did not know he had. With discovery, he can search for ways to develop it. Efficiency increases when natural talent is in harmony with assigned tasks.

— Where workers only follow orders-unique skills, natural talent and discovery of capabilities are lost to the company and its employees.

Skill level - The ability and desire to share knowledge with coworkers influences the continuing education level of the workforce, thereby, increasing skill level and the value of their services. Workplace education is dead for people who only follow orders.

Technology - Today's technology is reducing the time it takes to get jobs done. Workplace education is the only way to stay on technology's leading edge. Visionary leadership, not standard, is the only way for the organization to be a leader in its field.

Getting the job done - Projects only have value when the job is completed, until then, it is garbage. Competitive value depends on the efficiency of getting the job done, which is based on keeping elementary problems to a minimum. Efficiency is also a by product of employees' attitude towards their job. Leadership, opportunity and responsibility influence attitude.

ELEMENTS TO CONSIDER

— *Ethical policies* - Ethical policies at the organization's top filter down to the frontline. It is not possible to have unethical policies at the top and enforce ethical policies at the bottom. Leaders' ethical policies become the mindset of the organization. A person with high ethical standards will not stay long in an organization with low ethical standards, they will quit or be fired. A potential whistle blower becomes a threat, yet, this type of person makes an organization efficient. Success of workplace responsibility requires high ethical policies from top to bottom.

— *Exception to the rule* - The military uses command-and-control leadership, yet the troops are highly skilled, motivated and morale is high. This is opposite the statements stated above. The difference - military organizations are team orientated with continuous training. Troops expanding their skills and experiencing capabilities they never dreamed possible, produces a highly motivated and efficient organization. Learning opportunity and responsibility is the key.

— *Hiring a visionary leader* - Very often, an organization realizes it needs to upgrade its leadership. Management can recognize quality in an applicant, but they do not know how to manage them, should they be hired. The first thing current leadership does is tell the new leader how to manage subordinates using their policies. They are in the habit of giving orders and expect them to do as they say while getting desired results. Current leadership does not want to change - they want the front line to change their attitudes. Attitudes are reflections of leadership. If leadership wants subordinates to change, current leaders must first change their attitudes and develop quality leadership skills, then they can adapt and benefit from the experiences of visionary leadership.

— *Self-education* - Man has the ability to educate himself without instructors - commonly known as self-education. Employees, of organizations that stay on the leading edge of technology, know how to educate themselves. This is the only way to adapt new technology as it comes on the market. The education system waits for market demand before it is offered in classrooms. Organizations that wait for classroom instruction are on the trailing edge of technology.

— *Resources* - Efficiency is as effective as available resources-tools, supplies, work environment-to complete tasks. Employees will work hard to get jobs done, but they need quality resources to be efficient. Resources influence pride, which affects efficiency.

— *Self-fulfilling prophecy* - If leaders want to control workers, they will lead in such a way that self-fulfilling prophecy will condition workers to do nothing unless closely supervised. If leaders want workers to assume responsibility, they must lead in such a way that self-fulfilling prophecy will condition workers to assume responsibility. Employee turnover sorts personalities, attracting people who fit the leader's image and rejecting those who do not, thus fulfilling the self-fulfilling prophecy.

— *Social prejudice* believes other people are less capable than we are. If we are managers and we think other people are less capable, then we will establish a management policy that reflects that belief. Through employee turnover and self-fulfilling prophecy, our opinion will be proven right.

5

Maslow's Hierarchy of Needs

Abraham H. Maslow, was an American psychologist and leading exponent of humanistic psychology. He developed a theory of motivation describing the process by which an individual progresses from basic needs (such as food) to the highest needs of what he called self-actualization — the fulfillment of one's greatest human potential. Five stages make up Maslow's hierarchy. Before one can move up to the next stage in the hierarchy, one needs to feel reasonably secure in having achieved all of the previous stages.

The five stages, starting from the bottom of the hierarchy, are:

1 *Physiological Needs*: These include food, water, oxygen, and the like. The needs at this stage include anything one needs to survive. These are very fundamental life or death needs.

2 *Safety Needs*: Even the open water is far from safe when The Horde is nearby.

   If the physiological needs are reasonably well satisfied (the exact meaning of reasonably well depends upon the individual), the next level (Safety Needs) becomes apparent. Safety Needs include things like security; stability; freedom from fear, anxiety, and chaos; need for structure, order, law, and limits; and so on.

3 Belongingness and Love Needs: If the physiological and the safety needs are well gratified, there will emerge the Belongingness and Love needs. The needs at this stage involve giving and receiving affection. Attaining a place on this level will now matter more than anything else will.

The individual might even forget that once, when hunger was foremost, belongingness and love seemed unimportant. For Xena, fulfilling these needs in THE PRICE were the most personally difficult of them all.

4 Esteem Needs: Once the first three stages in the hierarchy are relatively satisfied, one has the need or desire for self-esteem and for the esteem of others. These may take various forms. The form this stage takes for Xena is prestige.

5 Self-actualization Need: Even if all these other needs are satisfied, one experiences discontent or restlessness unless the individual is doing what he or she, individually, is fitted for. Musicians must make music, artists must paint, and a Warrior Princess has gotta do what a Warrior Princess has gotta do, if they are to be ultimately at peace with themselves. That is, one needs to be true to one's own nature.

XENA'S JOURNEY THROUGH THE HIERARCHY

THE PRICE is a wonderful and complex story open to analysis on a number of different levels. Some might contend that The Price is a morality play that examines the question of good vs. evil, war vs. peace, or even Xena vs. Gabrielle. The Price might also be seen as a story in which violence is used to achieve peace. Each of these views is certainly worth investigating. The theme we shall be discussing here deals with the psychology of Xena having to deal with being thrust into an unexpected and desperate reality.

The calm before the storm.

The Price's opening scene depicts Xena at the top of the

hierarchy. She has all the food and water she needs. She feels safe and secure. She shares belongingness and love with Gabrielle. She knows that she is respected by her friends and enemies alike, and she is feeling reasonably self-actualized. (There is still that little thing about Redemption, but she is working on it!). This is not to say that Xena recites these five stages to herself like some mantra. Like the rest of us, the ease or unease she feels through all of this is buried deep within her psyche.

Just a few minutes into the episode, however, Xena starts her tumble down the stages of Maslow's hierarchy. The Horde attacks; men are being tortured and killed; and Xena and Gabrielle find themselves in the Athenian garrison. Safe? Hardly! That stage of the hierarchy is long past. Worse, Xena finds that she has to come to terms with some basic physiological needs. Food and water, she is told, are in desperately short supply.

Once Xena and Gabrielle enter the Athenian garrison, THE PRICE becomes a textbook study of Xena's struggle to climb back up the hierarchy stages. Her unconscious goal through all of this is to regain the "self-actualized" stage from which she started at the beginning of the episode. The fact that Gabrielle does not see the situation in the way that Xena does adds a vital element of strain to the episode. Let us see how all of this happens.

Physiological Needs

Xena's solution to the shortage of food and water is, as usual, simple and to the point. The available food and water is to go only to those who can still fight. Xena, in a bold and seemingly hard-hearted stroke, has brought herself and the rest of the garrison through stage one of the hierarchy. Their immediate physiological needs have been satisfied. (Of course, this is true only so long as you are not counted among the badly wounded!)

Behavior reflects personality. Xena's personality is that of a Warrior Leader. Gabrielle's personality is that of an artist. As a result, Xena's course of action is not Gabrielle's idea of a solution, and the disagreement between them adds fuel to the smoldering tension.

Safety Needs

Once Xena has achieved as much of the physiological needs as is possible under these conditions (including the self-limiting time available for the episode), she turns next to fulfilling the need for safety. The garrison is running short on arrows. Worse, the Athenian soldiers, convinced that they are going to die, have simply lost the will to defend themselves. Xena comes up with a plan to lure some of the Horde inside the fortifications. She and the Athenians trap and kill as many of the Horde as they can. The Horde quickly realize that they are no longer facing a demoralized band waiting for their own death. They find instead that they now face an organized and very lethal fighting force. Xena has gained some tentative footing on level two of the hierarchy: Safety. Of course, safety under the conditions depicted in the Athenian garrison, is a highly relative term!

The soldiers cheer Xena. From the look of triumph on Xena's face, it looks as though she has passed right by the (stage three) need for belongingness and love. She seems to have attained her stage four need for esteem. Yet, without achieving the third stage, Maslow would say, Xena could never *truly* rise any higher than stage two on the hierarchy.

Gabrielle is unable to disguise her horror at seeing the return of "Dark Xena" (TM).

This is where Gabrielle acts as a major force in the study. In fact, this episode could *not* have been made at all (at least, not as a good psychological study) without Gabrielle. It is Xena's eventual reconciliation with Gabrielle that will allow Xena to achieve the third and, therefore, subsequent stages.

However, Xena is not there yet. The look of triumph we see on Xena's face as the soldiers cheer her victory visibly drains away under Gabrielle's disapproving gaze.

After the fight, Xena talks to Gabrielle (berates her might be a more accurate description of their encounter). Gabrielle sees the changes that have come over Xena, and does not understand how all this could happen. When they part, it is hardly on friendly terms.

Later, during a meeting to determine how the garrison is to get reinforcements, Menticles tells Xena that she cannot be the one to get help because the soldiers would lose hope if she left. Xena shows us that she is still unable to feel prestige and appreciation. Xena's response is simple. All she can say to that is, "He's right."

In the meantime, Gabrielle discovers that Kaltaka is not the name of the Horde's god of war after all. It is their word for water! Enough is enough, she thinks, and Gabrielle finds a way to convince the gate guards to let her out of the fortification to bring water to the wounded who had been left lying on the field. Xena, ever protective of Gabrielle, is desperate. Xena finds, however, that Gabrielle's humanitarian act has created a de facto truce. She tries talking to Gabrielle again, but Gabrielle ends the conversation with a verbal slap at Xena. She tells Xena, "It looks like you've got your battle to the death!"

Belongingness and Love Needs

This slap wakens Xena enough for her to move to enter the third stage of the hierarchy, and she sends some soldiers to help Gabrielle in the hospital. It is not much of a reconciliation, but it is honest and heartfelt. Xena has made her first halting steps through the third stage: Belongingness and Love.

Esteem Needs

Xena finds a live one out on the battlefield.

Xena then tries an experiment with a captured Horde soldier. Xena finds that the soldier will fight anyone else, but will not fight her believing himself to be unworthy. She realizes that this due, not to her prowess as a fighter, but to her apparent leadership position in the garrison. As Xena says, "He thinks that I'm in charge and he's not worthy of my sword." It is only now that Xena can honestly acknowledge achieving the fourth stage: Prestige.

Self-actualization Need

Things are now driving hard and fast toward the apex of the hierarchy as well as the climax of the story. Xena's acceptance of the prestige and esteem she feels not only from the Athenians but also from the Horde soldier leads her to contrive a new and dangerous plan. The stage is set for Xena finally to achieve the fifth level of the hierarchy: Self-actualization.

In order to achieve the fifth stage Xena must now act in a manner true to her own nature. Her core nature — the thing that drives her to do so many of the things she does — is her quest for Redemption. Put 'very' simply, she was "bad" and she wants to be good. In fact, Xena is even willing to sacrifice herself to achieve this goal — this quest.

Xena decides to try to end the siege once and for all. She challenges the Horde's leader to single combat. He, of course, accepts. He probably feels that he himself is at stage five of the hierarchy and is more than willing to face this new threat!

Xena goes out to fight the Horde leader. After a tense and sometimes pitched battle, she defeats him in front of his own men. Xena has the chance to kill him. Instead, she throws down her weapon, turns her back on him, and walks away. Now it is the Horde leader's turn to slide down the stages of Maslow's hierarchy. His men do not like this. Showing their displeasure, they kill him. The Horde, apparently, took Maslow's hierarchy 'very' seriously!

Let us suppose that the Horde leader is himself a student of Maslow. If we could have listened in on his thoughts at the end of the battle, they might have sounded something like this.

"By the gods, she beat me! Well, lay on, Warrior-Witch. You can kill me, but you cannot destroy my spirit! What is this?! She has thrown down the weapon? She turned her back on me? She is walking away! Well, this is embarrassing. I must admit that I am not feeling particularly self-actualized any more. My men were watching too. I have lost face! Hmmm, I guess my prestige has dimmed a bit in their eyes, but we are still a team, right? Sure, I am still one of the guys! No, that does not work. By our own custom, the tribe will ostracize me. No, that is not right either. That only works for common soldiers! If the *leader* is defeated in single combat....Oh no! I am not feeling terribly safe anymore! I might as well try to kill the — [Sound and sensation of three well-aimed axes thudding their way into the leader's back.] Gasp! Well...I am sure everything will work out just fine if I can just satisfy this sudden physiological need to stop bleeding to death! Arrrgh..."

There is a saying that "Success is how you bounce on the bottom." Xena hit bottom and "bounced" back up through the five hierarchy stages. The Horde leader just hit bottom.

XENA'S FULL CIRCLE

Xena spares the Horde Chieftain, only to see his own people kill him moments later.

By the episode's end, we seem to have come full circle. Xena has overcome the threat of hunger and thirst. The Horde's immediate danger is past. Xena is again able to enjoy feelings of belongingness and love with Gabrielle. She accepts the esteem and respect that both the Athenian garrison and the Horde band hold for her. Finally, she has passed through the fire of single combat with the Horde leader on her quest for Redemption. Yes, in many ways, Xena is as she was at the start of the episode. However, she will be forever changed. Xena's climb back up the hierarchy was full of lessons that even a Warrior Princess cannot ignore. As usual, a consummate and persistent teacher taught many of those lessons: Gabrielle. Maslow would have been proud!

B-VALUES

Maslow understood that when man was at his best he had what he called "B-Values." Maslow identified these B-values as:

— Truth

— Goodness

— Beauty

— Unity

— Transcendence

— Aliveness

— Uniqueness

— Perfection

— Justice

— Order

— Simplicity

Not too long ago, perhaps within the last fifty years, behaviorism and Freudism prevailed. Maslow was one of the key figures that changed a prevailing atmosphere of subconscious demons and heavy emphasis on psychological measurement. The more enlightned deeper side of man was put aside. It was just not scientific or helpful to the people with sick brains.

Both the B-Values and Hierarchy of Needs were in sharp contrast to the simple mechanics of behaviorism introduced by Watson in 1919 and later by Skinner. Behaviorism was strictly observational and based solely on measurements. "If you don't see it, don't think about it" was the premise. Behaviorism was soulless and based merely on stimuli and reinforcement.

Behaviorism was one of many schools of psychology that debased man. For example, psychoanalysis taught that man was ruled by an unconscious mind and energized solely by animal instincts.

Maslow's introduction of B-values and related concepts changed psychology forever. Maslow elevated psychology to study a deeper and more complex man. Instead of sick man study, Maslow did great man study. In studied the greatest people in history and cataloged what they had in common that made them great.

Maslow drew his famous Hierarchy of Needs Pyramid in the late 1960's.

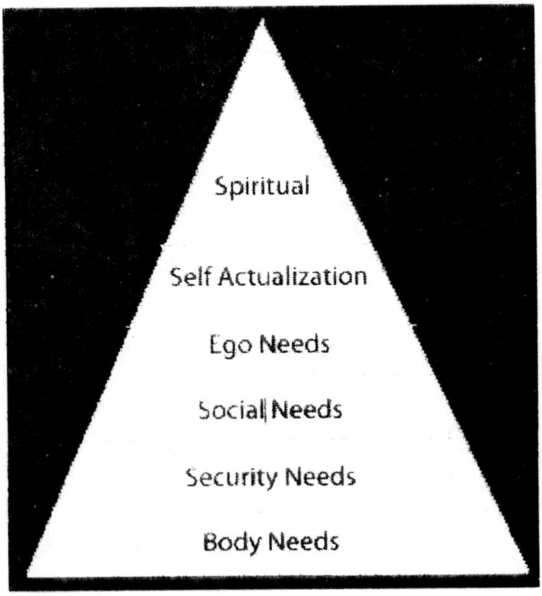

Maslow layers are defined as:

Body (Physiological) Needs such as air, warmth, food,

sleep, stimulation and activity. The Body needs are biological. These needs can be very strong because if deprived over time, the person will die.

Security (Safety) Needs such as living in a safe area away from threats. This level is more likely to be found in children as they have a greater need to feel safe

Social (Love and Belongingness) Needs such as the love of family and friends

Ego (Self esteem) Needs such as healthy pride The Ego needs focus on our need for self-respect, and respect from others.

Self Actualization (Fulfillment) Needs such as purpose, personal growth and realization of potentials. The point where people become fully functional, acting purely on their own volition and having a healthy personality. The Self-Actualization is described by Maslow as an ongoing process involved in a cause outside their own skin. People on this level work at something very precious, call it a vocation or calling in the old priestly sense. These people are very fine, healthy, strong, sagacious (very smart) and creative. Maslow included saintly people on this level.

But Mallow's hierarchy is of great historical importance. His statements of needs, moved psychology forward, replacing ideas that treated man as a mechanism,driven by the Id or long forgotten experiences. With Maslow man can elevate himself so that he is driven by what he feels is his as his own truth and his own ideas.

Self actualization is a mixture of the spiritual life and also the beginning of the true spiritual life. In self actualization Maslow said there is a need to be somebody different, or have some sort of calling. Spirituality is a matter of knowing that there is guidance from above, that is, a Being that knows more then we do.

Looking at some of the self actualization attributes we find:

— Wholeness, unity integration, oneness -this is part of the spiritual experience

— Perfection, just rightness - this is taught in classes in spirituality

— Completion, ending, destiny, fate -fate is not taught in classes on spirituality.

— Justice, search for truth, orderliness, oughtness -this is part of spirituality

— Simplicity, beauty, goodness, uniqueness, effortlessness, playfulness, truth, self sufficiency -again this part of spirituality

Some of the missing spiritual needs include:

— Need to feel close to God

— Need to Prayer

— Need to Meditate

— Need of Purity

If one visits a bookstore they might observe people picking up different types of books. People with lower needs have more identifiable needs. Those with body needs might fall asleep in a chair, or be readying about emergency planning, first aid.

Those with security needs might be in the self help area looking for books on how to make more money, how to protect themselves and might be very watchful.

Those with social needs might be in the self help area browsing the manuals on how to find a mate, feeling accepted. They might pick up a novel to at least live in a make believe world where people love them.

Those with ego needs might also read novels, putting themselves in the star role. They also might be found in the magazine area, looking to improve their looks, learning what car and clothes to buy..

Self Actualizing people might be anywhere. They might have their own books in the store. They would also be in learn mode sometimes, so the books on hobbies, politics, science, psychology might come in their possession. Maslow believed that once a person is self actualized, he is in a position to follow his calling. A musician must make music, an artist must paint and a poet must write. If these needs are not met, the person feels on edge and lacking something.

Those with spiritual needs might be in the religious and new age sections of the store. Maslow believed that people move through the needs to the highest level they can based their surroundings and education.

Some of the changes in the educational process that Maslow espoused:

People should:

— Be authentic.

— Transcend their cultural conditioning and become world citizens.

— Find their vocation and right mate.

— Know that life is precious.

— Be good and joyous in all kinds of situations.

— Learn from their inner nature.

— See that basic needs are satisfied.

— Refreshen their consciousness, appreciate beauty and other good things in life.

— Understand that controls are good, and complete abandon is bad.

— Transcend trifling problems: Grapple with serious problems such as injustice, pain suffering and death

— Be good choosers: Be given practice in making choices of goodies, then making choices in their religious beliefs.

According to Maslow, an individual is ready to act upon the growth needs if and only if the deficiency needs are met. Maslow's initial conceptualization included only one growth need—self-actualization. Self-actualized people are characterized by:

1) being problem-focused;
2) incorporating an ongoing freshness of appreciation of life;
3) a concern about personal growth; and
4) the ability to have peak experiences.

Maslow later differentiated the growth need of self-actualization, specifically naming two lower-level growth needs prior to general level of self-actualization and one beyond that level.

5) *Cognitive*: to know, to understand, and explore;
6) *Aesthetic*: symmetry, order, and beauty;
7) *Self-actualization*: to find self-fulfillment and realize one's potential; and
8) *Self-transcendence*: to connect to something beyond the ego or to help others find self-fulfillment and realize their potential.

Maslow's basic position is that as one becomes more self-actualized and self-transcendent, one becomes more wise (develops wisdom) and automatically knows what to do in a wide variety of situations. Daniels suggests that Maslow's ultimate conclusion that the highest levels of self-actualization are transcendent in their nature may be one of his most important contributions to the study of human behavior and motivation.

Norwood proposes that Maslow's hierarchy can be used to describe the kinds of information that individual's seek at different levels. For example, individuals at the lowest level seek *coping information* in order to meet their basic needs. Information that is not directly connected to helping a person meet his or her needs in a very short time span is simply left unattended. Individuals at the safety level need *helping information*.

They seek to be assisted in seeing how they can be safe and secure. *Enlightening information* is sought by individuals seeking to meet their belongingness needs. Quite often this can be found in books or other materials on relationship development. *Empowering information* is sought by people at the esteem level. They are looking for information on how their ego can be developed. Finally, people in the growth levels of cogntive, aesthetic, and self-actualization seek *edifying information*.

While Norwood does not specifically address the level of transcendence. Maslow published his first conceptualization of his theory over 50 years ago and it has since become one of the most popular and often cited theories of human motivation. An interesting phenomenon related to Maslow's work is that in spite of a lack of evidence to support his hierarchy, it enjoys wide acceptance.

The few major studies that have been completed on the hierarchy seem to support the proposals of William James and Mathes that there are three levels of human needs. James hypothesized the levels of material, social (belongingness, esteem), and *spiritual*. Mathes proposed the three levels were physiological, belonginess, and self-actualization; he considered security and self-esteem as unwarranted.

Alderfer developed a comparable hierarchy with his ERG (existence, relatedness, and growth) theory. His approach modified Maslow's theory based on the work of Gordon Allport who incorporated concepts from systems theory into his work on personality. Maslow recognized that not all personalities followed his proposed hierarchy. While a variety of personality dimensions might be considered as related to motivational needs, one of the most often cited is that of introversion and extroversion. Reorganizing Maslow's hierarchy based on the work of Alderfer and considering the introversion/extraversion dimension of personality results in three levels, each with an introverted and extroverted component. This organization suggests there may be two aspects of each level that differentiate how people relate to each set of needs.

Different personalities might relate more to one dimension than the other. For example, an introvert at the level of Other/ Relatedness might be more concerned with his or her own perceptions of being included in a group, whereas an extrovert at that same level would pay more attention to how others value that membership.

There is little agreement about the identification of basic human needs and how they are ordered. For example, Deci and Ryan also suggest three needs, although they are not necessarily arranged hierarchically: the need for autonomy, the need for competence, and the need for relatedness. Thompson, Grace and Cohen state the most important needs for children are connection, recognition, and power. Nohria, Lawrence, and Wilson provide evidence from a sociobiology theory of motivation that humans have four basic needs:

(1) acquire objects and experiences;

(2) bond with others in long-term relationships of mutual care and commitment;

(3) learn and make sense of the world and of ourselves; and

(4) to defend ourselves, our loved ones, beliefs and resources from harm. There are nine basic human needs: (1) security, (2) adventure, (3) freedom, (4) exchange, (5) power, (6) expansion, (7) acceptance, (8) community, and (9) expression.

Notice that bonding and relatedness are a component of every theory. However, there do not seem to be any others that are mentioned by all theorists. Franken suggests this lack of accord may be a result of different philosophies of researchers rather than differences among human beings. In addition, he reviews research that shows a person's explanatory or attributional style will modify the list of basic needs. Therefore, it seems appropriate to ask people what they want and how their needs could be met rather than relying on an unsupported theory.

For example, Waitley advises having a person imagine what life would be like if time and money were not an object in a person's life. That is, what would the person do this week, this month, next month, if you had all the money and time needed to engage in the activities and were secure that both would be available again next year. With some follow-up questions to identify what is keeping the person from happening now, this open-ended approach is likely to identify the most important needs of the individual.

There is much work still to be done in this area before we can rely on a theory to be more informative than simply collecting and analyzing data. However, this body of research can be very important to parents, educators, administrators and others concerned with developing and using human potential. It provides an outline of some important issues that must be addressed if human beings are to achieve the levels of character and competencies necessary to be successful in the information age.

6

INTELLIGENCE: MEANING AND NATURE

Intelligence is a complex topic. Howard Gardner, David Perkins, and Robert Sternberg have all been quite successful in helping spread knowledge about the meaning of "intelligence" and applications of this knowledge to education. The study and measurement of intelligence has been an important research topic for nearly 100 years IQ is a complex concept, and researchers in this field argue with each other about the various theories that have been developed. There is no clear agreement as to what constitutes IQ or how to measure it.

The following definition is a composite from various authors. Intelligence is a combination of the ability to:

— *Learn*: This includes all kinds of informal and formal learning via any combination of experience, education, and training.

— *Pose problems*: This includes recognizing problem situations and transforming them into more clearly defined problems.

— *Solve problems*: This includes solving problems, accomplishing tasks, fashioning products, and doing complex projects.

This definition of intelligence is a very optimistic one. It says that each of us can become more intelligent. We can become more intelligent through study and practice, through access to appropriate tools, and through learning to make effective use of these tools.

PBL can be used as a vehicle in which students can use and improve their intelligence. More detail on the work of Gardner, Sternberg, and Perkins is given in the next three subsections.

Some researchers in the field of intelligence have long argued that people have a variety of different intelligences. A person may be good at learning languages and terrible at learning music—or vice versa. A single number (a score on an IQ test) cannot adequately represent the complex and diverse capabilities of a human being.

Howard Gardner has proposed a theory of multiple intelligences. He originally identified seven components of intelligence. He argues that these intelligences are relatively distinct from each other and that each person has some level of each of these seven intelligences. More recently, he has added an eighth intelligence to his list.

Many PBL-using teachers have studied the work of Howard Gardner and use some of his ideas in their teaching. For example, in creating a team of students to do a particular project, a teacher may select a team whose collective "highest" talents encompass most of the eight areas of intelligence identified by Gardner. The teacher may encourage a team to divide up specific tasks in line with specific high levels of talents found on a team. Alternatively, a teacher may encourage or require that team members not be allowed to work in their areas of highest ability in order to encourage their development of knowledge and skills in other areas.

The following table lists the eight intelligences identified by Howard Gardner. It provides some examples of the types of professionals who exhibit a high level of an intelligence. The eight intelligences are listed in alphabetical order.

You might want to do some introspection. For each of the eight intelligences in the Howard Gardner list, think about your own level of talents and performance. For each intelligence, decide if you have an area of expertise that makes substantial use of the intelligence. For example, perhaps you are good at music. If so, is music the basis of your vocation?

Students can also do this type of introspection, and it can become a routine component of PBL lessons. Students can come to understand that they are more naturally gifted in some areas than in others, but that they have some talent in all of the eight areas identified by Howard Gardner. Curriculum and instruction can be developed to help all students make progress in enhancing their talents in each of these eight areas of intelligence.

Many teachers have provided testimonial evidence that PBL encourages participation on the part of their students who do not have a high level of "school smarts." They report that some of their students who were not doing well in school have become actively engaged and experienced a high level of success in working on projects. These observations are consistent with and supportive of the research of Robert Sternberg.

Different researchers have identified different components of intelligence. Sternberg focuses on just three main components:

— Practical intelligence—the ability to do well in informal and formal educational settings; adapting to and shaping one's environment; street smarts.

— Experiential intelligence—the ability to deal with novel situations; the ability to effectively automate ways of dealing with novel situations so they are easily handled in the future; the ability to think in novel ways.

— Componential intelligence—the ability to process information effectively. This includes metacognitive, executive, performance, and knowledge-acquisition components that help to steer cognitive processes.

Sternberg provides examples of people who are quite talented in one of these areas but not so talented in the other two. In that sense, his approach to the field of intelligence is somewhat like Howard Gardner's. However, you can see that Sternberg does not focus on specific components of intelligence that are aligned with various academic disciplines. He is far more concerned with helping people develop components of intelligence that will help them to perform well in whatever they chose to do.

Sternberg strongly believes that intelligence can be increased by study and practice. Quite a bit of his research focuses on such endeavors. Some of Sternberg's work focuses specifically on "street smarts" versus "school smarts." He notes that some people are particularly talented in one of these two areas, and not in the other. This observation is consistent with the work of Lev Vygotsky who argues that the type of learning that goes on outside of school is distinctly different than the type of learning that goes on in school. While some students are talented in both informal and formal education, others are much more successful in one rather than the other. A teacher who is skillful in developing PBL can help students to design projects that are consistent with their learning abilities and interests.

In his 1992 book, *Smart Schools*, David Perkins analyzes a number of different educational theories and approaches to education. His analysis is strongly supportive of Gardner's theory of multiple intelligences. Perkins' book contains extensive research-based evidence that education can be considerably improved by more explicit and appropriate teaching for transfer, focusing on higher-order cognitive skills, and the use of project-based learning.

Perkins examines a large number of research studies both on the measurement of IQ and of programs of study designed to increase IQ. He presents detailed arguments that IQ has three major components or dimensions:

Neural intelligence: This refers to the efficiency and precision of one's neurological system.

Experiential intelligence: This refers to one's accumulated knowledge and experience in different areas. It can be thought of as the accumulation of all of one's expertises.

Reflective intelligence: This refers to one's broad-based strategies for attacking problems, for learning, and for approaching intellectually challenging tasks. It includes attitudes that support persistence, systemization, and imagination. It includes self-monitoring and self-management.

There is substantial evidence to support the belief that a child's neural intelligence can be adversely affected by the mother's use of drugs such as alcohol and cocaine during pregnancy. Lead (such as from lead-based paint) can do severe neural damage to a person. Vitamins, or the lack thereof, can affect neural intelligence.

Moreover, there is general agreement that neural intelligence has a "use it or lose it" characteristic. It is clear that neural intelligence can be maintained and, indeed, increased, by use.

Experiential intelligence is based on years and years of accumulating knowledge and experience in both informal and formal learning environments. Such knowledge and experience can lead to a high level of expertise in one or more fields. People who live in "rich" learning environments have a significant intelligence advantage over people who grow up in less stimulating environments. Experiential intelligence can be increased by such environments.

Reflexive intelligence can be thought of as a control system that helps to make effective use of neural intelligence and experiential intelligence. A person can learn strategies that help to make more effective use of neural intelligence and experiential intelligence. The habits of mind included under reflexive intelligence can be learned and improved. Metacognition and other approaches to reflecting about one's cognitive processes can help.

TYPES OF INTELLIGENCE

There are different intelligences that help us deal with particular problems and solutions. The scientific community is divided on the issue.

Testing intelligence

One of the main tenet's underpinning the idea of a single entity 'intelligence' is the concept of 'General Intelligence', or 'g'. Devised by English Psychologist, Charles Spearman, in the early 20th Century 'g' was a statistical measure of performance across a variety of tests.

Spearman found that the same people who did well in a variety of mental tests tended to use a part in their brains that he termed 'g'. This 'g' laid the foundation for the notion of a single intelligence, which enables us to undertake everyday mental tasks.

A recent study seems to endorse Spearman's theory. Research has found that a part of the brain called the 'lateral prefrontal cortex' is the only area of the brain to increase in blood flow when volunteers tackle complicated puzzles.

Spearman's concept, however, is still highly controversial with many people questioning both the statistical process and the simplistic nature of 'g'. There is also a body of research that states that our mental ability is a function of social factors such as education and not one's inherent biological make-up.

Intelligence and the brain

The early Greeks thought the brain was the home of your soul, rather than your intellect. They believed that thinking happened somewhere around the lungs! Not until the seventeenth and eighteenth centuries was the brain seen as an organ of intelligence and thought, when the concept of the mind emerged.

Using new forms of technology, scientists have been able to look at how the brain performs when we undertake different tasks. Roll the pointer over the brain below to find out how our brain processes language. Intelligence as an overall ability or attribute of a person. That is, we tend to classify people as either bright, average or dull. It is much less common to hear someone differentiate between conditions of intelligence.

Of course, anyone who wishes to develop an intelligence test must come to grips with this problem. Is there such a thing as general intelligence as distinct from specific abilities, or is intelligence just a collection of abilities? Binet saw intelligence as one basic quality Binet assumed that intelligence was essentially unitary; that is, he maintained that the mind possesses one overriding quality, which he believed to beability to effectively adjust to the environment. In devising his test he assumed that this unitary factor could be manifested in three ways.

(1) As the ability to maintain a definite direction.

(2) In choosing means appropriate to ends.

(3) In objectively evaluating one's own actions.

Charles Spearman, an English statistician, looked at intelligence differently. He devised a two-factor theory. On the basis of his correlational studies he concluded that intelligence could be divided into a general factor (G) and a group of specific factors (S1, S2, S3, etc.). His theory was that "G" played a part in all intellectual activities, but also that any particular activity was affected by one or more of the specific factors.

E. L. Thorndike rejected the notion that there was such a thing as a general intelligence factor. He formulated the multifactor theory. This theory stated that intelligence is made up of many independent components, all of which, when added together, form intelligence. Thorndike took the position that a person could be very strong in one factor and very weak in another, and be just as intelligent as someone else who had the reverse capabilities.

A fourth theory, proposed by L. L. Thurstone, which is somewhere in between those just presented. According to his theory, intelligence is not just a matter of "G" plus "S" but a primary group of factors (6 or 7) and one general or "G" factor. Thurstone arrived at this position as a result of his factor analysis studies of intelligence. .

Thurstone's work indicated that a number of factors go into making up intelligence and further that each of the factors are In part related to each other and to some general intelligence factor (G).

Factor analysis is a statistical technique designed to identify and isolate the elemenrs that make up any complex trait. A psychologist involved in factor analysis gives different tests to the same people and calculates correlations between responses on subtests or individual items. When all the possible correlations are ready, procedures of statistical analysis are used to find out which items seem to be in clusters and which seem relatively independent. For example, several subtests or items dealing with words may correlate highly with each other, but not at all with subtests or items concerned with numbers. In this example, the statistics indicate that a verbal factor and a numerical factor are relatively independent.

Thurstone conducted an extensive study of the factors of intelligence. This study, which involved factor analyses of dozens of tests administered to schoolchildren, identified seven intelligence factors:

— Verbal comprehension—the ability to define and understand words
— Word fluency—the ability to produce words rapidly
— Number—the ability to solve arithmetic problems .

— Space—the ability to visualize relationships
— Memory—the ability to memorize and recall
— Perception—the ability to see differences and similarities among objects
— Reasoning—the ability to find rules

After deciding that these seven factors made up intelligence, Thurstone rearranged the existing subtests and devised some new ones. He referred to these sets as: "Tests of Primary Mental Abilities," which he used to investigate the question as to whether there was such a thing as "general" intelligence. His Tests of Primary Mental Abilities were administered to a large group of children, and correlations were computed between scores on the various tests. If there were no such thing as general intelligence, each factor would be independent.

However, there were positive correlations among all the tests, with some more highly correlated than others, which indicated that primary mental abilities share some common factor. Thurstone concluded that each primary factor is composed of an Independent primary factor and a general factor (G) that is shared by all of the primary factors; in other words, intelligence consists of both general ability and a number of specific abilities.

Today, many psychologists prefer theories by Sternbeg and by Gardner. Both of these psychologists reject the emphasis on a general intelligence. Robert Sternberg put forward a triarchic theory, proposing that intelligence embodies a wide variety of skills important for efective living. His observation of Yale graduate students, yeilded what he believed were components of intelligence: componential ntelligence (sovling problems; experiential intelligence (adapting creatively); and contextual intelligence (making the environment fit your strengths).

Gardner's theory is similar to Thurstone's theory. Gardner believes that there are seven separate intelligences: logical-mathematical, linquistic, spatial, musical, kinesthetic, interpersonal, and intrapersonal intelligences. Later, a group of investigators devised some finely differentiated tests that indicated the existence of at least 80, and perhaps as many as 120, separate factors that should be considered elements of intelligence.

ADULT INTELLIGENCE

As we saw in the last module, test scores purporting to define "mental age" increase up to the middle teens. But what happens then? After late adolescence, it appears that intelligence no longer improves and in fact may even deteriorate. Some studies have shown declining intelligence as people grow older. An early cross-sectional study included almost all the inhabitants from age 10 to age 60 in a New England community.

The average scores on the First World War army test rose rapidly until about age 18, and then declined steadily from 18 to 60. The scores on separate factors on the test, however, did not all show this same pattern. The scores on the reasoning test showed a sharp decline from age 18 to 30. Thereafter it continued to decline but at a much slower rate. The vocabulary test, however, showed no decline as a factor of age. The rise was rapid until age 20 and then continued to rise very slowly until it reached its highest point at age 60.

Another cross-sectional study that showed a decline in overall IQ scores took place during standardization of the WAIS The peaks were different but the overall picture was similar. That is, the peak of verbal intelligence came in the 25-34 age range and declined more rapidly after age 44. These data support the hypothesis that we become less intelligent as we grow older but some people have questioned this conclusion. They argue that the tests are biased against older people, particularly performance tests that place strong emphasis on speed.

Other studies revealed increased intelligence except in skills older people have little reason to use. Other data lends support to the hypothesis that perhaps the apparent decline in intelligence with age is an artifact of the tests used to measure it. Owens conducted a longitudinal study with a group of men who had taken the army's group intelligence test during the First World War and then took the same test again thirty years later. Their scores were higher on everything but arithmetic.

One interpretation of all these findings is that each generation grows up in an environment that is more conducive to intellectual growth than the generation before. This would be consistent with the declines observed in cross-sectional studies and the improvements in the longitudinal studies. More longitudinal studies are needed for a better understanding of the relationship between intelligence and age.

TWO MODELS OF INTELLIGENCE

Classic Hierarchical Model

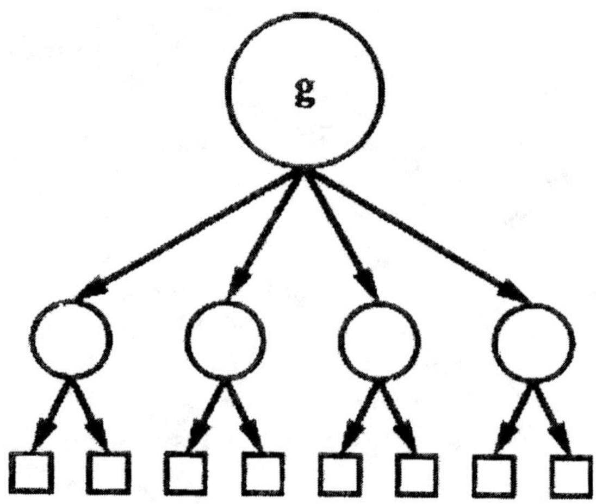

Two different *structural models* of intelligence can be distinguished, the hierarchical model and the bifactor model. In a structural model, squares represent *observables* (such as specific tests, or the specific items of which a test is comprised), and circles represent *unobservables* (factors, the hypothetical entities that explain the correlations among the observables). The arrows represent the correlations of the tests with the factors; such correlations are known as *factor loadings*.

Classic Bifactor Model

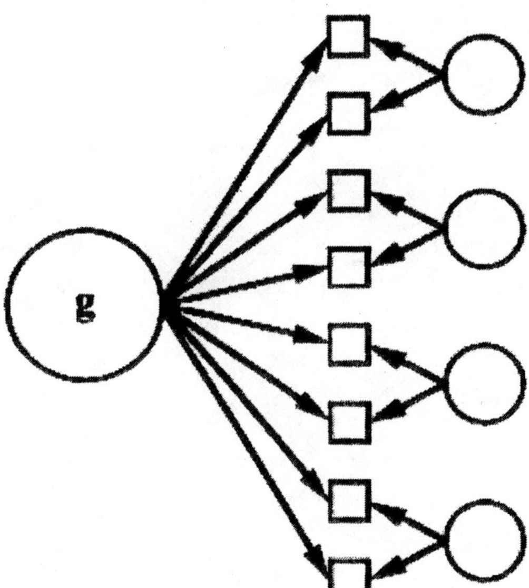

The hierarchical model is more efficient because it uses fewer parameters than the bifactor model. Counting arrows (parameters) in the figures above will reveal that the hierarchical model uses twelve parameters, and the bifactor model uses sixteen. Thus, the hierarchical model is more efficient.

However, the bifactor model allows one to talk about independent components or independent factors. The factors in the bifactor model (but not in the hierarchical model) are pure, uncorrelated, non-redundant. One would rather include independent factors in a regression equation than non-independent factors.

An example of the hierarchical model of intelligence is a model in which verbal and spatial abilities correlate $r = .6$. An example of the bifactor model of intelligence is a model in which verbal and spatial abilities do not correlate (i.e., they are *orthogonal*). Of course, this empirical difference in verbal and spatial abilities in a hierarchical model and a bifactor model would require that verbal and spatial abilities also differ conceptually between the two models.

Beyond the question of structure lies the deeper question, what is the meaning in terms of understandability or theoretical utility of these different models? If *g* is brain size, and everything else is an independent cognitive module, then the bifactor model makes sense. If *g* is the common variance of verbal and spatial abilities, then a hierarchical model is better.

VALIDITY OF INTELLIGENCE TESTS

IQ tests are reliable predictors of school success. Usually, we want an intelligence test to have predictive validity. That is, it would be desirable for a test of intelligence to predict how well someone will do on a task that involves intellectual ability. The most frequent use of IQ tests is to predict school success and, in this application, IQ tests generally have high predictive validity. In fact intelligence tests are such good predictors that teachers often become concerned if there is a discrepancy between IQ scores and school success. Students who score high on IQ tests, but who are not doing well in school, are often called "underachievers," reflecting the difference between actual achievement and potential achievement as revealed in the IO test score

However, we should remember that validity is defined as the answer to the question, "Does the test measure what it claims to measure?" In part, that question depends upon how the person constructing the test defines intelligence. For example, if one sees intelligence as the ability to do conceptual thinking, then those test items which require a student to formulate ideas and verbal symbols would be the most appropriate kinds of items to measure this ability. Thus we can talk of a test as having logical validity, which means only that the items we have selected fit our definition of intelligence.

INTELLIGENCE ACROSS CULTURES

Monitor staff

In recent years, researchers in Africa, Asia and elsewhere have found that people in non-Western cultures often have ideas about intelligence that differ fundamentally from those that have shaped Western intelligence tests.

Research on those differences is already providing support for some of the more inclusive Western definitions of intelligence, such as those proposed by APA President Robert J. Sternberg, PhD, of Yale University and Howard Gardner, PhD, of Harvard University's Graduate School of Education (see related article). Eventually, it may also help researchers design new intelligence tests that are sensitive to the values of the cultures in which they are used.

Researchers of cultural differences in intelligence face a major challenge, however: balancing the desire to compare people from various cultures according to a standard measure with the need to assess people in the light of their own values and concepts, says Elena Grigorenko, PhD, deputy director of the Center for the Psychology of Abilities, Competencies and

Expertise at Yale. "On the one hand, mindless application of the same tests across cultures is desired by no one," she suggests. "On the other, everyone would like to be able to do at least some comparisons of people across cultures."

Thinking about thinking

Some cultural differences in intelligence play out on a global scale. In "The Geography of Thought", Richard Nisbett, PhD, co-director of the Culture and Cognition Program at the University of Michigan, argues that East Asian and Western cultures have developed cognitive styles that differ in fundamental ways, including in how intelligence is understood.

People in Western cultures, he suggests, tend to view intelligence as a means for individuals to devise categories and to engage in rational debate, while people in Eastern cultures see it as a way for members of a community to recognize contradiction and complexity and to play their social roles successfully.

Other researchers have come to similar conclusions. In a study published in Intelligence, Sternberg and Shih-ying Yang, PhD, of National Chi-Nan University in Taiwan, found that Taiwanese-Chinese conceptions of intelligence emphasize understanding and relating to others--including knowing when to show and when not to show one's intelligence. Such differences between Eastern and Western views of intelligence are tied, says Nisbett, to differences in the basic cognitive processes of people in Eastern and Western cultures.

University of California, Berkeley, psychologist Kaiping Peng, PhD, who has collaborated with Nisbett on a number of studies, also believes that there are differences between the cognitive styles of people raised in Eastern and Western cultures. But, like Nisbett, he cautions against the simplistic idea that everyone raised in a particular culture will share equally in that culture's style of thinking, or that someone raised in one culture will be unable to learn the cognitive style of another.

"I don't believe that simply because you are born Asian means you will think like Asians," says Peng. "Culture is not just race, nationality or any particular social category--culture is experience."

The distinction between East Asia and the West is only one of many cultural distinctions that separate different ways of thinking about intelligence. Robert Serpell, PhD, who is returning this year to the University of Zambia after 13 years at the University of Maryland, Baltimore County, has studied concepts of intelligence in rural African communities since the 1970s.

Serpell and others have found that people in some African communities--especially where Western schooling has not yet become common--tend to blur the Western distinction between intelligence and social competence. In rural Zambia, for instance, the concept of nzelu includes both cleverness (chenjela) and responsibility (tumikila). "When rural parents in Africa talk about the intelligence of children, they prefer not to separate the cognitive speed aspect of intelligence from the social responsibility aspect," says Serpell.

Over the past several years, Sternberg and Grigorenko also have investigated concepts of intelligence in Africa. Among the Luo people in rural Kenya, Grigorenko and her collaborators have found that ideas about intelligence consist of four broad concepts: rieko, which largely corresponds to the Western idea of academic intelligence, but also includes specific skills; luoro, which includes social qualities like respect, responsibility and consideration; paro, or practical thinking; and winjo, or comprehension. Only one of the four--rieko--is correlated with traditional Western measures of intelligence.

In another study in the same community, Sternberg and his collaborators found that children who score highly on a test of knowledge about medicinal herbs--a measure of practical intelligence--tend to score poorly on tests of academic intelligence.

The results, published in the journal Intelligence, suggest that practical and academic intelligence can develop independently or even in conflict with each other, and that the values of a culture may shape the direction in which a child develops.

They also agree with studies in a number of countries, both industrialized and nonindustrialized, that suggest that people who are unable to solve complex problems in the abstract can often solve them when they are presented in a familiar context.

The end result of this research is twofold. As Sternberg has pointed out, lay theories of intelligence often lack the precision of scientific theories, but they can suggest new avenues of research, shed light on how people use intelligence in everyday life and highlight aspects of intelligence that scientific theories have ignored. Studying intelligence in different cultures can thus be a way of challenging conventional Western ideas about intelligence.

Research in non-Western cultures can also be directly useful to people in those cultures. It indicates the extent to which Western intelligence tests measure what those cultures are interested in measuring, and it may suggest alternative, culturally appropriate methods of assessing skills and abilities.

'Culture free?'

Are "culture-free" or "culture-fair" intelligence tests possible, or is success on a test inevitably influenced by familiarity with the culture in which the test was developed? Moreover, is it desirable--or even possible--to adapt Western tests to non-Western cultures, or should new tests be designed from the ground up to measure skills and abilities valued by the culture in which they are to be used?

Many psychologists believe that the idea that a test can be completely absent of cultural bias--a recurrent hope of test developers in the 20th century--is contradicted by the weight of the evidence. Raven's Progressive Matrices, for example, is one of several nonverbal intelligence tests that were originally advertised as "culture free," but are now recognized as culturally loaded.

Patricia Greenfield, PhD, of the University of California, Los Angeles, argues that nonverbal intelligence tests are based on cultural constructs, such as the matrix, that are ubiquitous in some cultures but almost nonexistent in others. In societies where formal schooling is common, she says, students gain an early familiarity with organizing items into rows and columns, which gives them an advantage over test-takers in cultures where formal schooling is rare.

Similarly, says Greenfield, media technologies like television, film and video games give test-takers from cultures where those technologies are widespread an advantage on visual tests, while test-takers from cultures where the language-based media are more common have advantages on verbal tests.

"I think it's important to point out that nonverbal tests or visual tests are the most culture-bound of all," she says. "They are not 'culture free' and they are not 'culture fair'; in fact, they are less fair than verbal tests."

Greenfield does not, however, believe that administering valid tests of ability in other cultures is impossible--just that it requires a deep familiarity with each culture's values and practices.

Recently, she and Ashley Maynard, PhD, now a professor of psychology at the University of Hawaii, conducted studies of cognitive development among children in a Zinacantec Mayan village in Chiapas, Mexico, using toy looms, spools of thread and other materials drawn from the local environment. The research convinced Greenfield that the children's development can be validly compared to the progression described by Western theories of development, but only by using testing materials and experimental designs based on the Zinacantec culture.

According to Serpell, simply translating a Western test into the local language is not enough. Instead, it is critical to tailor each test to the needs and values of the culture in which it is to be used.

Unless that happens, says Serpell, "you're just going to be able to pick out more efficiently those individuals who would be considered intelligent by Western standards, but you're not going to be able to answer the question of whether you're picking out people who are most intelligent according to the standards of their culture."

EMOTIONAL INTELLIGENCE

Ever since the publication of Daniel Goleman's first book on the topic in 1995, emotional intelligence has become one of the hottest buzzwords in corporate America. For instance, when the Harvard Business Review published an article on the topic two years ago, it attracted a higher percentage of readers than any other article published in that periodical in the last 40 years. When the CEO of Johnson & Johnson read that article, he was so impressed that he had copies sent out to the 400 top executives in the company worldwide.

Given that emotional intelligence is so popular in corporate America, and given that the concept is a psychological one, it is important for I/O psychologists to understand what it really means and to be aware of the research and theory on which it is based. Emotional intelligence represents a way in which I/O psychologists can make particularly significant contributions to their clients in the future.

When psychologists began to write and think about intelligence, they focused on cognitive aspects, such as memory and problem-solving. However, there were researchers who recognized early on that the non-cognitive aspects were also important. For instance, David Wechsler defined intelligence as "the aggregate or global capacity of the individual to act purposefully, to think rationally, and to deal effectively with his environment". As early as 1940 he referred to "non-intellective" as well as "intellective" elements, by which he meant affective, personal, and social factors. Furthermore, as early as 1943 Wechsler was proposing that the non-intellective abilities are essential for predicting one's ability to succeed in life. He wrote:

> The main question is whether non-intellective, that is affective and conative abilities, are admissible as factors of general intelligence. (My contention) has been that such factors are not only admissible but necessary. I have tried to show that in addition to intellective there are also definite non-intellective factors that determine intelligent behaviour. If the foregoing observations are correct, it follows that we cannot expect to measure total intelligence until our tests also include some measures of the non-intellective factors.

Wechsler was not the only researcher who saw non-cognitive aspects of intelligence to be important for adaptation and success. Robert Thorndike, to take another example, was writing about "social intelligence" in the late thirties . Unfortunately, the work of these early pioneers was largely forgotten or overlooked until 1983 when Howard Gardner began to write about "multiple intelligence." Gardner proposed that "intrapersonal" and "interpersonal" intelligences are as important as the type of intelligence typically measured by IQ and related tests.

Now let us switch our historical lens to I/O psychology. In the 1940s, under the direction of Hemphill, the Ohio State Leadership Studies suggested that "consideration" is an important aspect of effective leadership. More specifically, this research suggested that leaders who are able to establish "mutual trust, respect, and a certain warmth and rapport" with members of their group will be more effective. At about the same time, the Office of Strategic Services developed a process of assessment based on the earlier work of Murray that included the evaluation of non-cognitive, as well as cognitive, abilities. This process evolved into the "assessment center," which was first used in the private sector at AT&T in 1956. Many of the dimensions measured in assessment centers then and now involve social and emotional competencies such as communication, sensitivity, initiative, and interpersonal skills.

When Salovey and Mayer coined the term emotional intelligence in 1990, they were aware of the previous work on non-cognitive aspects of intelligence. They described emotional intelligence as "a form of social intelligence that involves the ability to monitor one's own and others' feelings and emotions, to discriminate among them, and to use this information to guide one's thinking and action". Salovey and Mayer also initiated a research program intended to develop valid measures of emotional intelligence and to explore its significance.

For instance, they found in one study that when a group of people saw an upsetting film, those who scored high on emotional clarity (which is the ability to identify and give a name to a mood that is being experienced) recovered more quickly. In another study, individuals who scored higher in the ability to perceive accurately, understand, and appraise others' emotions were better able to respond flexibly to changes in their social environments and build supportive social networks.

In the early 1990's Daniel Goleman became aware of Salovey and Mayer's work, and this eventually led to his book, *Emotional Intelligence*. Goleman was a science writer for the New York Times, whose beat was brain and behaviour research. He had been trained as a psychologist at Harvard where he worked with David McClelland, among others. McClelland was among a growing group of researchers who were becoming concerned with how little traditional tests of cognitive intelligence told us about what it takes to be successful in life.

IQ by itself is not a very good predictor of job performance. Hunter and Hunter estimated that at best IQ accounts for about 25 percent of the variance. Sternberg has pointed out that studies vary and that 10 percent may be a more realistic estimate. In some studies, IQ accounts for as little as 4 percent of the variance.

An example of this research on the limits of IQ as a predictor is the Sommerville study, a 40 year longitudinal investigation of 450 boys who grew up in Sommerville, Massachusetts. Two-thirds of the boys were from welfare families, and one-third had IQ's below 90. However, IQ had little relation to how well they did at work or in the rest of their lives. What made the biggest difference was childhood abilities such as being able to handle frustration, control emotions, and get along with other people.

Another good example is a study of 80 Ph.D.'s in science who underwent a battery of personality tests, IQ tests, and interviews in the 1950s when they were graduate students at Berkeley. Forty years later, when they were in their early seventies, they were tracked down and estimates were made of their success based on resumes, evaluations by experts in their own fields, and sources like American Men and Women of Science. It turned out that social and emotional abilities were four times more important than IQ in determining professional success and prestige.

Now it would be absurd to suggest that cognitive ability is irrelevant for success in science. One needs a relatively high level of such ability merely to get admitted to a graduate science program at a school like Berkeley. Once you are admitted, however, what matters in terms of how you do compared to your peers has less to do with IQ differences and more to do with social and emotional factors. To put it another way, if you're a scientist, you probably needed an IQ of 120 or so simply to get a doctorate and a job. But then it is more important to be able to persist in the face of difficulty and to get along well with colleagues and subordinates than it is to have an extra 10 or 15 points of IQ. The same is true in many other occupations.

We also should keep in mind that cognitive and non-cognitive abilities are very much related. In fact, there is research suggesting that emotional and social skills actually help improve cognitive functioning. For instance, in the famous "marshmallow studies" at Stanford University, four year olds were asked to stay in a room alone with a marshmallow and wait for a researcher to return. They were told that if they could wait until the researcher came back before eating the marshmallow, they could have two. Ten years later the researchers tracked down the kids who participated in the study. They found that the kids who were able to resist temptation had a total SAT score that was 210 points higher than those kids who were unable to wait.

Granted that cognitive ability seems to play a rather limited role in accounting for why some people are more successful than others, what is the evidence that emotional and social factors are important? In doing the research for his first book, Goleman became familiar with a wealth of research pointing to the importance of social and emotional abilities for personal success. Some of this research came from personality and social psychology, and some came from the burgeoning field of neuropsychology.

The Value of Emotional Intelligence

Martin Seligman has developed a construct that he calls "learned optimism" . It refers to the causal attributions people make when confronted with failure or setbacks. Optimists tend to make specific, temporary, external causal attributions while pessimists make global, permanent, internal attributions. In research at Met Life, Seligman and his colleagues found that new salesmen who were optimists sold 37 percent more insurance in their first two years than did pessimists. When the company hired a special group of individuals who scored high on optimism but failed the normal screening, they outsold the pessimists by 21 percent in their first year and 57 percent in the second. They even outsold the average agent by 27 percent.

In another study of learned optimism. Seligman tested 500 members of the freshman class at the University of Pennsylvania. He found that their scores on a test of optimism were a better predictor of actual grades during the freshman year than SAT scores or high school grades.

The ability to manage feelings and handle stress is another aspect of emotional intelligence that has been found to be important for success. A study of store managers in a retail chain found that the ability to handle stress predicted net profits, sales per square foot, sales per employee, and per dollar of inventory investment.

Emotional intelligence has as much to do with knowing when and how to express emotion as it does with controlling it. For instance, consider an experiment that was done at Yale University by Sigdal Barsade . He had a group of volunteers play the role of managers who come together in a group to allocate bonuses to their subordinates. A trained actor was planted among them. The actor always spoke first. In some groups the actor projected cheerful enthusiasm, in others relaxed warmth, in others depressed sluggishness, and in still others hostile irritability. The results indicated that the actor was able to infect the group with his emotion, and good feelings led to improved cooperation, fairness, and overall group performance. In fact, objective measures indicated that the cheerful groups were better able to distribute the money fairly and in a way that helped the organization. Similar findings come from the field. Bachman found that the most effective leaders in the US Navy were warmer, more outgoing, emotionally expressive, dramatic, and sociable.

One more example. Empathy is a particularly important aspect of emotional intelligence, and researchers have known for years that it contributes to occupational success. Rosenthal and his colleagues at Harvard discovered over two decades ago that people who were best at identifying others' emotions were more successful in their work as well as in their social lives. More recently, a survey of retail sales buyers found that apparel sales reps were valued primarily for their empathy. The buyers reported that they wanted reps who could listen well and really understand what they wanted and what their concerns were.

Some researchs suggesting that "emotional intelligence" is important for success in work and in life. However, this notion actually is somewhat simplistic and misleading. Both Goleman and Mayer, Salovey, & Caruso have argued that by itself emotional intelligence probably is not a strong predictor of job performance. Rather, it provides the bedrock for competencies that are. Goleman has tried to represent this idea by making a distinction between emotional intelligence and emotional competence. Emotional competence refers to the personal and social skills that lead to superior performance in the world of work. "The emotional competencies are linked to and based on emotional intelligence.

A certain level of emotional intelligence is necessary to learn the emotional competencies." For instance, the ability to recognize accurately what another person is feeling enables one to develop a specific competency such as Influence. Similarly, people who are better able to regulate their emotions will find it easier to develop a competency such as Initiative or Achievement drive. Ultimately it is these social and emotional competencies that we need to identify and measure if we want to be able to predict performance.

Emotional Intelligence and Competence

Assuming that emotional intelligence is important, the question of assessment and measurement becomes particularly pressing. What does the research suggest about the measurement of emotional intelligence and competence? In a paper published in 1998, Davies, Stankov, & Roberts concluded that there was nothing empirically new in the idea of emotional intelligence. However, most of those measures were new, and there was not yet much known about their psychometric properties.

Research now is emerging that suggests emotional intelligence, and particularly the new measures that have been developed to assess it, is in fact a distinct entity. However, there still is not much research on the predictive validity of such measures, and this is a serious lack.

The oldest instrument is Bar-On's EQ-I , which has been around for over a decade. This self-report instrument originally evolved not out of an occupational context but rather a clinical one. It was designed to assess those personal qualities that enabled some people to possess better "emotional well-being" than others. The EQ-I has been used to assess thousands of individuals, and we know quite a bit about its reliability and its convergent and discriminant validity. Less is known about its predictive validity in work situations. However, in one study the EQ-I was predictive of success for U.S. Air Force recruiters. In fact, by using the test to select recruiters, the Air Force saved nearly 3 million dollars annually . Also, there were no significant differences based on ethnic or racial group.

A second instrument is the Multifactor Emotional Intelligence Scale. The MEIS is a test of ability rather than a self-report measure. The test-taker performs a series of tasks that are designed to assess the person's ability to perceive, identify, understand, and work with emotion. There is some evidence of construct validity, convergent validity, and discriminant validity, but none for predictive validity.

A third instrument is the Emotional Competence Inventory. The ECI is a 360 degree instrument. People who know the individual rate him or her on 20 competencies that Goleman's research suggests are linked to emotional intelligence. Although the ECI is in its early stages of development, about 40 percent of the items come from an older instrument, the Self-Assessment Questionnaire, that was developed by Boyatzis . These earlier items had been "validated against performance in hundreds of competency studies of managers, executives, and leaders in North America," Italy. and Brazil. However, there currently is no research supporting the predictive validity of the ECI.

Another measure that has been promoted commercially is the EQ Map. Although there is some evidence for convergent and divergent validity, the data have been reported in a rather ambiguous fashion.

One other measure deserves mention, even though it is less well-known than the others. Schutte, Malouff, Hall, Haggerty, Cooper, Golden, & Dornheim have developed a 33-item self-report measure based on Salovey and Mayer's early work. There is evidence for convergent and divergent validity. Emotional intelligence scores on this measure were positively associated with first-year college grades and supervisor ratings of student counselors working at various mental health agencies. Also, scores were higher for therapists than for therapy clients or prisoners.

Finally, it might be helpful to keep in mind that emotional intelligence comprises a large set of abilities that have been studied by psychologists for many years. Thus, another way to measure emotional intelligence or competence is through tests of specific abilities. Some of these tests seem rather strong. To name just one example, there is Seligman's SASQ, which was designed to measure learned optimism and which has been impressive in its ability to identify high performing students, salespeople, and athletes, to name just a few.

TWO THEORIES ON THE NATURE OF INTELLIGENCE

There are two major schools of thought on the nature of intelligence. The first, supported by such psychologists as Eysenck, Galton, Jensen, and Spearman, believe that all intelligence comes from one general factor, known as *g*. The proponents of the other school of thought include Gardner, Sternberg, and Thurstone. These psychologists think that there is more than one general type of intelligence, or in other words, that there are different types of intelligences. An interesting note about this school of thought is that there is disagreement, even within that camp, on exactly how many different types of intelligences there are.

One General Intelligence

There are strong arguments to support the theory of one general type of intelligence. The most convincing evidence for a single general intelligence model is the fact that there is proof of a single general factor that governs the level of intelligence of an individual. This is also known as the positive manifold. Furthermore, there is a very high correlation between IQ and very simple cognitive tasks, which supports the theory of one general intelligence.

Positive manifold

The first argument in support of one general intelligence is the fact that there is a high positive correlation between different tests of cognitive ability. Spearman, in doing his research, administered to many people different types of tests, covering several different areas of cognitive ability. When he examined the results of these different tests, he found that there was a positive correlation between the tests for a given individual. In other words, if a certain person performed well on a test of verbal abilities, then that same person also performed well on another test of another cognitive ability, for instance, a mathematics test. Spearman named this positive correlation among tests the positive manifold.

This positive manifold was also called the general intelligence factor, or *g*. This is the single factor that determines the intelligence of the individual. Jensen supported the theory of one general intelligence by stating, "the positive correlation between all cognitive test items is a given, an inexorable fact of nature. The all-positive inter item correlation matrix is not an artifact of test construction or item selection, as some test critics mistakenly believe". This positive manifold led Spearman to find a large first factor that was dubbed general intelligence, or *g*.

Reaction time and g

Another strong argument in support of one general intelligence is the fact that there is a very high correlation between reaction time and IQ. According to Eysenck, "IQ correlates very highly (.8 and above, without correction for attenuation) with tests which are essentially so simple, or even directly physiological that they can hardly be considered cognitive in the accepted sense". For instance, an example of the type of tests used to measure reaction time is a test in which a light is turned on. The participant is asked to press a button as soon as he or she sees the light go on. From tests such as these, the reaction time can be measured. Given that only very simple sensory and motor movements are necessary to respond, it is difficult to argue that cultural, environmental, gender, socio-economic, or educational discrepancies will affect the participants ability to respond to the testers' questions.

Common definitions of intelligence are "success in problem solving, ability to learn, capacity for producing noegenetic solutions, understanding of complex instructions or simply all-round cognitive ability". A common thread in all of these definitions of intelligence is that they all require the nervous system, especially the brain, and sensory organs to be functioning properly. Furthermore, in order for these types of tasks to be completed, they require that the information processing that goes on within the bodily systems is relatively without error.

Jensen, as well as others, synthesized these facts and conjectured that "the most obvious hypothesis is that speed of information processing is the essential basis if *g*, and one possible neurological basis of speed of processing is the speed of transmission through nerve pathways". The speed of information transmission can be reasonably well measured or extrapolated from reaction time scores. Therefore, if an individual has faster neural processing speed, then he or she have a better reaction time. In turn, given that reaction time is highly correlated with IQ, then those individuals with faster neural processing speeds have higher IQ's. Consequently, neural processing speed determines the level of intelligence of the individual; this intelligence is the one general intelligence, *g*.

Sternberg and Gardner summarized the theory of one general intelligence by stating "general intelligence can be understood componentially as deriving in part from the execution of general components in information processing behavior". And Spearman concluded that "cognitive events do, like those of physics, admit throughout of being reduced to a small number of definitely formulatable principles in the sense of ultimate laws". These psychologists, as well as many others, believe that intelligence can be defined by a single factor. Whether that single factor be termed positive manifold, neural processing speed, or *g*, the complexities of the human mind and its processes can be reduced to a single factor, defined as intelligence.

Multiple Intelligences

The different proponents of one general intelligence all agree that there is a single factor that determines intelligence, and the proponents of multiple intelligences agree that there is more than one single type of intelligence. However, the different proponents of multiple intelligences do not agree on how many different intelligences there are, or could be. Both of them have their own theory on multiple intelligences; Gardner believes there are seven forms of intelligence; Sternberg believes there are three forms of intelligences.

Gardner's theory

Gardner's theory of multiple intelligences suggests that there are seven different forms of intelligence. They are linguistic, musical, spatial, bodily, interpersonal, intrapersonal and logico-mathematical. In developing his theory, Gardner attempted to rectify some of the errors of earlier psychologists who "all ignore[d] biology; all fail[ed] to come to grips with the higher levels of creativity; and all [were] insensitive to the range of roles highlighted in human society". So, Gardner based his own theory of intelligence on biological facts. Li summarizes Gardner's theory as follows:

— *Premise 1*: If it can be found that certain brain parts can distinctively map with certain cognitive functioning (A), then that cognitive functioning can be isolated as one candidate of multiple intelligences (B). (If A, then B).

— *Premise 2*: Now it has been found that certain brain parts do distinctively map with certain cognitive functioning, as evidenced by certain brain damage leading to loss of certain cognitive function. (Evidence of A).

Gardner's theory has a very solid biological basis. Premise two takes into account the brain as a major physical determinant of intelligence. By studying individuals who had speech impairment, paralysis, or other disabilities, Gardner could localize the parts of the brain that were needed to perform the physical function. He studied the brains of people with disabilities postmortem and found that there was damage in specific areas, in comparison to those who did not have a disability. Gardner found seven different areas of the brain, and so his theory consists of seven different intelligences, each related to a specific portion of the human brain.

Gardner looked to develop a theory with multiple intelligences also because he felt that the current psychometric tests only examined the linguistic, logical, and some aspects of spatial intelligence, whereas the other facets of intelligent behavior such as athleticism, musical talent, and social awareness were not included.

Sternberg's theory

The triarchic theory of intelligence developed by Sternberg is "a comprehensive theory, more encompassing. . . because it takes into account social and contextual factors apart from human abilities". Sternberg felt that the theories that preceded him were not incorrect, but, rather, incomplete. Consequently, his theory, like Gardner's, takes into account creative or musical intelligence. But as for the other six intelligences from Gardner's theory, Sternberg classifies them into two different types of intelligences: analytic (or academic) and practical.

These two types of intelligences differ and are defined as follows: Analytic problems tend to have been formulated by other people, be clearly defined, come with all information needed to solve them, have only a single right answer, which can be reached by only a single method, be disembodied from ordinary experience, and have little or no intrinsic interest. Practical problems tend to require problem recognition and formulation, be poorly defined, require information seeking, have various acceptable solutions, be embedded in and require prior everyday experience, and require motivation and personal involvement.

If an individual could solve one or the other of these types of problems well, then that individual would have a high analytic or practical intelligence, respectively. Also, there exist virtuosos, or individuals who are extremely talented in the fine arts, these people would have a high creative intelligence.

One reason why Sternberg's theory has received so much acclaim is that in real-life situations, is has proven itself. For example, Brazilian street children can do the math that they need to know in order to run their street businesses, but they are unable to pass a math class in school. Evidence such as this shows that there are two different types of mathematical intelligence, an academic classroom mathematical intelligence and a street wise practical intelligence.

Other theories

In addition to Gardner's and Sternberg's theories on multiple intelligences, there are other theories as well, including

Thurstone's and Guilford's. Both were proponents of multiple intelligences. Thurstone stated that "the biological function of intelligence is to protect the organism from bodily risk and to satisfy its wants with the least possible chance of recording failure on the environment". With this in mind, he found several primary mental abilities.

As expected, these abilities are those abilities that the individual uses in order to survive and succeed in society. He found this using factor analysis, like Spearman, but Thurstone took the factor analysis a step further and rotated the factors. He arrived at 13 different factors as opposed to Spearman's one and called these primary mental abilities. These factors included spatial, perceptual, numerical, logical, verbal, memory, arithmetical reasoning, and deductive abilities. Guilford found that the structure of intellect was composed of 4 contents, 5 operations, and 6 processes. Each of these was mixed and matched to come up with 120 different combinations of abilities.

7

THEORIES OF INTELLIGENCE

Intelligence theories have evolved through a succession of paradigms which have tried to explain and define intelligence. Many of these paradigms have been psychometric theories, cognitive theories, cognitive-contextual theories, and biological theories.

PSYCHOMETRIC THEORIES

Psychometric theories have sought to understand the structure of intelligence: the form it takes, its categories, and its composition. Underlying psychometric intelligence theory is a psychological model according to which intelligence is a combination of abilities that can be measured by mental testing. These tests often include analogies, classification/identification, and series completion. Each test score is equally weighted according to the evidence of underlying ability in each category.

British psychologist Charles E. Spearman published the first psychometric theory in 1904. His theory noted that people who excelled on one mental ability test often did well on the others, and people who did poorly on one of them tended to do poorly on the others. Using this concept, Spearman devised a technique of statistical analysis that examined patterns of individual differences in test scores. This analysis helped him discover what he believed to be the two sources of these individual differences: the "general factor" which is our general intellectual ability, and a test-specific factor.

American psychologist L. L. Thurstone disagreed with Spearman's theory and his isolation of the "general factor" of intelligence. Thurstone believed that the "general factor" resulted from Spearman's method of analysis, and that if analysis were more thorough, seven factors would emerge. These seven factors were collectively called the "primary mental abilities" and included verbal comprehension, verbal fluency, numbers, spatial visualization, inductive reasoning, memory, and perceptual speed.

To further complicate matters, a third theory was introduced by American Raymond Cattell and Canadian Philip Vernon. They combined ideas from Spearman and Thurstone's theories, stating that abilities are hierarchical. At the top of the hierarchy is our "general factor" of intellectual ability, and below are successive levels of narrowing abilities, ending with Spearman's "primary mental abilities".

Most psychologists agree that a broader subdivision of abilities than Spearman's classification is necessary, but only some agree with the hierarchical subdivision. It quickly became apparent to many psychologists that there were problems that could not be addressed by psychometric theories. The number of abilities could not be positively identified, and the differences between them could not be clearly defined due to the limitations of testing and analysis. However, the most significant problem extended beyond the number of abilities: what happens in someone's mind when they are using the ability in question? Psychometric theories had no means of addressing this issue, and cognitive theories began to fill this gap.

COGNITIVE THEORIES

During the era of psychometric theories, people's test scores dominated the study of intelligence. In 1957, American psychologist Lee Cronbach criticized how some psychologists study individual differences and others study commonalties in human behavior, but the two methods never meet. Cronbach voiced the need for the two methods to be united, which led to the development of cognitive theories of intelligence.

Without understanding the processes underlying intelligence, we cannot come to accurate conclusions when analyzing test scores or assessing someone's performance. Cognitive analysis helps the interpretation of test scores by determining to what degree the score reflects reasoning ability and the degree to which it is a result of not understanding the questions or vocabulary. Psychometric theories did not differentiate between these two factors, which have a significant effect on the determination of intelligence. Many people are excellent reasoners but have modest vocabularies, and vice versa.

Underlying the cognitive approach to intelligence is the assumption that intelligence is comprised of a set of mental representations of information, and a set of processes that operate the mental representations. It is assumed that a more intelligent person represents information better, and operates more quickly on these representations than does a less intelligent person.

Several different cognitive theories of intelligence have emerged over the years. One was introduced by Earl Hunt, Nancy Frost, and Clifford Lunneborg, who in 1973 showed one way in which psychometric and cognitive modeling could be combined. Instead of using conventional psychometric tests, they used tasks that allowed them to study the basis of cognition - perception, learning, and memory. Individual differences in the tasks became apparent, which they related to differing patterns of forming and operating mental representations.

Several years later, Robert Sternberg suggested an alternative approach to studying cognitive processes. He argued, based on evidence he had gathered, that there was only a weak relationship between basic cognitive tasks and psychometric test scores because the tasks being used were too simple. Although simple tasks involve cognitive processes, they are peripheral rather than central.

Although opposing cognitive theories exist, they are all based on the serial processing of information, which means that cognitive processes are executed one after another in a series. The assumption is that we process chunks of information one at a time, trying to combine the processes into an overall problem-solving strategy. Other psychologists have challenged this idea, arguing that cognitive processing is parallel, meaning that we process large amounts of information simultaneously. However, it has proved difficult to distinguish between serial and parallel models of information processing.

Despite evidence and support for cognitive intelligence theories, a major problem remains regarding the nature of intelligence. Cognitive theories do not take into account that the description of intelligence may differ from one cultural group to another. Even within mainstream cultures, it is well known that conventional tests do not reliably predict performance. Therefore in addition to cognition, the context in which the cognition operates also needs to be accounted for.

COGNITIVE-CONTEXTUAL THEORIES

Cognitive-contextual theories address the way cognitive processes operate. The two major cognitive-contextual theories are of Howard Gardner and Sternberg.

In 1983, Gardner proposed a theory of "multiple intelligences", arguing that there is no single intelligence. He identified what he believed to be the seven minimal intelligences, some of which are similar to the abilities proposed by psychometric theorists, but others not. Gardner devised his list of intelligences from a variety of sources, including studies of cognitive processing, brain damage, exceptional individuals, and cognition between cultures. He suggested that whereas most concepts of intelligence had been ethnocentric and culturally biased, his was universal.

Sternberg's "triarchic" theory of intelligence agreed with Gardner in terms of the conventional notions of intelligence being too narrow. However, he disagreed as to how to go beyond traditional notions. Sternberg suggested that some abilities are talents rather than intelligences, since they are specific and are not prerequisites for adaptation to a cultural environment. He proposed that intelligence has three aspects - not multiple intelligences, but independent aspects that relate intelligence to what goes on internally within someone, what goes on in the external world, and what mediates between the internal and external worlds.

BIOLOGICAL THEORIES

Biological theories are radically different approaches to intelligence, seeking to understand intelligence in terms of its biological basis instead of hypothetical factors or abilities. These theorists, called reductionists, believe that a full understanding of intelligence will only result from the identification of its biological substrates.

Those that oppose biological theories argue that they only seek to describe the fundamental behavior behind intelligence, not explain it. However, those in favor of these theories believe that the understanding of the biological basis of intelligence will compliment other investigations into intelligence, and will help unlock the mystery.

Every approach to thinking or the mind comes up with it's own different theory of what intelligence is, each from it's own different perspective, with it's own assumptions, and often contradicting at least one other theory.

The Behaviourists

The behaviourists seem to believe that there is no such thing as high level intelligence. The entire mind is built from the ground up from simple "Stimulus-Response" pairings, building higher and higher level functioning out of this simple technology. The surprising thing is that it seems to work as a model for some types of tasks. In fact it is this basic idea that is the basis for neural networks in artificial intelligence. Unfortunately, the further away you get from the initial input, the harder it is to get the neural nets to produce sensible answers. They are even managing to translate the structures of neural networks into higher level symbolic logic using the technology of fuzzy logic.

General Semantics

The people who are into General semantics have a different model of the nature of intelligence. Their founder Count Alfred Korzybsky believed that intelligence was an emergent property of life, which was an emergent property of complex chemistry. There is even some evidence to suport his belief with the discovery of auto-catalytic sets of chemicals, which confirms the first step in his theory. If you wish to learn more about his views, his book "science and sanity" sets out a wonderfully detailed step by step path to some quite remarkable conclusions. They are also doing detailed work at the institute of general semantics to try and find better ways of using the faculties that are inherent in the potential of the mind.

General Intelligence

Then there was the belief in an overall general intelligence, where your intelligence was composed of a single component that was easily measured on intelligence tests. While they proved to be partially right (about 70% of your IQ is this factor usually refered to as "g"), the improvement of the testing methods, combined with the direct measurement of "g" by a technique called Evoked Potential proved that they could not be totally right.

Gardener's multiple intelligences

This lead Howard Gardener, by 1980 to extend the theory of general intelligence to include a set of Specific Intelligences which make up the other 30% of your IQ score. There has been some sucess in finding evidense to support some of gardener's seven catagories, and the general technique of spotting extra components that go to make up your IQ is extendable to a lot more than 7 catagories.

THE G FACTOR: THE SCIENCE OF MENTAL ABILITY

The g factor is the highest-order common factor that can be extracted in a hierarchical factor analysis from a large battery of diverse tests of various cognitive abilities. It is the most important psychometric construct in the study of individual differences in human cognitive abilities. Since its discovery by Spearman in 1904, the g factor has become so firmly established as a major psychological construct in terms of psychometric and factor analytic criteria that further research along these lines is very unlikely either to disconfirm the construct validity of g or to add anything essentially new to our understanding of it.

In fact, g, unlike any of the primary, or first-order, factors revealed by factor analysis, cannot be described in terms of the knowledge content of cognitive test items, or in terms of skills, or even in terms of theoretical cognitive processes. It is not essentially a psychological or behavioral variable, but a biological one, a property of the brain. But although not itself a cognitive ability, g is what causes positive correlations among individual differences in performance, even on cognitive tasks that differ greatly with respect to sensory motor modality, brain modularity, and learned cognitive skills and knowledge.

The g factor derived from conventional nonspeeded psychometric tests shows higher correlations than any other factors independent of g with various measures of information-processing efficiency, such as working memory capacity, choice and discrimination reaction times, and perceptual speed. A test's g loading is the best predictor of its heritability and its sensitivity to inbreeding depression.

Psychometric g also has more direct biological correlates than any other independent source of test variance, for example brain size, brain evoked potentials, nerve conduction velocity, and the brain's glucose metabolic rate during cognitive activity. The ultimate arbiter among various "theories of intelligence" must be the physical properties of the brain itself.

The current frontier of g research is the investigation of the anatomical and physiological features of the brain that cause g. Research has reached the point at which the only direction left in which to go is that presaged by Spearman himself, who wrote that the final understanding of g must come from the most profound and detailed direct study of the human brain in its purely physical and chemical aspects".

The g factor arises from the empirical fact that scores on a large variety of independently designed tests of extremely diverse cognitive abilities all turn out to be positively correlated with one another. The g factor appears to be a biological property of the brain, highly correlated with measures of information-processing efficiency, such as working memory capacity, choice and discrimination reaction times, and perceptual speed.

It is highly heritable and has many biological correlates, including brain size, evoked potentials, nerve conduction velocity, and cerebral glucose metabolic rate during cognitive activity. It remains to investigate and explain its neurobiological basis. Commentary is invited from psychometricians, statisticians, geneticists, neuropsychologists, psychophysiologists, cognitive modellers, evolutionary psychologists and other specialties concerned with cognitive abilities, their measurement, and their cognitive and neurobiological basis.

Discovery of G

Spearman invented factor analysis, a method which permitted a rigorous statistical test of Spencer's and Galton's hypothesis that a general mental ability enters into every kind of activity requiring mental effort. A well established empirical method of finding positive correlations among measures of various mental abilities is putative evidence of a common factor in all of the measured abilities. Factor analysis makes it possible to determine the degree to which each of the variables is correlated (or loaded) with the factor that is common to all the variables in the analysis. Spearman gave the label "g" to this common factor, which is manifested in individual differences on all mental tests, however diverse.

Spearman's two-factor theory held that every mental test, however diverse in terms of the contents or skills called for, measures only two factors: g and s, a factor specific to each test. But later research based on larger numbers of tests than were available in Spearman's early studies showed that g alone could not account for all of the correlations between tests. So Spearman had to acknowledge that there are other factors besides g, called groupfactors, which different groups of tests, each with similar task demands (such as being either verbal, spatial, numerical, or mechanical), have in common.

By comparing tests with high and low g factor loadings, Spearman concluded that g is most strongly reflected in tests which call for the "eduction of relations and correlates," for example, reasoning to solve novel problems, as contrasted with recalling previously acquired knowledge or using already well learned skills.

Spearman thought of g metaphorically as "mental energy" that could be applied to any and every kind of mental task, and likened group factors and specificity to specialized "engines" for the performance of certain types of tasks. According to Spearman, individual differences in potential performance on any mental task result from two sources: differences in the amount of mental "energy" that can be delivered to the specific "engine" that mediates performance of the task, and differences in the efficiency of energy utilization by the "engine." The efficiency of the various "engines" differs independently within the same person.

Although Spearman remained agnostic concerning the biochemical and physiological basis of this energy, it was his fervent hope that scientists would eventually discover a physical basis for g.

TROUBLE WITH INTELLIGENCE

The word "intelligence" as an intraspecies concept has proved to be either undefinable or arbitrarily defined without a scientifically acceptable degree of consensus. The suggested remedy for this unsatisfactory condition is to dispense with the term "intelligence" altogether when referring to intraspecies' individual differences in the scientific context, and focus on specific mental abilities, which can be objectively defined and measured. The number of mental abilities, so defined, is unlimited, but the major sources of variance (i.e., individual differences) among myriad abilities are relatively few, because abilities are not independent, but have sources of variance in common.

The empirical fact that all mental abilities are positively correlated calls for an analytic taxonomy of mental abilities based on some form of correlation analysis. Factor analysis has proven to be the most suitable tool for this purpose. By means of factor analysis it is possible to describe the total variance of various abilities in terms of a smaller number of independent dimensions (i.e., factors), or components of variance, that differ in their degree of generality. "Generality" refers to the number of abilities that are correlated with a particular factor. The common factors in the abilities domain can be represented hierarchically in terms of their generality, with a large number of the least general factors (called first-order or primary factors) at the base of the hierarchy and the single, most general, factor at the apex.

Ability measurements can be represented geometrically and mathematically as vectors in space, with a common origin and with the angles between them related to their intercorrelations. Factors are the "reference axes" in this space, and the number of orthogonal axes, or independent dimensions, needed to represent the ability measurements, defines the number of factors. The dimensions found in the factor analysis of the correlations among a large variety of mental ability measurements can be arranged hierarchically according to their generality.

This hierarchical structure typically has three tiers, or strata: a large number of narrow (i.e., least general) first-order factors, a relatively small number (six to eight) of broad (i.e., more general) second-order factors, and, at the apex, a single third-order factor, conventionally symbolized as g. The g factor is the most general of all and is common to all mental abilities.

Models and Characteristics of G

The general factor, g, can be extracted from the correlation matrix of a battery of mental ability tests by a number of different methods of factor analysis and according to different models of the factor structure of abilities. Provided the number of tests in the analyzed battery is sufficiently large to yield reliable factors and the tests are sufficiently diverse in item types and information content to reflect more than a single narrow ability, a g factor always emerges. The only exception occurs when orthogonal rotation of the principal axes is employed. That method expressly precludes the appearance of a g factor. With orthogonal rotation, the g variance remains in the factor matrix, but is dispersed among all of the group (or primary) factors. This method of factor analysis (for which the most common factor rotation method is known as varimax) is not appropriate to any domain of variables, such as mental abilities, in which substantial positive correlations among all the variables reveal a large general factor.

Among the various methods of factor analysis that do not mathematically preclude the appearance of g when it is actually latent in the correlation matrix, a hierarchical model is generally the most satisfactory, both theoretically and statistically. In a hierarchical analysis, a number of correlated group factors (first-order factors) are extracted first.

The g factor then emerges as a second-order factor (or as a third-order factor in some very large and diverse batteries) from the correlations among the first-order factors (or among the second-order factors when g is at the third order).

The g factor is found to be remarkably invariant across all the various methods of factor analysis, except those that mathematically preclude the appearance of a general factor.

The g factor is found to be relatively invariant across different batteries of diverse tests of mental ability. This fact justifies the postulation of a true g (analogous to true score in classical measurement theory), of which the g obtained in any empirical study is an estimate.

The g factor is also found to be ubiquitous and relatively invariant across various racial and cultural groups.

The form of the population distribution of g is not known, because g cannot yet be measured on a ratio scale, but there are good theoretical reasons to assume that the distribution of g approximates the normal, or bell-shaped, curve.

The g factor is ubiquitous in all mental ability tests, and tests' g loadings are a continuous variable, ranging from values that are slightly greater than zero on some tests, to values that are near the reliability coefficient of other tests.

Although certain types of tests consistently show higher g loadings than others, it is conceptually incorrect to regard characteristics (e.g., relation eduction and abstract reasoning) of such tests as the "essence" or "defining characteristic" of g.

These features of tests may indicate the site of g, but not its nature. Unlike the group factors, the g factor cannot be described in terms of the item characteristics and information content of tests. Nor is g a measure of test difficulty: a test's g loading and its difficulty are conceptually separate.

It is wrong to regard g as a cognitive process, or as an operating principle of the mind, or as a design feature of the brain's neural circuitry. At the level of psychometrics, ideally, g may be thought of as a distillate of the common source of individual differences in all mental tests, completely stripped of their distinctive features of information content, skill, strategy, and the like. In this sense, g can be roughly likened to a computer's central processing unit.

The knowledge and skills tapped by mental test performance merely provide a vehicle for the measurement of g. Therefore, we cannot begin to fathom the causal underpinning of g merely by examining the most highly g-loaded psychometric tests. At the level of causality, g is perhaps best regarded as a source of variance in performance associated with individual differences in the speed or efficiency of the neural processes that affect the kinds of behavior called mental abilities.

Challenges to G

Viewpoints and theories antithetical to, or in some cases mistakenly thought to be antithetical to, the large body of psychometric evidence supporting the presence of a predominant general factor, g, in the domain of mental abilities are reviewed below. The proponents of the specificity doctrine, which holds that mental tests measure only a collection of bits of knowledge and skills that happen to be valued by the dominant culture in a society, as well as those who hold that individual differences in mental abilities reflect only differences in opportunities for learning certain skills, largely of a scholastic nature, or the contextualists who claim that mental ability is not general but is entirely specific to particular tasks and circumstances, have not produced any empirical evidence that contradicts the existence of the ubiquitous g factor found in any large and diverse collection of mental tests. There are, however, more rigorous critiques of g.

Guilford's Structure-of-Intellect (SOI) model, which claims 150 separate abilities, is supported only by a type of factor analysis that mathematically forces a large number of narrow factors to be uncorrelated, even though all the various ability tests that are entered into the analysis are correlated with one another. Guilford's claim of zero correlations between ability tests is unsupported by evidence: the few zero and negative correlations that are found are attributable to sampling error and other statistical limitations.

Cattell's theory of fluid intelligence (Gf) and crystallized intelligence (Gc) is reflected as second-order factors in tests that are either highly culture-reduced (Gf) or highly culture-specific (Gc), and is particularly valid in culturally and educationally heterogeneous populations. The greater the homogeneity in the population, however, the higher is the correlation between Gf and Gc. The correlation between these second-order factors is represented in a hierarchical factor analysis as a single third-order factor, namely g. Typically there is a near-perfect correlation between Gf and g, so that when the second-order factors are residualized, thereby subsuming their common variance into g, the Gf factor vanishes. In other words, Cattell's Gf and the third-order factor, g, turn out be one and the same.

Guttman's radex model, a multidimensional scaling method for spatially representing the relations between diverse mental tests, perfectly parallels the relationships shown in a hierarchical factor analysis. Tests' g loadings derived from factor analysis are displayed spatially in the radex model by the tests' proximity to the center of the circular array, with the most highly g-loaded tests being closest to the center.

Gardner's theory of seven independent "intelligences" is contradicted by the well established correlations between at least four of these "intelligences", verbal, logical-mathematical, spatial, and musical, all of which are substantially g loaded. The factorial structure of two of the "intelligences", interpersonal and intrapersonal, has not been determined, so their g loadings remain unknown, and one ability, kinesthetic, probably does not fall into the mental abilities domain as defined in Section III. There is no incompatibility between g and the existence of neural modules that control particular abilities.

Sternberg's componential and triarchic theories, which are sometimes mistakenly thought to be incompatible with g theory, are shown to be entirely consistent with it. Sternberg's theory explains the existence of g in terms of information processing components and metacomponents rather than in terms of any unitary process or property of the brain. Virtually all present day researchers in psychometrics now accept as a well established fact that individual differences in all complex mental tests are positively correlated, and that a hierarchical factor model, consisting of a number of group factors dominated by g at the apex (or the highest level of generality), is the best representation of the correlational structure of mental abilities.

Biological Correlates of G

The fact that psychometric g has many physical correlates proves that g is not just a methodological artifact of the content and formal characteristics of mental tests or of the mathematical properties of factor analysis, but is a biological phenomenon. The correlations of g with physical variables can be functional (causal), or genetically pleiotropic (two or more different phenotypic effects attributable to the same gene), or genetically correlated through cross-assortative mating on both traits, or the nongenetic result of both being affected by some environmental factor (e.g., nutrition). The physical characteristics correlated with g that are empirically best established are stature, head size, brain size, frequency of alpha brain waves, latency and amplitude of evoked brain potentials, rate of brain glucose metabolism, and general health.

The general factor of learning and problem-solving tasks in infrahuman animals has some properties similar to the g factor in humans, and experimental brain lesion studies suggest that a task's loading on the general factor is directly related to task complexity and to the number of neural processes involved in task performance.

It is clear that since it is a product of human evolution, g is strongly enmeshed with many other organismic variables.

The Heritability of G

Individual differences in mental test scores have a substantial genetic component indexed by the coefficient of heritability (in the broad sense), that is, the proportion of the population variance in test scores attributable to all sources of genetic variability. The broad heritability of IQ is about .40 to .50 when measured in children, about .60 to .70 in adolescents and young adults, and approaches .80 in later maturity.

Environmental variance can be partitioned into two sources: (1) environmental influences that are shared by children reared in the same family but that differ between families, and (2) nonshared environmental influences that are specific to each child in the same family, and therefore differ within families. The shared environmental variance diminishes from about 35 percent of the total IQ variance in early childhood to near zero percent in late adolescence.

The non-shared environmental variance remains nearly constant at around 20 to 30 percent from childhood to maturity. That is, virtually all of the nongenetic variance in adult IQs is attributable to within-family causes, while virtually none is attributable to the kinds of environmental variables that differ between families. The specific sources of much of the within-family environmental variance are still not entirely identified, but a large part of the specific environmental variance appears to be due to the additive effects of a large number of more or less random and largely physical events - developmental "noise" - with small, but variable positive and negative influences on the neurophysiological substrate of mental growth. More of the genetic variance in test scores is associated with g than with any other common factor. Hence the relative g loadings of various tests predict their relative heritability coefficients (the proportion of genetic variance in the test scores).

Traits that show genetic dominance provide evidence that they have been subjected to natural selection as a Darwinian fitness character over the course of evolution. IQ, and particularly its g component, manifest the theoretically predictable effects of genetic dominance: inbreeding depression in the offspring of consanguineous parents, and the opposite effect, hybrid vigor (or heterosis), that shows up in the offspring when each parent has a different racial ancestry.

Tests' relative g loadings significantly predict the degree to which various tests manifest both inbreeding depression and heterosis. These data support the hypothesis that the g factor of psychometric tests has arisen through natural selection over the course of human evolution and therefore can be regarded as a fitness character in the Darwinian sense.

Information Processing and G

Psychometric g can be studied more analytically by means of elementary cognitive tasks (ECTs) than is possible with the conventional IQ tests, with items based on past acquired knowledge, reasoning, and problem solving requiring the concerted action of a number of relatively complex cognitive processes. A particular ECT is intended to measure a few relatively simple cognitive processes, independently of specific knowledge or information content. Each ECT is devised to tap a somewhat different set of cognitive processes, and performance on two or more different ECTs yields data from which individual differences in distinct processes can be measured, such as stimulus apprehension, discrimination, choice, visual search, scanning of short term memory (STM), and retrieval of information from long term memory (LTM).

Typically ECTs nvolve no past learned information content, and in those that do, the content is so familiar and over learned as to be common to all persons taking the ECT, as can be shown on a nonspeeded version of the ECT. Most ECTs are so simple that every person in the study can perform them easily, and individual differences in performance must be measured in terms of response time (RT). The theoretically most interesting ECTs are those with RTs of less than one second and with response error rates close to zero. The subject's median RT (over n number of trials) and the subject's intraindividual variability of RTs (measured as the standard deviation of RT, or RTSD, over n trials) are of particular interest. Another type of ECT, known as Inspection Time (IT), measures sheer speed of perceptual discrimination (visual or auditory) independently of RT.

Measures of RT, RTSD, and IT derived from the various ECTs are correlated with IQ. For single ECTs, the correlations average about -.35, ranging from about -.10 to -.50, depending on the complexity or number of distinct processes involved in the ECT. Some processes are more strongly correlated with IQ than others. ECTs that strain the capacity of working memory generally have larger correlations with IQ. A composite score based on the RTs and RTSDs from several different ECTs, thereby sampling a greater number of different processes, typically correlates between .50 and .70 with IQ. (Recall that the average correlation between various standard IQ tests is about .80.) Factor analysis and the method of correlated vectors show that it is the g component of IQ (or of any other kind of cognitive test) that is almost entirely responsible for the correlations between ECTs and conventional psychometric tests.

RT and RTSD show only negligible loadings on group factors independent of g.

The RT x g correlation is not explained by speed-accuracy tradeoff, use of strategies, or motivation. Nor can the correlation be attributed to correlating RT with speeded psychometric tests. Most studies of the RT X g correlation are based on untimed or nonspeeded IQ tests. Moreover, the RTs of ECTs have near-zero loadings on the speed-of test-taking factor that emerges from some factor analyses of test batteries that include speeded tests.

The RT X g correlation reflects individual differences in the speed and efficiency (i.e., trial-to-trial consistency of RT, as measured by RTSD) of information processing. As there is a general factor of speed of processing common to virtually all ECTs, and as this general speed-of-information-processing factor is highly loaded on psychometric g, it is hypothesized that g is explainable, at least in part, in terms of the speed and efficiency of information processing.

The physiological properties of the brain that might account for the speed-of-processing aspect of g are not yet known completely, but it seems safe to say that they would have to be properties that are common to all regions and modules of the brain that subserve cognitive functions in which there are reliable individual differences in the neurologically normal population. One obvious candidate is individual differences in nerve conduction velocity (NCV). Brain NCV increases along with measurements of mental growth from childhood to maturity and decreases along with mental decline in old age.

NCV is also significantly correlated with IQ (Raven matrices) in college students. (The great theoretical importance of this finding, based on a single study, absolutely demands its replication.) It has been hypothesized that periodic oscillation of the synchronized action potentials of groups of neurons may account for intraindividual variability (RTSD) in ECTs. It has also been hypothesized that random biological "noise" in the neural transmission of information in the brain causes slower and less efficient information processing, individual differences in which constitute some part of g.

NCV and "noise" in neural transmission are related to the degree of myelination of nerve fibers, which may be the major physiological variable underlying g. Considerable empirical evidence indicates a relationship between myelin and other physiological and behavioral phenomena that are correlated with g. Structural, neural net, or "design" features of the brain have scarcely been investigated in relation to g in normal persons and cannot be evaluated in this respect at present.

At the level of complex psychometric tests the g factor is unitary. But it now appears most unlikely that g is unitary at the level of its causal underpinnings, as indicated by the timed measurements of performance on various ECTs and by neurophysiological measurements of variables such as NCV, rate of glucose metabolism (PET scan), and degree of myelination (MRI) of nerve fibers.

The Practical Validy of G

Practical validity is indicated by a significant and predictively useful correlation of a measurement with some educational, economic, or social criterion that is deemed important by many people. The g factor (and highly g-loaded test scores, such as the IQ) shows a more far-reaching and universal practical validity than any other coherent psychological construct yet discovered. It predicts performance to some degree in every kind of behavior that calls for learning, decision, and judgment. Its validity is an increasing monotonic function of the level of cognitive complexity in the predicted criterion. Even at moderate levels of complexity of the criterion to be predicted, g is the sine qua non of test validity. The removal of g (by statistical regression) from any psychometric test or battery, leaving only group factors and specificity, absolutely destroys their practical validity when they are used in a population that ranges widely in general ability.

The validity of g is most conspicuous in scholastic performance, not because g-loaded tests measure specifically what is taught in school, but because g is intrinsic to learning novel material, grasping concepts, distinctions, and meanings. The pupil's most crucial tool for scholastic learning beyond the primary grades - reading comprehension - is probably the most highly g-loaded attainment in the course of elementary education.

In the world of work, g is the main cognitive correlate and best single predictor of success in job training and job performance. Its validity is not nullified or replaced by formal education (independent of g), nor is it decreased by increasing experience on the job.

Although g has ubiquitous validity as a predictor of job performance, tests that tap other ability factors in addition to g may improve the predictive validity for certain types of jobs, tests of spatial ability for mechanical jobs and of speed and accuracy for clerical and secretarial jobs.

Meta-analyses of hundreds of test validation studies have shown that the validity of a highly g-loaded test with demonstrated validity for a particular job in a particular organizational setting is generalizable to virtually all other jobs and settings, especially within broad job categories.

The g factor is also reflected in many broad social outcomes. Many social behavior problems, including dropping out of school, chronic welfare status, illegitimacy, child neglect, poverty, accident proneness, delinquency, and crime, are negatively correlated with g or IQ independently of social class of origin. These social pathologies have an inverse monotonic relation to IQ level in the population, and show, on average, nearly five times the percentage of occurrence in the lowest quartile (IQ below 90) of the total distribution of IQ as in the highest quartile (IQ above 110).

Construct, Vehicles, and Measurements

As a construct, the g factor can be represented with varying degrees of convenience, efficiency, and validity by a wide variety of vehicles (psychometric tests, laboratory techniques, physiological indices) which yield measurements that have different scale properties. These three key concepts are related to one another, but do not all represent the same thing. It is important to recognize the distinctions between them when considering the nature of empirically observed changes in objective mental measurements. These may be spontaneous changes in test scores within an individual, or a secular trend in the mean of a population, or score gains induced by training or other interventions.

The critical question, then, is the locus of the change. Does it represent a change in the construct itself? Or is the change more attributable to properties of the vehicle, or to properties of the scale of measurement? The item content of the Stanford-Binet IQ tests, for example, differs from one age level to the next. Several different highly g-loaded tests differ in other factors unrelated to g. What exactly has changed, the level of g or the non-g sources of variance? Is a unit change in one range of the measuring scale equivalent to a unit change in another range, that is, are the measurements an interval scale throughout their range? A change in the measurement is not necessarily a change in the level of the construct; it could reflect any one (or a combination) of several different sources of variance in the measurements.

Evidence for an authentic change in the construct g requires broad transfer or generalizability across a wide variety of cognitive performance. Anything less implies changes in lower-order factors, or in test specificity, or in conditions peculiar to the tests, or the conditions of administration, or the measurement scales.

The practice effect from taking a given g-loaded test, as indicated by the amount of test-retest gain in score, appears to be unrelated to g. Test-retest gains probably reflect only the source of variance known as the test's specificity.

Some persons show large, apparently spontaneous changes in IQ from one testing to another. They are a small minority of all persons who have been tested. All but about 10 percent of this group showing large changes in IQ (or in other g-loaded test scores) can be accounted for by the normal distribution of measurement errors. The 10 percent or so not so accounted for by measurement error are not attributable to any specific systematic causes and are statistically unpredictable for any given individual. The kinds of events and life experiences typically invoked post hoc to explain large IQ changes are in fact not significantly correlated with IQ change but occur with the same frequency among persons who have shown little or no change in IQ.

Over the past half-century or so, a secular upward trend in IQ averaging three IQ points per decade has been observed in many developed countries. The gain has been greater on tests of fluid abilities (Gf) than of crystallized abilities (Gc), and it is generally greater in the lower than in the upper half of the IQ distribution. It is uncertain to what extent the rise in IQ represents a real change in g itself.

Several different theories have been propounded to account for the secular rise in IQ, involving changing attitudes (e.g., risk taking, guessing tendencies) toward mental tests, effects of extended schooling and more widespread education throughout all strata of society, and improvements in nutrition and medical and health care. That many such biological factors could be a major cause of the IQ gains is suggested by the fact that, over the same period of time, the average physical stature of the population has shown a comparable increase (measured in standard deviation units).

Experimental attempts to raise IQ have not produced large or lasting effects. The most intensive and extensive psychological interventions, beginning shortly after birth and continuing until five or six years of age, when the treated children enter regular schools, have produced gains of twenty to thirty or more IQ points above that of a control group at the peak of their effectiveness. But these large gains diminish greatly over time. Moreover, the almost negligible generalizability, or transfer, of the training effect to scholastic performance during the years following treatment suggests that it is not the level of g, but only the test scores that were raised, and suggests that most of the training effect resulted from "teaching to the test". The IQ gain is thus "hollow" with respect to g. However, the most recent and best-conducted intensive intervention experiment showed a lasting gain equivalent to about five IQ points (at age twelve), and a significant transfer to scholastic achievement and to unconventional g-loaded Piagetian tests, which suggest that the expected outcome is a real change in the level of g.

INTELLIGENCE IN SEVEN STEPS

The concept of intelligence, a very old one, has been employed in the most varied ways over the centuries. During the past century, there has been considerable movement on the "intelligence front," and this trend shows no sign of abating.

Until this century, the word "intelligence" has been used primarily by ordinary individuals in an effort to describe their own mental powers as well as those of other persons. Consistent with ordinary language usage, "intelligence" has been deployed in anything but a precise manner. Forgetting about homonyms which denote the gathering of information, individuals living in the West were called "intelligent" if they were quick or eloquent or scientifically astute or wise. In other cultures, the individual who was obedient, or well behaved, or quiet, or equipped with magical powers, may well have been referred to by terms which have been translated as "intelligent."

For the most part, the word "intelligent" was used in a beneficent way; however, its imprecision can be readily displayed by a recognition that it has been applied to nearly all of the American presidents in this century, even though it is doubtful that any two of our presidents exhibited similar kinds of minds. Perhaps ironically, Herbert Hoover and Jimmy Carter, two of Americas least successful presidents, both of whom were engineers, probably came closest to the lay idea of "intelligence." It may be worth noting that they have become distinguished by their behaviours as ex-presidents.

THE SCIENTIFIC TURN

In a sequence of events that is by now familiar, Alfred Binet responded to requests from Parisian ministers at the turn of the century by creating the first intelligence test. It then became possible to estimate an individual's "intelligence" by noting his or her performance on a deliberately heterogeneous set of items, ranging from sensory discrimination to vocabulary knowledge. Used first clinically for "at risk" Parisian elementary schoolchildren, the intelligence test became "normed" on Californian middle-class children and was administered quite widely, thanks in large part to the efforts of Lewis Terman at Stanford University. By the 1920's and 1930's, intelligence tests (and their product, an individual's IQ) had become deeply ensconced not only in American society but also in many other parts of the world.

PLURALIZATION OF INTELLIGENCE

While intelligence was initially perceived as a unitary (if overarching) concept, which could be captured by a single number, a debate soon arose about whether the concept could legitimately be broken into components. Such researchers as L.L. Thurstone and J.P. Guilford argued that intelligence was better conceived of as a set of possibly independent factors. In recent years, buoyed by findings from fields as disparate as artificial intelligence, developmental psychology, and neurology, a number of investigators have put forth the view that the mind consists of several independent modules or "intelligences."

CONTEXTUALIZATION

As initially put forth, most theories of intelligence-whether singular or multiple-have assumed that intelligences are simply biological entities or potentials, which exist "in the head" (and "in the brain") and can be measured reliably, independent of context. While the theory of multiple intelligences was deliberately formulated to take into account the unfolding of intelligence in different cultures, it nevertheless suffered in its early formulations from an "individual-centered" bias. Most students of intelligence, however, are now coming to the realization that intelligence cannot be conceptualized, or measured with accuracy, independent of the particular contexts in which an individual happens to live, work, and play, and of the opportunities and values provided by that milieu. Bobby Fischer might inherently have had the potential to be a great chess player, but if he had lived in a culture without chess, that potential would never have been manifested, let alone actualized. Intelligence is always an interaction between biological proclivities and opportunities for learning in a particular cultural context.

Project Spectrum, a curriculum-and-assessment project for young children, is one reflection of this view. We initially designed the project to determine whether young children exhibit distinctive profiles of intelligences, but we soon came to realize that intelligences could not be measured in the abstract; instead we had to create new environments, contexts more like children's museums than like traditional schoolrooms, in which children's intellectual proclivities had an opportunity to be elicited and practiced. Only then could some kind of meaningful assessment become possible.

INTELLIGENCE AS DISTRIBUTED

Closely related to the trend toward the contextualization of intelligence is the realization that significant parts of intelligence are distributed. The essential insight here is, again, that not all intelligence is in the head. But rather than residing simply in the general context wherein a person lives, much of everyday intelligence can be located in the human and non-human resources with which individuals work, and on which they come to depend in their productive work. Typically these resources are thought of as non-human artifacts, such as books, notebooks, computer files, and the like. And it is true that in a literate world, much on which the productive individual depends inheres in these materials.

It is also appropriate, however, to think of other individuals as part of one's "distributed intelligence." Most workers do not depend exclusively on their own skills and understanding; rather, they assume the presence of others in their work environments with whom they can regularly interact. This view is brought home vividly when one considers an office that is being computerized. Rarely does all relevant knowledge reside with a single individual; much more commonly, different office members exceed the novice level in different areas of hardware or software expertise. In our terms, intelligence about computers is "widely distributed" across individuals under such circumstances.

Our own efforts to examine the "distributed nature" of intelligence can be seen in two of our projects. In Arts Propel, a cooperative project in arts and humanities assessment, we ask students to keep detailed "processfolios" - complete records of their involvement in a project, from initial conception through interim sketches and drafts, ultimately to new plans that grow out of the final completed project. We believe that students' learning is significantly enhanced when they can have an ongoing dialogue with the record of their previous efforts, as captured in these constantly evolving processfolios.

In the Key School, an Indianapolis elementary school, children are exposed each day to contexts that nurture each of the intelligences. As part of their regular work at this experimental public school, students carry out each year three theme-related projects. Our research interest is in developing methods whereby these projects can be evaluated in a fair and comprehensive way. Part of that evaluation centres on the ways in which participation in a project has been cooperative: the human and non-human resources involved in preparation of the project, the help given by others in the presentation of the project, and the reactions of other individuals-peers as well as experts-to the final project. By deliberately including these "extra-individual" elements in our evaluations, we hope to bring home to the community the importance of "distributed aspects of intelligence." At the same time we want to undercut the common notion that all skill and learning must exist within a single brain, be that brain at home, at school, or at the work place.

NURTURANCE OF INTELLIGENCE

Even though our efforts to understand intelligence have been advancing, we still know very little about how to nurture intelligence, be it conceptualized in unitary or pluralistic fashion, in individual-centered, contextualized, or distributed form. Yet surely our efforts to understand intelligence as scientists can best be crowned by a demonstration that intelligence can be nurtured in particular educational settings, using strategic pedagogical or facilitating techniques. Here lies one important challenge for the future.

HUMANIZING INTELLIGENCE

Understanding the nature of the human mind in all of its complexity is no mean feat, and a complete understanding may well exceed human investigative capacities. But understanding intelligence-and even knowing how better to develop it-does not suffice in itself. Any human capacity can be used for ill as well as for good; and it is part of our responsibility as human beings living on a single troubled planet to try to use our competences, our intelligences, in morally responsible ways. This assignment cannot fall exclusively on the shoulders of researchers; nor can we simply afford to pass this responsibility on to others.

The human being is also more than his or her intellectual powers. Perhaps more crucial than intelligence in the human firmament are motivation, personality, emotions, and will. If we are ever to obtain a comprehensive and fully integrated picture of human beings, we need to meld our insights about cognition with comparable insights in respect to these other aspects of the human being. Perhaps, indeed, a different view of human nature will result from this activity of synthesis.

Obviously so grand an undertaking requires the highest degree of "distributed collaboration" among researchers, educators, and the general citizenry. Although the task is formidable, the advances made in understanding over the past decade give one some reason for optimism.

DEVELOPMENT OF MI THEORY

After years of research, Howard Gardner proposed a new theory and definition of intelligence in his 1983 book entitled Frames of Mind: The Theory of Multiple Intelligences. The basic question he sought to answer was: Is intelligence a single thing or various independent intellectual faculties? Gardner is Professor of Cognition and Education at the Harvard Graduate School of Education. He also holds an adjunct faculty post in psychology at Harvard and in neurology at Boston University School of Medicine. He is best known for his work in the area of Multiple Intelligences, which has been a career-long pursuit to understand and describe the construct of intelligence.

Gardner describes his work with two distinct populations as the inspiration for his theory of Multiple Intelligences. Early in his career, he began studying stroke victims suffering from aphasia at the Boston University Aphasia Research Center and working with children at Harvard's Project Zero, a laboratory designed to study the cognitive development of children and its associated educational implications. In Intelligence Reframed, Gardner states,

> Both of the populations I was working with were clueing me into the same message: that the human mind is better thought of as a series of relatively separate faculties, with only loose and nonpredictable relations with one another, than as a single, all-purpose machine that performs steadily at a certain horsepower, independent of content and context.

Gardner concluded from his work with these two populations that strength in one area of performance did not reliably predict comparable strength in another area. With this intuitive conclusion in mind, Gardner set about studying intelligence in a systematic, multi-disciplinary, and scientific manner, drawing from psychology, biology, neurology, sociology, anthropology, and the arts and humanities.

This resulted in the emergence of his Theory of Multiple Intelligences (MI Theory) as presented in Frames of Mind. Since the publication of that work, Gardner and others have continued to research the theory and its implications for education in general, curriculum development, teaching, and assessment. For the purposes of this Hot Topic, the focus will be on a description of the theory, major criticisms, and the implications for assessment.

Definition of MI Theory

According to Gardner, intelligence is much more than IQ because a high IQ in the absence of productivity does not equate to intelligence. In his definition, "Intelligence is a biopsychological potential to process information that can be activated in a cultural setting to solve problems or create products that are of value in a culture". Consequently, instead of intelligence being a single entity described psychometrically with an IQ score, Gardner's definition views it as many things. He endeavored to define intelligence in a much broader way than psychometricians. To achieve this goal Gardner established several criteria for defining intelligence. In identifying capabilities to be considered for one of the "multiple intelligences" the construct under consideration had to meet several criteria rather than resting on the results of a narrow psychometric approach.

To qualify as an "intelligence" the particular capacity under study was considered from multiple perspectives consisting of eight specific criteria drawn from the biological sciences, logical analysis, developmental psychology, experimental psychology, and psychometrics. The criteria to consider "candidate intelligences" are:

1) the potential for brain isolation by brain damage,
2) its place in evolutionary history,
3) the presence of core operations,
4) susceptibility to encoding,
5) a distinct developmental progression,
6) the existence of idiot-savants, prodigies and other exceptional people,
7) support from experimental psychology, and
8) support from psychometric findings.

To illustrate the specifics of these criteria, a brief description and example of each is provided.

The potential for brain isolation by brain damage means that one "candidate intelligence" can be dissociated from others. This criterion came from Gardner's work in neuropsychology. For example, stroke patients who are left with some forms of "intelligence" intact despite damage to other cognitive abilities such as speech. From an evolutionary perspective, the candidate intelligence has to have played a role in the development of our species and its ability to cope with the environment. In this case, Gardner uses inference to conclude that spatial abilities were critical to the survival of our species. Early hominids had to be able to navigate diverse terrains using spatial abilities. The pressure of the environment then resulted in selection for this ability. Both of these criteria emerged from the biological sciences.

From the perspective of logical analysis, an intelligence must have an identifiable core set of operations. Acknowledging the fact that specific intelligences operate in the context of the environment, Gardner argues that it is crucial to specify the capacities that are central to the intelligence under consideration. For example, linguistic intelligence consists of core operations such as recognition and discrimination of phonemes, command of syntax and acquisition of word meanings.

In the area of musical intelligence, the core operations are pitch, rhythm, timbre, and harmony. Another criteria related to logical analysis states that an intelligence must be susceptible to encoding in a symbol system. According to Gardner, symbol systems are developed versus occurring naturally, and their purpose is to accurately and systematically convey information that is culturally meaningful. Some examples of encoding include written and spoken language, mathematical systems, logical equations, maps, charts and drawings.

Gardner established two criteria from developmental psychology. The first is the presence of a developmental trajectory for the particular ability toward an expert end-state. In other words, individuals do not necessarily exhibit their "intelligence" in its raw state. Rather, they prepare to use their intelligence by passing through a developmental process. Thus, people who want to be mathematicians or physicists, spend years studying and honing their logical/mathematical abilities in a distinctive and socially relevant way.

The second criteria borrowed from the discipline of developmental psychology, is the existence of idiot-savants, prodigies and exceptional people. Gardner refers to these as accidents of nature that allow researchers to observe the nature of a particular intelligence in great contrast to other average or impaired abilities. One example of this type of highlighted intelligence is the autistic person who excels at numerical calculations or musical performance.

Finally, Gardner draws his last two criteria from traditional psychology and psychometrics to determine if a candidate intelligence makes it onto the list of specific abilities he calls Multiple Intelligences. There must be support from experimental psychology that indicates the extent to which two operations are related or different. Observing subjects who are asked to carry out two activities simultaneously can help determine if those activities rely on the same mental capacities or different ones.

For example, a person engaged in working a crossword puzzle is unlikely to be able to carry on a conversation effectively, because both tasks demand the attention of linguistic intelligence, which creates interference. Whereas, the absence of this sort of competition allows a person to be able to walk and converse at the same time suggesting that two different intelligences are engaged. In spite of the fact that Gardner proposed his theory in opposition to psychometrics, he recognizes the importance of acknowledging psychometric data.

From the preceding eight criteria, Gardner proposed and defined seven intelligences.

Logical-mathematical intelligence is the ability to detect patterns, think logically, reason deductively and carry out mathematical operations.

Linguistic intelligence involves the mastery of spoken and written language to express oneself or remember things. These first two forms of intelligence are typically the abilities that contribute to strong performance in traditional school environments and to producing high scores on most IQ measures or tests of achievement.

Spatial intelligence involves the potential for recognizing and manipulating the patterns of both wide spaces such as those negotiated by pilots or navigators, and confined spaces such as those encountered by sculptors, architects or championship chess players.

Musical intelligence consists of the capacity to recognize and compose musical pitches, tones, rhythms, and patterns and to use them for performance or composition.

Bodily-Kinesthetic intelligence involves the use of parts of the body or the whole body to solve problems or create products. Athletes, dancers, surgeons and craftspeople are likely to have highly developed capacity in this area.

The last two intelligences are the personal intelligences: interpersonal and intrapersonal. Interpersonal intelligence indicates a person's ability to recognize the intentions, feelings and motivations of others. People who possess and develop this quality are likely to work well with others and may choose fields like sales, teaching, counseling or politics in order to use them.

Intrapersonal intelligence is described as the ability to understand oneself and use that information to regulate one's own life. According to Gardner each of these seven "intelligences" has a specific set of abilities that can be observed and measured.

More recently, Gardner has nominated three additional candidate intelligences: Naturalist, Spiritual and Existential intelligence and evaluated them. He defines a naturalist as a person "who demonstrates expertise in recognition and classification of the numerous species - the flora and fauna - of her or his environment." Gardner is comfortable with declaring that a Naturalist intelligence meets the criteria he set forth, however he is less sure about how to define and incorporate Spiritual and Existential intelligences.

> "...the monopoly of those who believe in a single general intelligence has come to an end."

Criticism of MI Theory

When reviewing criticism of Multiple Intelligences theory, addressing the historically ever-present question of whether intelligence is one thing or many things is unavoidable. The fundamental criticism of MI theory is the belief by scholars that each of the seven multiple intelligences is in fact a cognitive style rather than a stand-alone construct. Morgan, refers to Gardner's approach of describing the nature of each intelligence with terms such as abilities, sensitivities, skills and abilities as evidence of the fact that the "theory" is really a matter of semantics rather than new thinking on multiple constructs of intelligence and resembles earlier work by factor theorists of intelligence like L.L. Thurstone who argued that a single factor (g) cannot explain the complexity of human intellectual activity.

According to Morgan, identifying these various abilities and developing a theory that supports the many factors of intelligence has been a significant contribution to the field. Furthermore, he believes that MI theory has proven beneficial to schools and teachers and it may help explain why students do not perform well on standardized tests but it in Morgan's opinion it does not warrant the complete rejection of g.

Gardner admittedly avoided addressing criticism of his theory for nearly a decade after the publication of Frames of Mind. However, in a 1995 article that appeared in Phi Delta Kappan he responds to several "myths" about the Theory of Multiple Intelligences. These myths provide a summary of the major commentary on and criticism of Gardner's theory. The first myth is that if there are seven intelligences we must be able to measure them with seven specific tests. Gardner is vocal about his disdain for a singularly psychometric approach to measuring intelligence based on paper and pencil tests. Secondly, he responds to the belief that an intelligence is the same as a domain or a discipline.

Gardner reiterates his definition of an intelligence and distinguishes it from a domain which he describes as a culturally relevant, organized set of activities characterized by a symbol system and a set of operations. For example, dance performance is a domain that relies on the use of bodily-kinesthetic and musical intelligence.

Other criticisms include the notion that MI theory is not empirical, is incompatible with g, heritability, and environmental influences, and broadens the construct of intelligence so widely as to render it meaningless. Gardner staunchly defends the empiricism of the theory by referring to the numerous laboratory and field data that contributed to its development and the ongoing re-conceptualization of the theory based on new scientific data. Regarding the claim that Multiple Intelligences theory cannot accommodate g, Gardner argues that g has a scientific place in intelligence theory but that he is interested in understanding intellectual processes that are not explained by g.

In response to the criticism that MI theory is incompatible with genetic or environmental accounts of the nature of intelligence, Gardner states that his theory is most concerned with the interaction between genetics and the environment in understanding intelligence. Finally, the notion that MI theory has expanded the definition of intelligence beyond utility produces a strong reaction from Gardner. He argues passionately that the narrow definition of intelligence as equal to scholastic performance is simply too constrictive. In his view, MI theory is about the intellectual and cognitive aspects of the human mind. Gardner is careful to point out that MI theory is not a theory of personality, morality, motivation, or any other psychological construct.

Implications

The two most widely used standardized tests of intelligence are the Wechsler scales and the Stanford-Binet. Both instruments are psychometrically sound, but Gardner believes that these tests measure only linguistic and logical/mathematical intelligences, with a narrow focus within content in those domains. According to Gardner, the current psychometric approach for measuring intelligence is not sufficient. In his view, assessment must cast a wider net to measure human cognitive abilities more accurately. Gardner proposes several improvements for the development of intelligence measures. Before enumerating those improvements, it is important to understand how Gardner defines assessment.

In his view, the purpose of assessment should be to obtain information about the skills and potentials of individuals, and provide useful feedback to the individuals and the community at large. Furthermore, Gardner draws a distinction between testing and assessment. Assessment elicits information about an individual's abilities in the context of actual performance rather than by proxy using formal instruments in a de-contextualized setting.

Gardner argues for making assessment a natural part of the learning environment. Assessment is then built into the learning situation much like the constant assessment of skills that occurs in apprenticeship or the self-assessment that occurs in experts who have internalized a standard of performance based on the earlier guidance of teachers. The ecological validity of assessment is also at issue according to Gardner. Predictive validity of traditional intelligence tests may be psychometrically sound, but its usefulness beyond predicting school performance is questionable.

Therefore, prediction could be improved if assessments more closely approximated real working conditions. Instruments for measuring intelligence should also be "intelligence-fair". Consequently, we need to reduce the bias toward measuring intelligence through logical/mathematical and linguistic abilities and move toward looking more directly at a specific intelligence in operation (e.g., assessing for spatial intelligence by having an individual navigate his or her way around unfamiliar territory). Gardner acknowledges that this approach to assessment may be difficult to implement.

Gardner emphasizes two additional points about assessment that are critical. The first is that the assessment of intelligence should encompass multiple measures. Relying on a single IQ score from a WISC-III (Wechsler Intelligence Scale for Children) without substantiating the findings through other data sources does the individual examinee a disservice and produces insufficient information for those who provide interventions. Secondly, all assessments and resulting interventions must be sensitive to individual differences and developmental levels. Finally, Gardner is in favour of assessment for the primary purpose of helping students rather than classifying or ranking them.

While these views about assessment are intuitively sensible, Sternberg argues that the naturalistic approach is a "psychometric nightmare". Quantifying performance on these sorts of assessments is difficult, objectivity is questionable, and cultural bias is still a problem. Hard data is the scientific "gold standard" and psychometric soundness is a prerequisite. Therefore, Sternberg hesitates endorsing this approach to assessment on the basis that we would simply be replacing one flawed system of measurement with an approach that is equally problematic. Recent research on MI Theory-based assessments provides evidence in support of Sternberg's concern about psychometric quality.

Future Research Directions

The future research agenda for MI Theory and intelligence is likely to encompass a multidisciplinary approach. While intelligence is usually researched through the lens of psychology, future discoveries are likely to come from the cross-pollination of ideas in neuroscience, cellular biology, genetics, and anthropology to name a few. Gardner also favours gathering ethnographic data and cross-cultural information to see intelligence in action and in context. The use of information processing techniques and computer simulations is another relevant approach for gaining new insight into human intellectual capacities. At this point in history, the study of intelligence has moved well beyond the realm of psychometrics. As Gardner writes, "The theory of multiple intelligences has helped break the psychometricians century long stranglehold on the subject of intelligence."

ALTERNATIVE APPROACHES TO COGNITIVE ABILITIES

In the last decade of the nineteenth century, a French physician named Alfred Binet was commissioned by the school system to develop a way to differentiate those students who were uneducable, or severely mentally handicapped, from the other students. He developed an intelligence test to do so. The very first intelligence tests, introduced a decade earlier, emphasized sensory tasks, physical measures, and simple processes. Unlike these tests, Binet developed an intelligence test that consisted of items that required complex processes of the mind and examined the comprehensive individual.

Consequently, the results from Binet's scales were successful in discriminating between the two types of students. The success of Binet's test led to a much greater question to be asked: what exactly are these tests measuring? What the tests claimed to measure was intelligence. But, if they measured intelligence, then the next question that arose was this: what exactly is intelligence? It is at this point that the great debate on the definition of intelligence began.

There is a general consensus that there are different levels of intelligence, and that different individuals have different capacities of intelligence. In other words, "individuals differ from one another in their ability to understand complex ideas, to adapt effectively to the environment, to learn from experience, to engage in various forms of reasoning, to overcome obstacles by taking thought". But, how many and what kinds of different types of intelligences exist, and how to define intelligence, is still at debate.

NEW AND EMERGING THEORIES OF INTELLIGENCE

The study of intelligence has proved to be a continuously

evolving, dynamic field, with the breadth of the field expanding rapidly over the past 25 - 30 years. Many individuals, such as Gardner, Naglieri, and Goleman, argue that our view of human intelligence is far too narrow, leading the way to an expanded view of what intelligence is and what constitutes an intelligence. Several of the new and emerging intelligences are noted in the following sections.

Moral Intelligence

Moral Intelligence is the ability to distinguish between right and wrong. Broadly conceived, moral intelligence represents the ability to make sound decisions that benefit not only yourself, but others around you.

Social Intelligence

Interpersonal intelligence is the ability to understand other people: what motivates them, how they work, how to work cooperatively with them. Successful salespeople, politicians, teachers, clinicians, and religious leaders are all likely to be individuals with high degrees of interpersonal intelligence. At the same time, social intelligence probably draws on specific internal abilities. For example, in a recent study of incompetence, Kruger and Dunning found that incompetent people assessed themselves as being highly competent. This lack of ability to self-assess may be due to a combination of internal (poor metacognition) and external factors (poor ability to compare oneself to others). Social intelligence appears to be receiving the most attention in the management and organizational psychology literatures.

Emotional Intelligence

Emotional intelligence, on the other hand, "is a type of social intelligence that involves the ability to monitor one's own and others' emotions, to discriminate among them, and to use the information to guide one's thinking and actions". According to Goleman, "Emotional intelligence, the skills that help people harmonize, should become increasingly valued as a workplace asset in the years to come". EI may subsume Gardner's inter- and intrapersonal intelligences, and involves abilities that may be categorized into five domains:

— *Self-awareness*: Observing yourself and recognizing a feeling as it happens.

— *Managing emotions*: Handling feelings so that they are appropriate; realizing what is behind a feeling; finding ways to handle fears and anxieties, anger, and sadness.

— *Motivating oneself*: Channeling emotions in the service of a goal; emotional self control; delaying gratification and stifling impulses.

— *Empathy*: Sensitivity to others' feelings and concerns and taking their perspective; appreciating the differences in how people feel about things.

— *Handling relationships*: Managing emotions in others; social competence and social skills.

INTELLIGENCE THEORY AND GIFTED EDUCATION

The study of giftedness has closely paralleled the study of intelligence. Many scholars who were concerned with matters of intelligence also focused on manifestations of talent and genius: Kant, William James, Galton, Terman, and Hollingworth, to name just a few. The interrelationship between intelligence and gifted education continues today. Intelligence theory influences the way we identify and assess students, our attitudes toward giftedness and gifted students, the models upon which we base our programs and interventions, and many other aspects of gifted education.

Yet with the surge in new intelligence theories, many of these theories and their potential applications remain underexamined. The purpose of this Hot Topic is to identify theories that have significant potential for gifted education or that, for various reasons, have been underutilized.

But how to organize the multitude of intelligence theories? Both Sternberg and Gardner, Kornhaber, and Wake propose classification schemes in their texts on intelligence. Sternberg suggests that we view intelligence theories in terms of the metaphors on which they are based: geographic, computational, biological, epistemological, anthropological, sociological, and systems.

Gardner et al. take the more traditional approach to classify these theories based on their dominant perspective: psychometric, developmental, biological, cognitive, and recent.

The unitary, entity view of intelligence ("*g*") has been by far the most influential conception of intelligence since Spearman first provided evidence of its existence early in the 20th century. Although *g* is much maligned in educational circles, anyone concluding that unitary entity perspectives are out of fashion should note the passion surrounding the publication of *The Bell Curve*. This book, which is among the most exhaustive defenses of g, elicited a great deal of debate within gifted education.

Indeed, Jensen goes so far as to argue that Sternberg's Triarchic Theory is fully compatible with the idea of *g*. The death of *g* has been exaggerated. However, the debate about the existence of unitary theories of intelligence is unfortunate for another reason: Several other theories of intelligence that emerged prior to 1980 received little application in gifted education. These theories include the conception of Fluid and Crystallized Intelligences and the Structure of the Intellect model. These theories have seen different degrees of application in schools, but not to the degree one would have expected given their considerable empirical support.

Several "new" approaches to intelligence theory have become rather widespread in their acceptance and application.

Foremost among these theories are the Theory of Multiple Intelligences and the Triarchic Theory of Intelligence. MI Theory has enjoyed widespread application since its inception, but the popularity of the theory in educational circles has peaked. Triarchic Theory, which has received much less attention from educators primarily due to its complexity, is well-known and may be gaining momentum — the work of Sternberg and his colleagues applying the theory in educational settings (in conjunction with Sternberg's theories of successful intelligence and mental self-government) has produced promising results.

Interestingly, two approaches to intelligence theory that are often cited in the psychological literature are much less popular by educators of the gifted. Ceci's extension of Sternberg's theory to incorporate bio-ecological elements receives very little attention among educators, as does Carroll's Three-Stratum Theory of Cognitive Abilities. These conceptualizations of intelligence are worthy of further investigation.

A major goal of this special issue is to introduce emerging theories of intelligence and ability. Some of these theories (e.g., PASS Theory) have had longer incubation periods than others, but all provide alternative perspectives on the nature of human intellect. For example, many educators are exploring the potential applications of emotional intelligence, implicit theories of intelligence, and similarly alternative perspectives.

Determining the relative worth of these theories is a difficult process. After all, who would have expected MI Theory to have such a pervasive influence on gifted education, and education in general, back in 1983? And who would have expected the potential applications of Triarchic Theory to become more readily apparent a decade after its introduction? As Sternberg and Lubart (1995) note in their investment theory of creativity, when considering the value of ideas, "buying low" and "selling high" has considerable value.

Educators and psychologists have begun to "buy" the value of PASS Theory, emotional intelligence, and implicit theories. The other, even more recent perspectives have similar potential.

Intelligence is meant to be a generalised measure of overall ability, or potential ability: its proponents claim that it is getting at an underlying feature which is independent of specific skill development or learning achievement.

The problem is that it is difficult to get a consensus about what "intelligence" actually is:

— The power of good responses from the point of view of truth or fact" (Thorndike)

— A biological mechanism by which the effects of a complexity of stimuli are brought together and given a somewhat unified effect in behavior" (Peterson)

— The ability to carry on abstract thinking" (Terman)

— The ability to adapt oneself adequately to relatively new situations in life" (Pintner)

— The capacity for knowledge, and knowledge possessed" (Henmon)

— The capacity to acquire capacity" (Woodrow)

— Viewed narrowly, there seem to be almost as many definitions of intelligence as there were experts asked to define it" (Sternberg)

— Francis Galton measured head size, reaction time etc., but found no correlations

Alfred Binet (1905 on) devised tests to determine ineducability (to meet the requirements of a new French law prescribing schooling for all educable children) and formulated the idea of "Mental Age" from which developed the idea of the "Intelligence Quotient".

Lewis Terman (at Stanford University) adapted and standardised the Binet tests for American children known as the "Stanford-Binet" tests.

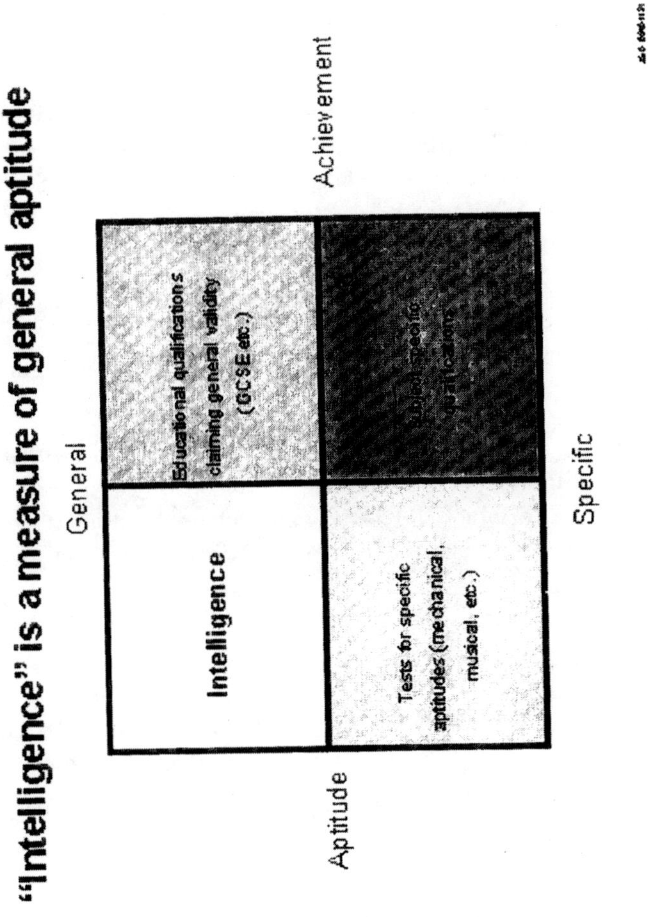
"Intelligence" is a measure of general aptitude
General
Specific
Aptitude
Achievement
Intelligence
Educational qualifications claiming general validity (GCSE etc.)
Tests for specific aptitudes (mechanical, musical, etc.)

David Wechsler developed the Wechsler Adult Intelligence Scale in 1939

INTELLIGENCE QUOTIENT (IQ)

$$IQ = \frac{\text{Mental Age x 100}}{\text{Chronological Age}}$$

So if the Mental Age = Chronological Age, IQ = 100, the notional average. The distribution of IQ supposedly follows a normal distribution curve (or "Bell Curve"), and assessment of "superiority" and "inferiority" is determined by the number of statistical Standard Deviations above and below the mean.

However, the "Flynn effect" suggests that IQ scores have been rising over time, so that the initial norm of 100 is no longer valid. This is of course problematic because of different approaches to measurement.

The Bell curve referred to in Herrnstein and Murray's (1995) famous (or notorious) book is simply the normal distribution curve which IQ tests were set up to plot. 68% of the population come within one standard deviation of the mean, and 95% within two standard deviations.

Components

The 1986 Stanford-Binet Test—one of the accepted standard tests—examines four broad areas of intelligence, which are *supposed to be* independent of each other, and not culture bound.

— verbal reasoning

— abstract/visual reasoning

— quantitative reasoning

— short-term memory

However, there is considerable argument as to whether these are simply more specific manifestations of a more general underlying feature, known as the *g* factor.

Spearman's g *Factor*

The *g* (for "general") factor is arrived at by factor analysis of results from tests and is suggested as the main underlying component, supplemented by components relating to more specific aptitudes. Critics suggest **g** is an artefact of method, since Spearman was a statistician rather than a psychologist, although it is conceded that "intelligence" may have a hierarchical structure. At the other end of the scale is the notion of multiple intelligences, suggested by Howard Gardner.

FACTORS IN EDUCATIONAL ACHIEVEMENT

As the correlation figures show, intelligence alone is not sufficient to account for academic achievement: it is certainly necessary, but beyond a certain threshold, it is by no means clear how much.

As education progresses, other factors come into play, such that the limits are determined by the strength of the weakest link in the chain.

Political issues

- Intelligence has been a fraught political issue, ever since Francis Galton attempted to measure ability to support his eugenic theories. Early abuses in the United States included compulsory sterilisation of people with low IQ
- In the UK, Sir Cyril Burt's work on IQ was the basis of selection at 11+, in the 1944 Education Act. In the 1970s, Burt was accused of fraudulent results because some of his findings were *too* significant: he appears to have been rehabilitated, but there are still some unanswered questions.
- Arthur Jensen (1969) was accused of racism when he suggested that white children were more intelligent than blacks (and that Asian children were brighter than either). Latterly, the controversy has been revived by Herrnstein

Chain of factors influencing educational achievement

and Murray (1995) and publication of Chris Brand's book *The g Factor* was abandoned at the last minute in 1996 because of concerns about his self-confessed "scientific racism"

CAN INTELLIGENCE BE TAUGHT?

There is considerable debate over the hereditary component in intelligence, and the picture is getting more complicated all the time, but at least one school believes that intelligence can largely be identified with "problem-solving skills" or even forms of pattern recognition and that as such it can be taught.

8

MEASUREMENT OF INTELLIGENCE

Although there are many different ways of measuring intelligence, most methods fall within two traditions. The first tradition is that of English scientist Sir Francis Galton. The second and most prominent tradition is that of French psychologist Alfred Binet. From 1884 to 1890, Sir Francis Galton maintained a laboratory at the South Kensington Museum in London, where people could have themselves tested against a variety of psychophysical tasks, such as weight discrimination, and sensitivity to sound frequencies. Galton believed that psychophysical abilities were the basis of intelligence, and therefore his tests were indirect measures of intelligence.

IQ TESTS

The IQ test is the most influential tradition of intelligence testing, and was developed in France by Alfred Binet and Theodore Simon. In 1904, the minister of public instruction in Paris named a commission to test children, ensuring that mentally handicapped children would receive adequate education and that children with behavior problems would not be mislabeled as mentally handicapped. Binet was in charge of developing the test, and strongly opposed the Galtonian tradition, believing that his tests only measured trivial abilities.

Binet instead proposed that intelligence tests should measure skills such as judgement, comprehension, problem-solving, and reasoning. Binet's test became the basis of most modern intelligence tests. Shortly after its completion, Binet's test was brought to the United States by Stanford University psychologist Lewis Terman, who then modified the test. The new version of the IQ test was named the Stanford-Binet test, which is still occasionally used today. The Stanford-Binet and similar tests yield an overall score referred to as an intelligence quotient, or IQ. Newer tests, such as the Wechsler Adult Intelligence Scale and the Wechsler Intelligence Scale for Children yield not only an overall IQ, but also separate IQs for verbal and performance sub-tests.

IQ was originally derived as the ratio of mental age to chronological age, multiplied by 100. Therefore, if a 10-year-old had a mental age of 12 (the average mental age of a 12-year-old), the child's IQ was 120. However, in recent years the concept of mental age has come under much controversy, and few tests continue to use this method. Today most tests determine IQ based on statistical distribution. Scores are assigned based on what percentage of people would be expected to have a certain IQ.

Some IQ tests focus on verbal ability, some on spatial skills, and others on reasoning and analytical skills. Some tests depend on reaction time, or the amount of time it takes to recognize a specific stimulus. Many IQ tests incorporate all of these factors in sub-tests to test a wide range of abilities. It is believed that despite the nature of the test, a general statistical factor can be extracted from the results using a technique called factor analysis, which is a general measurement of intelligence.

However, not all psychologists agree that there is a general, measurable intelligence factor. Some believe that this general statistical factor only reflects some types of intelligence, but not others. Other psychologists believe that there are multiple intelligences that cannot be measured.

Distribution of IQs

Intelligence scores follow normal distribution or a bell curve, meaning that most people score near the middle and fewer scores occur as you move farther away from the middle. Scores are usually converted to a scale where the average is 100 and the standard deviation is 15. Ninety-five percent of the population falls within two standard deviations of the mean (between 70 and 130).

It has become common to associate certain IQs with labels. At the upper end of the scale, people with IQs over 130 are often labeled as "gifted". At the lower end, scores of 70-84 have been classified as borderline retarded, 55-69 as mildly retarded, 40-54 as moderately retarded, and 25-39 as severely retarded. However, placing these labels has its downside, and some people even believe that labeling according to IQ is dangerous.

Before we can assign labels, it must be assumed that IQ tests provide adequate and accurate information. Most experts believe that this is not the case, since conventional intelligence tests only test a narrow range of abilities according to specific types of questions. Labeling someone according to a single test score can potentially cause an injustice to that person. Secondly, other factors are generally recognized as part of intelligence and need to be taken into account when labeling someone as gifted or mentally handicapped.

There are many degrees of intelligence, some of which are believed to develop over time and according to our experiences. It is also widely believed that IQ only reflects part of our overall intelligence. Thirdly, external factors contribute to the outcome of an intelligence test. People who are "test-anxious" rarely perform well on standardized tests, and people who do not have an extensive knowledge of the language they are being tested in often perform well below their potential. For these reasons, it has come to be believed that IQ scores need to be interpreted carefully and on an individual basis.

MEASUREMENT OF VERBAL ABILITY

Assumption 1

The psychometric measurement of verbal ability with students who live in a bilingual environment is not possible using traditional psychometric technique.

One reason for the difficulty is the absence of a normative sample which can be used as a peer group. The peer group will be very difficult to find, because each student's language history varies, and so does the opportunity to acquire a given language. A related problem is that the bilingual student experiences a change in the method of processing information when the second language is learned subsequent to the first. As they experience a prolonged period of not understanding the details of language, they begin to process information (both verbal and nonverbal) by getting the gist or gestalt of the information. Details are no longer something to which they attend, both verbally and nonverbally.

If it were possible to measure the verbal ability, one could consider this a partial measurement of "g". "g" is understood to be the innate ability of an individual. This concept was developed to predict academic success in the general population, and has been used in order to predict vocational success. An average "g" would be 100 (Standard Deviation is assumed to be 15), with a mentally deficient measure of "g" having an upper limit at 69 and a gifted measure of "g" begins at 130 and goes up. "g" is usually expressed in this numeric way, and is commonly thought of as being equivalent to an IQ score. On the most widely accepted IQ tests, Verbal ability is included as a major factor in the measurement of "g".

School Psychologists have been assigned the duty of finding this number, and we take this responsibility very seriously. Unfortunately, we have begun to believe that we really can find "g", that it is accurately measured by Wechslers, Binets, and Kaufmans. We frequently have taken the mistaken position that educational disadvantage does not exist, that lower socio-economic populations have lower "g" than middle to upper socio-economic groups because the IQ test results say so. We translate IQ tests from one language to another because we believe that responses to certain key questions or tasks will permit us to know "g". Some of us have begun to believe that the IQ test score really is "g", even though "g" can not be measured directly. This mistaken notion of "g" has resulted in a wide variety of educational errors, which typically "blame" the child for educational deficits. These errors also include programming which is directed at accepting the deficits, tending to perpetuate the learning problems.

For example, the child who has a Verbal IQ score of 75 and a performance IQ of 100 is said to learn better visually, so all instruction should include visual materials. The material used by teachers with which to teach continues to include that which the student cannot learn due to the absence of prerequisite skills, and the student's relative educational status amongst peers (verbal IQ) continues to fall. If this kind of intervention fails, educators are justified in placing the child in Special Education. In these classes, all too frequently the academic oral (or manual) language that the student needs to learn is even more difficult to encounter.

Instead of this "Visual Learner" mentality, it would be preferable to adjust the material to that which the student is ready to learn, and to provide more opportunities for discussion. It is verbal interaction and discussion that will raise the student's verbal IQ (relative academic status amongst peers), not passive visual reception of information. As the Oral language facility with academic language increases (Verbal IQ), the student's reading ability increases, and the reading skills can improve.

Most commonly, IQ scores are obtained from the results of Intelligence tests which purport to use a normative sample that is representative of the population evaluated. Typically, normative samples of the tests which attempt to measure "g" include only monolingual speakers of the language sampled, or fluent speakers if the language sampled is different from the native language of the individual considered in the sample. This is done in an effort to control for factors which don't relate to intelligence, including limited language training and major cultural variations.

For example, a student whose native language is Spanish and who is not fluent in English, would not be included in the normative sample of an IQ test in English. Also, a mentally handicapped student who is a monolingual speaker of the language sampled could be included in the sample. Since Mentally handicapped students are not fluent speakers, no mentally handicapped students who have a native language other than English are included in the normative samples of IQ tests standardized in English. This means that normative statistics are skewed too high when considering second language students. It is clear that "g" in bilingual students is not possible to measure with existing tests, so procedures to approximate "g" may be essential. Two reasons for this are:

1) that Verbal abilities are not measured by verbal tests due to the omission of these students in the normative samples, and the different way of processing the information preferred by this population. Additionally, these students have not had the same opportunity to learn a given language like monolingual speakers, and they should not be compared to monolinguals for this specific reason. They are educationally disadvantaged during the early years of introduction of a second language, and this symptom can only be overcome by hard work on the part of the individual.
2) that neither Verbal abilities nor skills are assessed by nonverbal tests, and to predict academic success, measurement of verbal skill is essential (some of the most important prerequisites for reading include verbal skills).

Assumption 2

Elementary students who live in a bilingual world have an

average Verbal Ability Score which is depressed by some quantity. It is assumed that this quantity is one standard deviation.

As mentioned elsewhere, peer groups of second language students are varied, so that no one group should be used as a basis for normative data. It has been observed that second language students seem to have verbal ability scores about one standard deviation below the monolingual mean, and so it is assumed that this guideline is adequate when considering the verbal ability part of "g" in the second language student. Therefore, a second language student who scores 85 on verbal ability tests is considered to have a verbal "g" score of 100. Further, a verbal score of 61 is equivalent to a verbal "g" score of 70, and a score of 111 is considered to be equal to a verbal "g" score of 130.

For those who may be offended by the relative status of these scores, it should be clear that the Second Language Student would show "g" verbal measurements in their native language at a level far superior to their dominant language monolingual peers in that same native language. However, compared to monolingual speakers of the native language, these children would compare similarly as they do to their peers in English. Even in their native tongue, they are generally one standard deviation below monolingual native speaking peers. Again, "g" is impossible to measure in these students, but can be estimated based on monolingual performance.

To infer the "innate" verbal ability of a bilingual student, use actual standard score measurements on verbal (or Oral language) tests in the following way:

— 60-down is Intellectually Deficient or Very Low

— 61-68 is Borderline or Low

— 69-76 is Low Average

— 77-94 is Average

— 95-102 is Above Average

— 103-110 is Superior
— 111-up is Very Superior (gifted)

BILINGUAL IQ CONVERSION CHART

The following chart may be used to compute a student's "Bilingual Score" from a given Verbal Scale Standard score (or conversely):

Listed Score:	57	61	65	69	73	77	81	85	89	94	98	102	107	111
Bilingual Score:	65	70	75	80	85	90	95	100	105	110	115	120	125	130

Interpolate any other scores (Listed score of 75 = Bilingual score of about 88), and continue the table up or down by using the guide of up (or down) 4 in a listed score is the same as up (or down) 5 in a bilingual score.

Example: José has a measured score of 85 on the Batería oral language cluster. His ability to function in a bilingual academic world would be 100. Therefore, his K-ABC Simultaneous Processing Scale (similar to the WISC-III Performance Scale) score of 100 would be thought of as being equivalent. In fact, a pre-converted Batería score of 100 would be thought of as being at the same level as a K-ABC Simultaneous Processing score of 118, unless this student has only recently (within the last 2 years if primary or intermediate level) immigrated from a monolingual Spanish area. This leads to the conclusion that a student who scores 100 on the Batería and 100 on the K-ABC Simultaneous Processing scale shows a strength in the Oral Language area. This isn't obvious until converted scores are used.

Elementary Students who live in a bilingual world are not subjected to opportunities to expand their language skills in any one language like those who live in monolingual worlds.

Therefore, students that are from environments which tend to be monoiingual should be expected to be compared to other monolinguals (mean = 100), and those who have histories somewhat similar to Bilingual students should be compared to other bilingual students (mean = 85). Use the conversion chart above for more general guidance, adjustments would need to be made for the disadvantaged.

Typically, students that have lived in the United States for two years or more (one year or more at Kindergarten or First grade) should be compared to bilingual students due to the impact of the dominant (English) language in the child's environment. Limited availability of books and electronic media, the absence of Spanish language instruction, and the subtle messages from society which imply that English is better than Spanish contribute to this problem.

Fortunately, verbal ability can be inferred, based on typical environmental histories seen in bilingual students paired with oral language proficiency measurements. A familiarity with the student's language and educational histories is necessary. For example, a student who was raised in México until age 8 has had written language training in Spanish. This student should be compared to monolingual Spanish language speakers at age 8 when estimating verbal "g" (mean = 100) because he has not been raised in a bilingual environment.

However, he should be compared to bilingual students (mean = 85) at age 11 (assuming the student remains in the United States) because he would have exceeded the two years of being raised in a bilingual environment. When this student moved to the United States, measured verbal ability levels would be different from those of an eight year old student who was raised in the United States in a home where the family speaks Spanish and is educated in a classroom in English. In the latter case, the student should be compared to other bilingually affected students at age eight, when estimating verbal "g" (mean = 85). As this student first had to learn fluent English before learning written language, overall measured verbal ability in

Spanish would decline compared to peers, but rise compared to English speaking peers.

HISTORY OF THE MEASUREMENT OF INTELLIGENCE

The pursuit of an efficient and accurate way to attain comparative cognitive abilities in humans is not new. As long ago as 2200 B.C., it has been noted that Chinese emperors used large-scale "aptitude" testing for the selection of civil servants, and stories such as that of the Wild Boy of Averyon, in the 18th century, have captured our imagination regarding the relative difference between what is "normal" and "abnormal" thinking. At the end of the 19th century, the foundation was being further laid for how we assess intelligence today.

For example, Sir Francis Galton sought to predict one's intellectual capacity through tests of sensory discrimination and motor coordination. Although his belief that such capacities are necessarily correlated with intelligence was eventually seen as unfounded, he ushered in an age of individual psychology and the pursuit of measuring intelligence by quantifying those traits assumed to be correlated.

Shortly, Alfred Binet and his colleagues would publish what could be considered the precursor of most common intelligence measures. Although its main purpose at the time was to diagnose mental retardation, its basic characteristics are still used in today's tests. For example, Binet's scale (the Binet-Simon Scale) used items in order of difficulty with a mind to the typical developmental abilities of children of differing ages. For example, it would ask the participant to point out objects in a picture, or to discriminate between two weights.

Characteristics of Individually Administered IQ Tests

Intelligence tests are also sometimes called potential based assessments because they give us an educated guess as to how well a student may be expected to do in school (that is, their academic potential). In fact, there is much statistical data evidencing the power of such tests to predict future scholastic achievement. Discussions about them can often be confusing due to the technical wording and procedures that these tests use. It may help to briefly explain some basic characteristics common to most, if not all, potential based assessments.

Standardization

Most potential-based assessments are standardized. Standardized tests have a straightforward set of criteria that the examiner must follow. These criteria dictate the way that the test is administered as well as scored; the wording of questions, what responses are acceptable, etc. The goal of standardization is to control all of the elements involved in the testing process with the exception of the child's responses. The standardization can even extend to instructions about the testing environment, such as where the test should take place and who can be present.

Many potential-based tests are also *norm-referenced*. When a standardized test is *normed*, it means that it was initially administered to a large number of children, usually in the thousands. Ideally, this norm group is characteristic of the children who ultimately will be taking the standardized instrument. When looking at results from such a test, you have a degree of confidence in comparing that child's scores to the scores of other children the same age. In this way it is possible to say how well a child performed relative to his peers of the same age, or in the same grade.

Standardized tests use *standard* scores to report results. Although the name sounds like it would simplify interpretation, it can be confusing. This is because different test makers choose rather arbitrary numbers to represent what is average, as well as the size of the numbers used.

THE TESTING PROCESS

The latest versions of the two most widely used tests are the SB-IV, and the WISC-III (although new versions of each test have recently been published). Table 1 shows a list of some of the more commonly used intelligence measures. Note that some of these are "nonverbal" instruments. These tests rely on little or no verbal expression and are useful for a number of populations, such as non-native speakers, children with poor expressive abilities, or hard of hearing students.

Table 1

Test	Age Range	Description
Stanford-Binet Intelligence Scale, Fifth Edition (SBIS-V)	2 – 90+	An update of the SB-IV. Inaddition to providing a Full Scale score, it assesses Fluid Reasoning, Knowledge, Quantitative Reasoning, Visual-Spatial Processing, and Working Memory as well as the ability to compare verbal and nonverbal performance.
Wechsler Intelligence Scale for Children, Fourth Edition (WISC-IV)	6 – 16-11	An update of the WISC-III, this test yields a Full Scale score and scores for Verbal Comprehension, Working Memory, Perceptual Reasoning, and Processing speed.
Woodcock-Johnson III Tests of Cognitive Abilities	2 – 90+	This test gives a measure of general intellectual ability, as well as looking at working memory and executive function skills.
Cognitive Assessment System (CAS)	5 - 17	Based on the "PASS" theory, this test measures 'P'lanning, 'A'ttention, 'S'imultaneous, and 'S'successive cognitive processes.

Wechsler Adult Intelligence Scale (WAIS)	16 - 89	An IQ test for older children and adults, the WAIS provides a Verbal, Performance, and Full Scale score, as well as scores for verbal comprehension, perceptual organization, working memory, and processing speed.
Comprehensive Test of Nonverbal Intelligence (CTONI)	6 – 18-11	Designed to assess children who may be disadvantaged by traditional tests that put a premium on language skills, the CTONI is made up of six subtests that measure different nonverbal intellectual abilities.
Universal Nonverbal Intelligence Test (UNIT)	5 - 17	Designed to assess children who may be disadvantaged by traditional tests that put a premium on language skills, this test is entirely nonverbal in administration and response style.
Kaufman Assessment Battery for Children (KABC)	2-6 to 12-5	This test measures simultaneous and sequential processing skills, and has subscales that measure academic achievement as well.

Following is information that will help you understand the process that your child will be going through when taking such tests.

Not an Ordinary "Test"

First, since IQ tests do not directly assess the same things that are taught in the classroom, it is difficult to "study" for them. Instead, preparation should probably consist of a good night's rest. In addition, it is sometimes necessary to put a child at ease as to the expectations of the session. Since children usually think of tests as something that they can do "well" or "poorly" on, it may be appropriate to explain that the test they will be taking is different. IQ tests can be described as ones that aren't concerned with "passing" and "failing." It should be explained that the test aims to get a better understanding of a child's unique abilities in a wide variety of areas

Tasks Involved

In order to get a fuller understanding a child's abilities, intelligence tests require him or her to perform a number of tasks that vary widely in what they are asking. For example, one task, often referred to as a subtest, may ask the child to answer questions about everyday knowledge. Another subtest may ask him or her to construct specific patterns of colored beads or blocks. Other subtests may tap into the child's ability to recognize similarities between concepts or even written symbols. The main idea is to measure many different abilities that may contribute to overall intelligence.

As Pleasant an Experience as Possible

Ideally, the actual testing session takes place in a room that is comfortable in environment and atmosphere, thereby reducing distractions. The test administrator for most major intelligence tests is required to be a trained professional regarding their administration. This person is often a licensed school psychologist. The psychologist and the child are usually the only people in the room during testing. One of the most important aspects of the testing session is for a comfortable rapport to be established before testing takes place. If the student is rushed right into a novel, and possibly intimidating, task, her performance may suffer. The examiner must also be adept at dealing with a variety of different personalities and student characteristics, and be responsive to their needs during testing (e.g. allowing bathroom breaks, recognizing when fatigue has set in, etc.).

Probable Length of Testing

The time it takes to complete an individually administered intelligence test can vary depending on a child's age, response style, and the amount of questions he/she answers acceptably. The questions on most subtests are designed to increase in complexity. For this reason, younger children will tend to "max" out more quickly than older students. In addition, more reticent or reflective students will tend to take longer. Whereas some subtests are timed, others allow ample time for the respondent to think through his answer before responding. On average, one should expect a single administration of such an instrument to take an hour and twenty minutes, give or take twenty minutes.

Reporting Irregularities

Since these tests are standardized, the examiner is obligated to adhere to the strict training that accompanies them. Any time that there are circumstances or variables that may impinge on the results of a test, the examiner is required to report this in her report on the testing session. For example, if a student appears overly guarded and shy, and this behaviour may have kept him from answering correctly or with confidence, this should be noted. Likewise, if for some reason the climate in the room is not acceptable (overly hot, cold, dark, etc.), there is an obligation to report these situations. The examiner may decide that the irregularities were such that the assessment results are invalid.

Testing for Assessment of a Reading Problem

The first step in the assessment of a reading problem is to determine if the reading level is delayed in comparison to intelligence. There are several different intelligence tests. The choice of which intelligence test to use should be informed by the suspected area of disability. That is, an intelligence test which allows for assessment in an area less affected by the suspected disability should be used. Otherwise, the estimate of intelligence will be contaminated by the disability and decision makers will be possibly caught in a dilemma of what is the level of a student's "real" intelligence.

For example, the Wechsler series of intelligence tests have two component scales which combine to make up the "Full Scale IQ" score: a Verbal Scale and nonverbal (Performance) Scale. The student with a language disability may score quite a bit lower on the Verbal Scale, thus lowering the overall "Full Scale" score. On the other hand, simply using the Comprehensive Test of Nonverbal Intelligence may substantially bypass the disability. Or, the Stanford Binet IV may allow providing credit for an answer the youngster has difficulty expressing, thereby providing a verbal intelligence score less dominated by expressive-language difficulties.

It should be realized, however, that there is no way to entirely bypass a cognitive disability. The brain functions as a unified organ and an injury in one location more or less affects the quality of thinking in all other areas. For example, the difficulty in sequential reasoning and memory which is common to language disorders may affect the ability to reason through a problem in constructing visual patterns. The student may attempt to sequentially think through the steps of a complex problem rather than rely on the innate intuition which might be sufficient for a simple problem. It is just that the "spatial" problems rely less on language or sequential processing skills than expressive-language tasks or other verbal tasks. Any specific test places more or less demand on particular skills but can never be assumed to be totally free of influence from a particular disability.

Once an estimate of intelligence is reached, it can then be used as a comparison for measuring the severity of delay in reading development. The traditional intelligence tests were developed to predict success in school and the achievement test scales are almost always placed on a similar measurement scale so the numbers should match with only slight adjustments.

The test for the assessment of reading level depends on the age of the child. Early elementary children whose curriculum is mainly involved in learning basic reading skills should be assessed in reading word mastery. The ability to rapidly pronounce words is essential for a reading level which can relied on for effortless reading. The Woodcock series reading tests are widely used for this purpose and are very useful in this regard. These tests require that a child correctly read a word within 5 seconds.

In another subtest in the Woodcock series, the student is asked to read "nonsense" words so that phonic mastery can be assessed independently of "naming" a word which is visually recognized without sounding out the word. In early grades, some children will have memorized words without really mastering the phonic code; this leaves them vulnerable to reading problems in later grades and ongoing spelling problems. In the need to save time, examiners will often administer the word reading list but not the nonsense word list thereby missing diagnosis of early nonreaders who are simply memorizing words.

The objective in choosing a test is to provide an objective, standardized assessment of the skills need for success in the classroom or curriculum. When an older student is being asked to read, the youngster is expected to read paragraphs or multiparagraph material. Therefore, an adequate reading assessment must include paragraph reading material. Otherwise, the student is not being assessed on the real requirements for success in the classroom. Success in the task of reading a paragraph or longer material in class or for homework depends on:

— reading speed,

— reading accuracy,

— the ability to sustain concentration while reading,

— comprehension of the material, and
— retention of what is read.

A weakness in any of these factors in reading will lower the likelihood of successful reading. For example, the slow reader will tend to avoid reading because it is too time consuming. Usually more than one reading test will be needed to cover all these areas of reading. The Gray Oral Reading Test-3 measures oral reading speed, reading accuracy, short-term retention, and comprehension. However, some students may be inhibited by the requirement for oral reading and comprehension must be measured through a test which allows for silent reading (such as the Kaufman Test of Education Achievement). However, silent reading does not allow for an assessment of reading accuracy or speed.

The Woodcock Paragraph Comprehension test is not recommended as a measure for paragraph comprehension as most items require reading only a single sentence. If your student is unable to comprehend meaning at this level, then the WJ-R Paragraph Comprehension test would be appropriate. Students with language disorders are prime candidates for this test as they often display difficulties in understanding the subtle meaning of phrases and the meaning carried in sentence structure. However, a paragraph reading test would still be in order to document difficulties at each level of complexity so that all levels can be addressed in the curriculum.

The next step in the assessment process is to specify the underlying cause of the reading problem. Often, an educated guess can be made on the basis of the intelligence test and its component subtests. Often, separate tests will have to be given to document that the impairment in reading is caused by an impaired cognitive process. The underlying problem is often a difficulty in sequential memory although sometimes inadequate hearing discrimination of sounds is the cause. In other cases, memory for what is seen or confusion in right-left directionality can be the culprit. There may be many underlying causes but most can be assessed through the testing process.

In many cases, an attention disorder can impair reading. An attention disorder which is inadequately treated can impair the rate of Teaming due to difficulties in "working" memory. Working memory is the ability to hold information in mind while you think and is considered to be a core problem for attention disorders. Even with adequate treatment, an attention disorder can also frequently cause disorganization in the expression of complex ideas in writing or impairments in paragraph reading comprehension through inadequate organization of ideas or impaired memory. Attention disorder is an especially important cause of reading problems in teenagers who have not been previously diagnosed with a reading disorder in elementary school.

Sometimes, the teacher reports grade-level reading even though all tests show the student to be a deficient reader. You can ask that the school examiner obtain a tape-recorded sample of reading of never previously read material and a sample that the class has already covered. The reading should be conducted with a awareness by the student that comprehension questions will be asked so that effort to comprehend the materials applied during the reading. You might also ask an independent reading specialist to conduct this assessment and compare performance to age-group expectations.

The student who has been retained presents a problem for examiners. Is the examination to be based on age-level or grade-level norms? Each basis of comparison has its advantages and disadvantages. The retained student should be compared to age-level norms as reading is less tied to specific academic instruction than, say, arithmetic. Much of learning is self-teaching. The instructor in the classroom can only present a brief exposure to material. A child's ability to learn in the classroom environment depends on the ability to register what the teacher is presenting and integrate that information into what is needed in the reading development process.

Emotional problems can interfere with learning. Often, emotional problems coexist with learning disabilities. It is important to discriminate whether the emotions cause the impairment in learning, are caused by the learning impairment, or are present independent of the Teaming impairment. To make this discrimination, a careful history and Assessment is needed to document the chronology of problems, the nature of the problems, and the situations under which the difficulties are observed. It is useful to document when symptoms are produced: only in the classroom or throughout the student's life. Frequently the learning disabled child will be much happier in the summer when not in school. Stomachaches and headaches may occur only on school days. Symptoms which are caused by school problems build up after school starts in September and usually occur only on school days, often after school rather than before school, but anticipatory anxiety can cause problems before school each day.

While it may be tempting to rely on a standard set of reading tests, it is important to use common sense in combination with technical expertise in assessing teaming disabilities. The professional can bring the technical expertise to the assessment but the parent can contribute common sense to the assessment plan. Together, a more meaningful assessment can be crafted.

Nonverbal intelligence tests (Leiter-Revised, Comprehensive Test Of Nonverbal Intelligence), because impaired communication limits scores on verbal IQ tests, and impaired attention/cooperation/task-orientation, as well as poor fine motor function, limit scores on timed, visual-motor tasks (Wechsler Performance IQ); with younger or more severely delayed kids, "infant/toddler" tests can determine competencies (Bayley, Merrill-Palmer).

Communication: a skilled speech pathologist and pediatric neuropsychologist should do detailed testing of language abilities (receptive and expressive, verbal and nonverbal communication; at the word, sentence, narrative, and discourse levels; assessing vocabulary, syntax, semantics, pragmatics).

Academics: use receptive/comprehension measures of academic skills, which ask the child to point to the answer (such as the Bracken or Peabody achievement tests), as well as measures that require more talking or paper-and-pencil work (such as the Woodcock-Johnson or Wechsler achievement tests)

Memory: verbal and visual memory testing (e.g, Wide Range Assessment of Memory and Learning, Children's Memory Scales) may highlight strengths in visual or rote verbal recall.

Visual-motor: drawing tests (Visual-Motor Integration), and motor tasks (Grooved Pegboard, Finger Sequencing, etc.) help document motor incoordination, often seen in high-functioning autism or Asperger's syndrome.

Interpersonal & play skills: the ADOS [Autism Diagnostic Observation Schedule] is a structured, systematic "test" that bases specific observational coding on administration of a series of play-like tasks -- e.g., trying to involve the child in blowing bubbles, acting out a doll's birthday party, etc. It requires special training and experience to administer and code reliably, so ADOS examiners need to be trained by someone already certified on this measure.

The CARS [Childhood Autism Rating Scale] is a structured rating form, based on examiner's, parent's, or teacher's observations of the child's behaviour over a period of time (at least 30 minutes of play observation). It is very interesting to see how different raters' impressions compare.

The ADI-R [Autism Diagnostic Interview-Revised] is a structured parent interview about the child's developmental history and current behaviour, which is also very useful in establishing the diagnosis. It is too long for most clinical uses (takes up to 3 hours to administer). I've borrowed ideas from the ADI-R, for a shorter clinical interview.

Elsa Shapiro's questionnaire about social and behavioral development; and the Australian Scale for Asperger's Syndrome (published in Tony Attwood's book), are useful in identifying social-emotional skills deficits.

Other questionnaires for autism symptoms (Krug, Gilliam) are useful in assessing the presence and intensity of specific symptoms (e.g., stereotyped behaviors, atypical sensory reactions, etc.).

Teacher's observations and ratings (e.g., Behaviour Assessment Scales for Children) are often helpful in understanding how children relate to peers and strangers.

Adaptive behaviour: A parent- or teacher-rated scale of adaptive behaviour (either the Vineland or the Woodcock-Johnson Scales of Independent Behaviour-Revised) measures "everyday" learning. About 50-60% of kids with autism also have mental retardation (which means a global developmental delay > 70% on both nonverbal IQ and adaptive behaviour tests).

The WJSIB scale of maladaptive behaviors is especially useful in identifying concerns about disruptive, withdrawn, self-stimulatory or other problem behaviour; adaptive behaviors can be measured separately from communication skills; and parents can complete this scale independently (it does not have to be administered in an interview format, once the parent understands the directions). The Child Development Inventory or Kent Infant Development Scale are useful ratings of behavioral competence in younger/more delayed children.

Always be a critical and skeptical consumer, especially with internet information. There are many, many "alternative therapies" for autism which have some enthusiastic supporters, in print and in parent groups, but which do not necessarily work for most children according to scientific studies and surveys. "Alternative" therapies include Sensory Integration Therapy, Auditory Integration Therapy, megavitamins, casein-free and gluten-free diets, secretin, ACTH, Igg, anti-yeast, etc.

Many of these therapies claim dramatic, sudden, improvements or even "cures." Experience over the years of many "fad treatments" for autism suggests that it is wise to question closely the theoretical basis and experimental evidence of effectiveness, as well as the cost, of any proposed treatments.

Similarly, various medications may be useful in treating overactivity, anxiety, impulsivity, perseverative/obsessive, or self-injurious behaviors, but no medication "cures" autism.

9

TYPES OF INTELLIGENCE TESTS

Tests of intelligence itself (in the psychometric sense) come in many forms. Some use only a single type of item or question; examples include the Peabody Picture Vocabulary Test (a measure of children's verbal intelligence) and Raven's Progressive Matrices (a nonverbal, untimed test that requires inductive reasoning about perceptual patterns).

Although such instruments are useful for specific purposes, the more familiar measures of general intelligence, such as the Wechsler tests and the Stanford-Binet, include many different types of items, both verbal and nonverbal. Test-takers may be asked to give the meanings of words, to complete a series of pictures, to indicate which of several words does not belong with the others, and the like. Their performance can then be scored to yield several subscores as well as an overall score.

By convention, overall intelligence test scores are usuallv converted to a scale in which the mean is 100 and the standard deviation is 15. (The standard deviation is a measure of the variability of the distribution of scores.) Approximately 95% of the population has scores within two standard deviations of the mean, i.e. between 70 and 130. For historical reasons, the term "IQ" is often used to describe scores on tests of intelligence.

It originally referred to an "intelligence Quotient" that was formed by dividing a so-called mental age by a chronological age, but this procedure is no longer used.

INTERCORRELATIONS AMONG TESTS

Individuals rarely perform equally well on all the different kinds of items included in a test of intelligence. One person may do relatively better on verbal than on spatial items, for example, while another may show the opposite pattern. Nevertheless, subtests measuring different abilities tend to be positively correlated: people who score high on one such subtest are likely to be above average on others as well. These complex patterns of correlation can be clarified by factor analysis, but the results of such analyses are often controversial themselves. Some theorists have emphasized the importance of a general factor, g, which represents what all the tests have in common; others focus on more specific group factors such as memory, verbal comprehension, or number facility.

There have been many disputes over the utility of IQ and g. Some theorists are critical of the entire psychometric approach, while others regard it as firmly established. The critics do not dispute the stability of test scores, nor the fact that they predict certain forms of achievement-especially school achievement—rather effectively. They do argue, however, that to base a concept of intelligence on test scores alone is to ignore many important aspects of mental ability. Some of those aspects are emphasized in other approaches reviewed below.

MULTIPLE FORMS OF INTELLIGENCE

Gardner's Theory

A relatively new approach is the theory of "multiple intelligences"; proposed by Howard Gardner. On this view conceptions of intelligence should be informed not only by work with normal children and adults but also by studies of gifted individuals (including so-called 'savants"), of persons who have suffered brain damage, of experts and virtuosos, and of individuals from diverse cultures. These considerations have led Gardner to include musical, bodlily-kinesthetic, and various forms of personal intelligence as well as more familiar spatial, linguistic, and logical mathematical abilities in the scope of his theory. He argues that psychometric tests address only linguistic and logical plus some aspects of spatial intelligence; other forms have been entirely ignored.

Moreover, the paper and-pencil format of most tests rules out many kinds of intelligent performance that matter in everyday life, such as giving an extemporaneous talk (linguistic) or being able to find one's way in a new town (spatial). While Gardner's arguments have attracted considerable interest, the stability and validity of performance tests in these new domains has yet to be conclusively demonstrated. It is also possible to doubt whether some of these abilities-bodily-kinesthetic," for example—are appropriately described as forms of intelligence rather than as special talents.

Sternberg's Theory

Robert Sternberg's triarchic theory proposes three fundamental aspects of intelligence-analytic, creative, and practical—of which only the first is measured to any significant extent by mainstream tests. His investigations suggest the need for a balance between analytic intelligence, on the one hand, and creative and especially practical intelligence on the other. The distinction between analytic (or "academic") and practical intelligence has also been made by others. Analytic problems, of the type suitable for test construction, tend to (a) have been formulated by other people, (b) be clearly defined, (c) come with all the information needed to solve them, (d) have only a single right answer, which can be reached by only a single method, (e) be disembodied from ordinary experience, and (f) have little or no intrinsic interest. Practical problems, in contrast, tend to (a) require problem recognition and formulation, (b) be poorly defined, (c) require information seeking, (d) have various acceptable solutions, (e) be embedded in and require prior everyday experience, and (f) require motivation and personal involvement.

As part of their study of practical intelligence, Sternberg and his collaborators have developed measures of "*tacit knowledge*" in various domains, especially business management. In these measures, individuals are given written scenarios of various work related situations and then asked to rank a number of options for dealing with the situation presented. The results show that tacit knowledge predicts such criteria such as job performance fairly well, even though it is relatively independent of intelligence test scores and other common selection measures. This work, too, has its critics.

Other investigators have also demonstrated the relative independence of academic and practical intelligence. Brazilian street children, for example, are quite capable of doing the math required for survival in their street business even though they have failed mathematics in school. Similarly, women shoppers in California who had no difficulty in comparing product values at the supermarket were unable to carry out the same mathematical operations in paper-and pencil tests. In a study of expertise in wagering on harness races, Ceci and Liker found that the skilled handicappers implicitly used a highly complex interactive model with as many as seven variables; the ability to do this successfully was unrelated to scores on intelligence tests.

CULTURAL VARIATION

It is very difficult to compare concepts of intelligence across cultures. English is not alone in having many words for different aspects of intellectual power and cognitive skill (*wise, sensible, smart, bright, clever; cunning, etc.*); if another language has just as many, which of them shall we say corresponds to its speakers' "concept of intelligence"? The few attempts to examine this issue directly have typically found that, even within a given society, different cognitive characteristics are emphasized from one situation to another and from one subculture to another. These differences extend not just to conceptions of intelligence but to what is considered adaptive or appropriate in a broader sense.

These issues have occasionally been addressed across subcultures and ethnic groups in America. In a study conducted in San Jose California, Okagaki and Sternberg asked immigrant parents from Cambodia, Mexico, the Philippines and Vietnam, as well as native-born Angle-Americans and Mexican-Americans, about their conceptions of child-rearing, appropriate teaching, and children's intelligence. Parents from all groups except Angle-Americans indicated that such characteristics as motivation, social skills, and practical school skills were as or more important than cognitive characteristics for their conceptions of an intelligent first-grade child.

Heath found that different ethnic groups in North Carolina have different conceptions of intelligence. To be considered as intelligent or adaptive, one must excel in the skills valued by one's own group. One particularly interesting contrast was in the importance ascribed to verbal vs. nonverbal communication skills—to saying things explicitly as opposed to using and understanding gestures and facial expressions. Note that while both these forms of communicative skill have their uses, they are not equally well represented in psychometric tests.

How testing is done can have different effects in different cultural groups. This can happen for many reasons, including differential familiarity with the test materials themselves. Serpell, for example, asked Zambian and English children to reproduce patterns in three media: wire models, clay models, or pencil and paper. The Zambian children excelled in the wire medium with which they were familiar, while the English children were best with pencil and paper. Both groups performed equally well with clay.

Piaget's Theory

The best-known developmentally-based conception of intelligence is certainly that of the Swiss psychologist Jean Piaget. Unlike most of the theorists considered here, Piaget had relatively little interest in individual differences. Intelligence develops in all children through the continually shifting balance between the assimilation of new information into existing cognitive structures and the accommodation of those structures themselves to the new information. To index the development of intelligence in this sense, Piaget devised methods that are rather different from conventional tests.

To assess the understanding of "conservation." for example, (roughly, the principle that material quantity is not affected by mere changes of shape), children who have watched water being poured from a shallow to a tall beaker may be asked if there is now more water than before. (A positive answer would suggest that the child has not yet mastered the principle of conservation.) Piaget's tasks can be modified to serve as measures of individual differences; when this is done, they correlate fairly well with standard psychometric tests.

Vygotsky's Theory

The Russian psychologist Lev Vygotsky argued that all intellectual abilities are social in origin. Language and thought first appear in early interactions with parents, and continue to develop through contact with teachers and others. Traditional intelligence tests ignore what Vygotsky called the "zone of proximal development." i.e., the level of performance that a child might reach with appropriate help from a supportive adult. Such tests are "static." measuring only the intelligence that is already fully developed. "Dynamic" testing, in which the examiner provides guided and graded feedback, can go further to give some indication of the child's latent potential. These ideas are being developed and extended by a number of contemporary psychologists.

BIOLOGICAL APPROACHES

Some investigators have recently turned to the study of the brain as a basis for new ideas about what intelligence is and how to measure it. Many aspects of brain anatomy and physiology have been suggested as potentially relevant to intelligence: the arborization of cortical neurons, cerebral glucose metabolism, evoked potentials, nerve conduction velocity, sex hormones, and still others. Advances in research methods, including new forms of brain imaging such as PET and MRI scans, will surely add to this list. In the not-too-distant future it may be possible to relate some aspects of test performance to specific characteristics of brain function.

This brief survey has revealed a wide range of contemporary conceptions of intelligence and of how it should be measured. The psychometric approach is the oldest and best established, but others also have much to contribute. We should be open to the possibility that our understanding of intelligence in the future will be rather different from what it is today.

INTELLIGENCE TESTS AND THEIR CORRELATES

The correlation coefficient, r, can be computed whenever the scores in a sample are paired in some way. Typically this is because each individual is measured twice: he or she takes the same test on two occasions, or takes two different tests, or has both a test score and some criterion measure such as grade point average or job performance.

The value of r measures the degree of relationship between the two sets of scores in a convenient way, by assessing how well one of them (computationally it doesn't matter which one) could be used to predict the value of the other. Its sign indicates the direction of relationship: when r is negative, high scores on one measure predict low scores on the other. Its magnitude indicates the strength of the relationship. If r=0, there is no relation at all; if r is 1 (or -1), one score can be used to predict the other score perfectly. Moreover, the square of r has a particular meaning in cases where we are concerned with predicting one variable from another. When r=.50, for example, r2 is .25: this means (given certain linear assumptions) that 25% of the variance in one set of scores is predictable from the correlated values of the other set, while the remaining 75% is not.

Basic Characteristics of Test Scores

Stability

Intelligence test scores are fairly stable during development. When Jones and Bayley tested a sample of children annually throughout childhood and adolescence, for example, scores obtained at age 18 were correlated r=.77 with scores that had been obtained at age 6, r=.89 with scores from age 12. When scores were averaged across several successive tests to remove short-term fluctuations, the correlations were even higher. The mean for ages 17 and 18 was correlated r=.86 with the mean for ages 5, 6 and 7, r=.96 with the mean for ages 11, 12 and 13. Nevertheless, IQ scores do change over time. In the same study, the average change between age 12 and age 17 was 7.1 IQ points; some individuals changed as much as 18 points.

Is it possible to measure the intelligence of young infants in a similar way? Conventional tests of "infant intelligence" do not predict later test scores very well, but certain experimental measures of infant attention and memory that were originally developed for other purposes have turned out to be more successful. In the most common procedure, a particular visual pattern is shown to a baby over and over again. The experimenter records how long the infant subject looks at the pattern on each trial; these looks get shorter and shorter as the baby becomes "habituated" to it. The time required to reach a certain level of habituation, or the extent to which the baby now "prefers" (looks longer at) a new pattern, are regarded as measures of some aspect of his or her information-processing capability.

These habituation-based measures, obtained from babies at ages ranging from three months to a year, are significantly correlated with the intelligence test scores of the same children when they get to be 2 or 4 or 6 years old. A few studies have found such correlations even at ages 8 or 11. A recent meta analysis, based on 31 different samples, estimates the average magnitude of the correlations at about r=.36. (The largest rs often appear in samples that include 'at risk' infants.) It is possible that these habituation scores (and other similar measures of infant cognition) do indeed reflect real cognitive differences, perhaps in 'speed of information processing". It is also possible, however, that - to a presently unknown extent - they reflect early differences in temperament or inhibition.

It is important to understand what remains stable and what changes in the development of intelligence. A child whose IQ score remains the same from age 6 to age 18 does not exhibit the same performance throughout that period. On the contrary, steady gains in general knowledge vocabulary, reasoning ability, etc. will be apparent. What does *not* change is his or her score in comparison to that of other individuals of the same age. A six-year old with an IQ of 100 is at the mean of six-year-olds; an 11 year-old with that score is at the mean of 18-year-olds.

Factors and g

The patterns of intercorrelation among tests (i.e. among different kinds of items) are complex. Some pairs of tests are much more closely related than others, but all such correlations are typically positive and form what is called a "positive manifold." Spearman showed that in any such manifold, some portion of the variance of scores on each test can be mathematically attributed to a "general factor," or g. Given this analysis, the overall pattern of correlations can be roughly described as produced by individual differences in g plus differences in the specific abilities sampled by particular tests.

In addition, however, there are usually patterns of intercorrelation among groups of tests. These commonalities, which played only a small role in Spearman's analysis, were emphasized by other theorists. Thurstone, for example, proposed an analysis based primarily on the concept of group factors. While some psychologists today still regard g as the most fundamental measure of intelligence, others prefer to emphasize the distinctive profile of strengths and weaknesses present in each person's performance.

A recently published review identifies over 70 different abilities that can be distinguished by currently available tests. One way to represent this structure is in terms of a hierarchical arrangement with a general intelligence factor at the apex and various more specialized abilities arrayed below it. Such a summary merely acknowledges that performance levels on different tests are correlated; it is consistent with, but does not prove, the hypothesis that a common factor such as g underlies those correlations. Different specialized abilities might also be correlated for other reasons, such as the effects of education. Thus while the g-based factor hierarchy is the most widely accepted current view of the structure of abilities, some theorists regard it as misleading. Moreover, as noted in Section 1, a wide range of human abilities, including many that seem to have intellectual components, are outside the domain of standard psychometric tests.

Tests as Predictors

School Performance

Intelligence tests were originally devised by Alfred Binet to measure children's ability to succeed in school. They do in fact predict school performance fairly well: the correlation between IQ scores and grades is about .50. They also predict scores on school achievement tests, designed to measure knowledge of the curriculum. Note, however, that correlations of this magnitude account for only about 25% of the overall variance. Successful school learning depends on many personal characteristics other than intelligence, such as persistence, interest in school, and willingness to study. The encouragement for academic achievement that is received from peers, family and teachers may also be important, together with more general cultural factors.

The relationship between test scores and school performance seems to be ubiquitous. Wherever it has been studied, children with high scores on tests of intelligence tend to learn more of what is taught in school than their lower-scoring peers. There may be styles of teaching and methods of instruction that will decrease or increase this correlation, but none that consistently eliminates it has yet been found.

What children learn in school depends not only on their individual abilities but also on teaching practices and on what is actually taught. Recent comparisons among pupils attending school in different countries have made this especially obvious. Children in Japan and China, for example, know a great deal more math than American children even though their intelligence test scores are quite similar. This difference may result from many factors, including cultural attitudes toward schooling as well as the sheer amount of time devoted to the study of mathematics and how that study is organized. In principle it is quite possible to improve the school learning of American children—even very substantially-without changing their intelligence test scores at all.

Years of Education

Some children stay in school longer than others; many go on to college and perhaps beyond. Two variables that can be measured as early as elementary school correlate with the total amount of education individuals will obtain: test scores and social class background. Correlations between IQ scores and total years of education are about .55, implying that differences in psychometric intelligence account for about 30% of the outcome variance. The correlations of years of education with social class background are also positive, but somewhat lower.

There are a number of reasons why children with higher test scores tend to get more education. They are likely to get good grades, and to be encouraged by teachers and counselors; often they are placed in "college preparatory" classes, where they make friends who may also encourage them.

In general, they are likely to find the process of education rewarding in a way that many low-scoring children do not. These influences are not omnipotent: some high scoring children do drop out of school. Many personal and social characteristics other than psychometric intelligence determine academic success and interest, and social privilege may also play a role. Nevertheless, test scores are the best single predictor of an individual's years of education.

In contemporary American society, the amount of schooling that adults complete is also somewhat predictive of their social status. Occupations considered high in prestige (e.g., law, medicine, even corporate business) usually require at least a college degree-16 or more years of education-as a condition of entry. It is partly because intelligence test scores predict years of education so well that they also predict occupational status, and even income to a smaller extent. Moreover, many occupations can only be entered through professional schools which base their admissions at least partly on test scores: the MCAT, the GMAT, the LSAT, etc. Individual scores on admission-related tests such as these are certainly correlated with scores on tests of intelligence.

Social Status and Income

How well do IQ scores (which can be obtained before individuals enter the labor force) predict such outcome measures as the social status or income of adults? This question is complex, in part because another variable also predicts such outcomes: namely, the socioeconomic status (SES) of one's parents. Unsurprisingly, children of privileged families are more likely to attain high social status than those whose parents are poor and less educated. These two predictors (IQ and parental SES) are by no means independent of one another; the correlation between them is around .33.

One way to look at these relationships is to begin with SES. According to Jencks, measures of parental SES predict about one-third of the variance in young adults' social status and about one-fifth of the variance in their income. About half of this predictive effectiveness depends on the fact that the SES of parents also predicts children's intelligence test scores, which have their own predictive value for social outcomes; the other half comes about in other ways.

We can also begin with IQ scores, which by themselves account for about one-fourth of the social status variance and one-sixth of the income variance. Statistical controls for parental SES eliminate only about a quarter of this predictive power. One way to conceptualize this effect is by comparing the occupational status (or income) of adult brothers who grew up in the same family and hence have the same parental SES. In such cases, the brother with the higher adolescent IQ score is likely to have the higher adult social status and income. This effect, in turn, is substantially mediated by education: the brother with the higher test scores is likely to get more schooling, and hence to be better credentialled as he enters the workplace.

Do these data imply that psychometric intelligence is a major determinant of social status or income? That depends on what one means by major. In fact, individuals who have the same test scores may differ widely in occupational status and even more widely in income. Consider for a moment the distribution of occupational status scores for all individuals in a population, and then consider the conditional distribution of such scores for just those individuals who test at some given IQ. Jencks notes that the standard deviation of the latter distribution may still be quite large; in some cases it amounts to about 88% of the standard deviation for the entire population. Viewed from this perspective, psychometric intelligence appears as only one of a great many factors that influence social outcomes.

Job Performance

Scores on intelligence tests predict various measures of job performance: supervisor ratings, work samples, etc. Such correlations, which typically lie between r=.30 and r=.50, are partly restricted by the limited reliability of those measures themselves. They become higher when ris statistically corrected for this unreliability: in one survey of relevant studies, the mean of the corrected correlations was .54. This implies that, across a wide range of occupations, intelligence test performance accounts for some 29% of the variance in job performance.

Although these correlations can sometimes be modified by changing methods of training or aspects of the job itself, intelligence test scores are at least weakly related to job performance in most settings. Sometimes IQ scores are described as the 'best available predictor" of that performance. It is worth noting, however, that such tests predict considerably less than half the variance of job-related measures. Other individual characteristics such as interpersonal skills, aspects of personality, etc., are probably of equal or greater importance, but at this point we do not have equally reliable instruments to measure them.

Social Outcomes

Psychometric intelligence is negatively correlated with certain socially undesirable outcomes. For example, children with high test scores are less likely than lower-scoring children to engage in juvenile crime. in one study, Moffitt, Gabrielli, Mednick & Schulsinger found a correlation of -.19 between IQ scores and number of juvenile offenses in a large Danish sample; with social class controlled, the correlation dropped to -. 17. The correlations for most "negative outcome" variables are typically smaller than .20, which means that test scores are associated with less than 4% of their total variance. It is important to realize that the causal links between psychometric ability and social outcomes may be indirect. Children who are unsuccessful in- and hence alienated from-school may be more likely to engage in delinquent behaviors for that very reason, compared to other children who enjoy school and are doing well.

Intelligence test scores predict a wide range of social outcomes with varying degrees of success. Correlations are highest for school achievement, where they account for about a quarter of the variance. They are somewhat lower for job performance, and very low for negatively valued outcomes such as criminality. In general, intelligence tests measure only some of the many personal characteristics that are relevant to life in contemporary America. Those characteristics are never the only influence on outcomes, though in the case of school performance they may well be the strongest.

Test Scores and Measures of Processing Speed

Many recent studies show that the speeds with which people perform very simple perceptual and cognitive tasks are correlated with psychometric intelligence. In general, people with higher intelligence test scores apprehend, scan, retrieve, and respond to stimuli more quickly than those who score lower.

Cognitive Correlates

The modern study of these relations began in the 1970s, as part of the general growth of interest in chronometric measures of cognition. Many of the new cognitive paradigms required subjects to make same/different judgments or other types of speeded responses to visual displays. Although those paradigms had not been devised with individual differences in mind, they could be interpreted as providing measures of the speed of certain information processes. Those speeds turned out to correlate with psychometrically-measured verbal ability. In some problem solving tasks, it was possible to analyze the subjects' overall response times into theoretically motivated 'cognitive components"; component times could then be correlated with test scores in their own right.

Although the size of these correlations was modest (seldom accounting for more than 10% of the variance), they did increase as the basic tasks were made more complex by requiring increased memory or attentional capacity. For instance, the correlation between paired associate learning and intelligence increased as the pairs were presented at faster rates.

Choice Reaction Time

In another popular cognitive paradigm, the subject simply moves his or her finger from a 'home" button to one of eight others arranged in a semicircle around it; these are marked by small lights that indicate which one is the target on a given trial. Various aspects of the choice reaction times obtained in this paradigm are correlated with scores on intelligence tests, sometimes with values of r as high as .30 or -.40 (r is negative because higher test scores go with shorter times). Nevertheless it has proved difficult to make theoretical sense of the overall pattern of correlations, and the results obtained in this paradigm are still hard to interpret. A later modification, the 'odd-man-out" procedure of Frearson and Eysenck, seems to be more promising.

Inspection Time

A more recently developed measure of processing speed, which seems relatively independent of response factors, is the method of "inspection time" (IT). In the standard version of this paradigm, two vertical lines are shown very briefly on each trial, followed by a pattern mask; the subject must judge which line was shorter. For a given subject, IT is defined as the minimum exposure duration (up to the onset of the mask) for which the lines must be displayed if he or she is to meet a preestablished criterion of accuracy - e.g., nine correct trials out of ten.

Inspection times defined in this way are consistently correlated with measures of psychometric intelligence. In a recent meta-analysis, Kranzler and Jensen reported an overall correlation of -.30 between IQ scores and IT; this rose to -.55 when corrected for measurement error and attenuation. More recent findings confirm this general result. IT usually correlates best with performance subtests of intelligence; its correlation with verbal intelligence is usually weaker and sometimes zero.

One apparent advantage of IT over other chronometric methods is that the task itself seems particularly simple. At first glance, it is hard to imagine that any differences in response strategies or stimulus familiarity could affect the outcome. Nevertheless, it seems that they do. Brian Mackenzie and his colleagues discovered that some subjects use apparent-movement cues in the basic IT task while others do not; only in the latter group is IT correlated with intelligence test scores.

Moreover, standard IT paradigms require an essentially spatial judgment; it is not surprising, then, that they correlate with intelligence tests which emphasize spatial ability. With this in mind, Mackenzie et al devised a verbal inspection time task based on Posner's classical same-letter/different-letter paradigm. As predicted, the resulting ITs correlated with verbal but not with spatial intelligence. It is clear that the apparently simple IT task actually involves complex modes of information processing that are as yet poorly understood.

Neurological Measures

Recent research has begun to explore what seem to be still more direct measures of neural processing. Reed and Jensen have used visual evoked potential (VEP) techniques to assess what they call "nerve conduction velocity" (NCV). To estimate this velocity, each subject's head length (a rough index of the distance between the eye and the occipital cortex) is divided by the mean latency of an early component (N70 or P100) in his or her VEP pattern.

In a study with 147 college-student subjects, this measure correlated $r = .26$ with scores on an unspeeded test of intelligence. (A statistical correction for the restricted subject range raised the correlation to $r = .37$.) Other researchers have also reported correlations between VEP parameters and intelligence test scores. Interestingly, however, the same "conduction velocities" were not correlated with the same subjects' choice reaction times. Other researchers have also reported correlations between VEP parameters and intelligence test scores.

Problems of Interpretation

Some researchers believe that psychometric intelligence, especially g, depends directly on the 'neural efficiency" of the brain. They regard the observed correlations between test scores and measures of processing speed as evidence for their view. If choice reaction times, inspection times, and VEP latencies actually reflect the speed of basic neural processes, such correlations are only to be expected. In fact, however, the observed patterns of correlation are rarely as simple as this hypothesis would predict.

Moreover, it is quite possible that high- and low-IQ individuals differ in other ways that affect speeded performance. Those variables include motivation, response criteria (emphasis on speed vs. accuracy), perceptual strategies, attentional strategies, and in some cases differential familiarity with the material itself. Finally, we do not know the direction of causation that underlies many of these correlations. Do high levels of neural efficiency" promote the development of intelligence, or do more intelligent people just find faster ways to carry out perceptual tasks? Or both? These questions are still open.

THE GENES AND INTELLIGENCE

We focus here on the relative contributions of genes and environments to individual differences in particular traits. To avoid misunderstanding, it must be emphasized from the outset that gene action always involves an environment—at least a biochemical environment, and often an ecological one. Thus all genetic effects on the development of observable traits are potentially modifiable by environmental input, though the practicability of making such modifications may be another matter. Conversely, all environmental effects on trait development involve the genes or structures to which the genes have contributed. Thus there is always a genetic aspect to the effects of the environment.

Sources of Individual Differences

Partitioning the Variation

Individuals differ from one another on a wide variety of traits: familiar examples include height. intelligence, and aspects of personality. Those differences are often of considerable social importance. Many interesting questions can be asked about their nature and origins. One such question is the extent to which they reflect differences among the genes of the individuals involved, as distinguished from differences among the environments to which those individuals have been exposed. The issue here is not whether genes and environments are both essential for the development of a given trait (this is always the case), and it is not about the genes or environment of any particular person. We are concerned only with the observed variation of the trait across individuals in a given population. A figure called the "heritability" (h2) of the trait represents the proportion of that variation that is associated with genetic differences among the individuals. The remaining variation (1 - h2] is associated with environmental differences and with errors of measurement. These proportions can be estimated by various methods described below.

Sometimes special interest attaches to those aspects of environments that family members have in common (for example, characteristics of the home). The part of the variation that derives from this source, called "shared" variation or c2, can also be estimated. Still more refined estimates can be made: c2 is sometimes subdivided into several kinds of shared variation; h2 is sometimes subdivided into so-called "additive" and "non-additive" portions /the part that is transmissible from parent to child vs. the part expressed anew in each generation by a unique patterning of genes.) Variation associated with correlations and statistical interactions between genes and environments may also be identifiable. In theory, any of the above estimates may vary with the age of the individuals involved.

A high heritability does not mean that the environment has no impact on the development of a trait, or that learning is not involved. Vocabulary size, for example, is very substantially heritable (and highly correlated with general intelligence) although every word in an individual's vocabulary is learned. In a society in which plenty of words are available in everyone's environment, especially for individuals who are motivated to seek them out, the number of words that individuals actually learn depends to a considerable extent on their genetic predispositions.

Behavior geneticists have often emphasized the fact that individuals can be active in creating or selecting their own environments. Some describe this process as active or reactive genotype-environment correlation. (The distinction is between the action of the organism in selecting its own environment and the reaction of others to its gene-based traits.) Others suggest that these forms of gene-environment relationship are typical of the way that genes are normally expressed, and simply include them as part of the genetic effect. This is a matter of terminological preference, not a dispute about facts.

How Genetic Estimates are Made

Estimates of the magnitudes of these sources of individual differences are made by exploiting natural and social 'experiments" that combine genotypes and environments in informative ways. Monozygotic (MZ) and dyzygotic (DZ) twins, for example, can be regarded as experiments of nature. MZ twins are paired individuals of the same age growing up in the same family who have all their genes in common; DZ twins are otherwise similar pairs who have only half their genes in common. Adoptions, in contrast, are experiments of society.

They allow one to compare genetically unrelated persons who are growing up in the same family as well as genetically related persons who are growing up in different families. They can also provide information about genotype-environment correlations: in ordinary families genes and environments are correlated because the same parents provide both, whereas in adoptive families one set of parents provides the genes and another the environment. An experiment involving both nature and society is the study of monozygotic twins who have been reared apart. Relationships in the families of monozygotic twins also offer unique possibilities for analysis. Because these comparisons are subject to different sources of potential error, the results of studies involving several kinds of kinship are often analyzed together to arrive at robust overall conclusions.

Results for IQ scores

Parameter Estimates. Across the ordinary range of environments in modern Western societies, a sizable part of the variation in intelligence test scores is associated with genetic differences among individuals. Quantitative estimates vary from one study to another, because many are based on small or selective samples. If one simply combines all available correlations in a single analysis, the heritability (h2) works out to about .50 and the between-family variance (c2) to about .25. These overall figures are misleading, however, because most of the relevant studies have been done with children. We now know that the heritability of IQ changes with age: h2 goes up and c2 goes down from infancy to adulthood. In childhood h2 and C2 for IQ are of the order of .45 and .35; by late adolescence h2 is around .75 and c2 is quite low (zero in some studies). Substantial environmental variance remains, but it primarily reflects within-family rather than between-family differences.

These adult parameter estimates are based on a number of independent studies. The correlation between MZ twins reared apart, which directly estimates h2, ranged from .68 to .78 in five studies involving adult samples from Europe and the U.S.. The correlation between unrelated children reared together in adoptive families, which directly estimates c2, was approximately zero for adolescents in two adoption studies and .19 in a third.

These particular estimates derive from samples in which the lowest socioeconomic levels were underrepresented (i.e., there were few very poor families), so the range of between family differences was smaller than in the population as a whole. This means that we should be cautious in generalizing the findings for betw en-family effects across the entire social spectrum. The samples were also mostly white, but available data suggest that twin and sibling correlations in African-American and similarly selected White samples are more often comparable than not.

Why should individual differences in intelligence (as measured by test scores) reflect genetic differences more strongly in adults than they do in children's One possibility is that as individuals grow older their transactions with their environments are increasingly influenced by the characteristics that they bring to those environments themselves, decreasingly by the conditions imposed by family life and social origins. Older persons are in a better position to select their own effective environments, a form of genotype-environment correlation. In any case the popular view that genetic influences on the development of a trait are essentially frozen at conception while the effects of the early environment cumulate inexorably is quite misleading, at least for the trait of psychometric intelligence.

Implications

Estimates of h2 and c2 for IQ (or any other trait) are descriptive statistics for the populations studied. (In this respect they are like means and standard deviations.) They are outcome measures, summarizing the results of a great many diverse, intricate, individually variable events and processes, but they can nevertheless be quite useful. They can tell us how much of the variation in a given trait the genes and family environments explain, and changes in them place some constraints on theories of how this occurs.

On the other hand they have little to say about specific mechanisms, i.e. about how genetic and environmental differences get translated into individual physiological and psychological differences. Many psychologists and neuroscientists are actively studying such processes; data on heritabilities may give them ideas about what to look for and where or when to look for it.

A common error is to assume that because something is heritable it is necessarily unchangeable This is wrong. Heritability does not imply immutability. As previously noted, heritable traits can depend on learning, and they may be subject to other environmental effects as well. The value of h2 can change if the distribution of environments (or genes) in the population is substantially altered. On the other hand, there can be effective environmental changes that do not change heritability at all. If the environment relevant to a given trait improves in a way that affects all members of the population equally, the mean value of the trait will rise without any change in its heritability (because the differences among individuals in the population will stay the same). This has evidently happened for height: the heritability of stature is high, but average heights continue to increase. Something of the sort may also be taking place for IQ scores the so-called "Flynn effect".

In theory, different subgroups of a population might have different distributions of environments or genes and hence different values of h2. This seems not to be the case for high and low IQ levels, for which adult heritabilities appear to be much the same. It is also possible that an impoverished or suppressive environment could fail to support the development of a trait, and hence restrict individual variation. This could affect estimates of h2, c2, Or both, depending on the details of the process. Again, an environmental factor that affected every member of a subgroup equally might alter the group's mean without affecting heritabilities at all.

Where the heritability of IQ is concerned, it has sometimes seemed as if the findings based on differences between group means were in contradiction with those based on correlations. For example, children adopted in infancy into advantaged families tend to have higher IQs in childhood than would have been expected if they had been reared by their birth mothers; this is a mean difference implicating the environment. Yet at the same time their individual resemblance to their birth mothers persists, and this correlation is most plausibly interpreted in genetic terms. There is no real contradiction: the two findings simply call attention to different aspects of the same phenomenon. A sensible account must include both aspects: there is only a single developmental process, and it occurs in individuals. By looking at means or correlations one learns somewhat different but compatible things about the genetic and environmental contributions to that process.

As far as behavior genetic methods are concerned, there is nothing unique about psychometric intelligence relative to other traits or abilities. Any reliably measured trait can be analyzed by these methods, and many traits including personality and attitudes have been. The methods are neutral with regard to genetic and environmental sources of variance: if individual differences on a trait are entirely due to environmental factors, the analysis will reveal this. These methods have shown that genes contribute substantially to individual differences in intelligence test performance, and that their role seems to increase from infancy to adulthood. They have also shown that variations in the unique environments of individuals are important, and that between-family variation contributes significantly to observed differences in IQ scores in childhood although this effect diminishes later on. All these conclusions are wholly consistent with the notion that both genes and environment, in complex interplay, are essential to the development of intellectual competence.

ENVIRONMENTAL EFFECTS ON INTELLIGENCE

The 'environment" includes a wide range of influences on intelligence. Some of those variables affect whole populations, while others contribute to individual differences within a given group. Some of them are social, some are biological; at this point some are still mysterious. It may also happen that the proper interpretation of an environmental variable requires the simultaneous consideration of genetic effects. Nevertheless, a good deal of solid information is available.

Social Variables

It is obvious that the cultural environment - how people live, what they value, what they do - has a significant effect on the intellectual skills developed by individuals. Rice farmers in Liberia are good at estimating quantities of rice; children in Botswana, accustomed to storytelling, have excellent memories for stories. Both these groups were far ahead of American controls on the tasks in question. On the other hand Americans and other Westernized groups typically outperform members of traditional societies on psychometric tests, even those designed to be "culture-fair."

Cultures typically differ from one another in so many ways that particular differences can rarely be ascribed to single causes. Even comparisons between subpopulations are often difficult to interpret. If we find that groups living in different environments differ in their test scores, it is easy to suppose that the environmental difference causes the IQ difference. But there is also an opposite direction of causation: individuals may come to be in one environment or another because of differences in their own abilities, including the abilities measured by intelligence tests. Waller has shown, for example, that sons whose IQ scores are above those of their fathers also tend to achieve a higher social class status; conversely, those with scores below their fathers' tend to achieve lower status.

Schooling

Attendance at school is both a dependent and an independent variable in relation to intelligence. On the one hand, children with higher test scores are less likely to drop out, more likely to be promoted from grade to grade and then to attend college. Thus the number of years of education that adults complete is roughly predictable from their childhood scores on intelligence tests. On the other hand schooling itself changes mental abilities, including those abilities measured on psychometric tests. This is obvious for tests like the SAT that are explicitly designed to assess school learning, but it is almost equally true of intelligence tests themselves.

The evidence for the effect of schooling on intelligence test scores takes many forms. When children of nearly the same age go through school a year apart (because of birthday-related admission criteria), those who have been in school longer have higher mean scores. Children who attend school intermittently score below those who go regularly, and test performance tends to drop over the summer vacation. A striking demonstration of this effect appeared when the schools in one Virginia county closed for several years in the 1960s to avoid integration, leaving most Black children with no formal education at all. Compared to controls, the intelligence-test scores of these children dropped by about 0.4 standard deviations (6 points) per missed year of school.

Schools affect intelligence in several ways, most obviously by transmitting information. The answers to questions like "Who wrote Hamlet?" and "What is the boiling point of water?" are typically learned in school, where some pupils learn them more easily and thoroughly than others. Perhaps at least as important are certain general skills and attitudes: systematic problem-solving, abstract thinking, categorization, sustained attention to material of little intrinsic interest, repeated manipulation of basic symbols and operations. There is no doubt that schools promote and permit the development of significant intellectual skills, which develop to different extents in different children. It is because tests of intelligence draw on many of those same skills that they predict school achievement as well as they do.

To achieve these results, the school experience must meet at least some minimum standard of quality. In very poor schools, children may learn so little that they fall farther behind the national IQ norms for every year of attendance. When this happens, older siblings have systematically lower scores than their younger counterparts. This pattern of scores appeared in at least one rural Georgia school system in the 1970s. Before desegregation, it must have been characteristic of many of the schools attended by Black pupils in the South. In a study based on Black children who had moved to Philadelphia at various ages during this period, Lee found that their IQ scores went up more than half a point for each year that they were enrolled in the Philadelphia system.

Interventions

Intelligence test scores reflect a child's standing relative to others in his or her age cohort. Very poor or interrupted schooling can lower that standing substantially; are there also ways to raise it? In fact many interventions have been shown to raise test scores and mental ability 'in the short run" (i.e. while the program itself was in progress), but long-run gains have proved more elusive. One noteworthy example of (at least short-run) success was the Venezuelan Intelligence Project, in which hundreds of seventh-grade children from underprivileged backgrounds in that country were exposed to an extensive, theoretically based curriculum focused on thinking skills. The intervention produced substantial gains on a wide range of tests, but there has been no follow-up.

Children who participate in "Head Start" and similar programs are exposed to various school-related materials and experiences for one or two years. Their test scores often go up during the course of the program, but these gains fade with time. By the end of elementary school, there are usually no significant I9 or achievement-test differences between children who have been in such programs and controls who have not. There may, however, be other differences. Follow-up studies suggest that children who participated in such programs as preschoolers are less likely to be assigned to special education, less likely to be held back in grade, and more likely to finish high school than matched controls.

More extensive interventions might be expected to produce larger and more lasting effects, but few such programs have been evaluated systematically. One of the more successful is the Carolina Abecedarian Project, which provided a group of children with enriched environments from early infancy through preschool and also maintained appropriate controls. The test scores of the enrichment-group children were already higher than those of controls at age two; they were still some five points higher at age twelve, seven years after the end of the intervention. Importantly, the enrichment group also outperformed the controls in academic achievement.

Family environment

No one doubts that normal child development requires a certain minimum level of responsible care. Severely deprived, neglectful, or abusive environments must have negative effects on a great many aspects of development, including intellectual aspects. Beyond that minimum, however, the role of family experience is now in serious dispute. Psychometric intelligence is a case in point. Do differences between children's family environments (within the normal range) produce differences in their intelligence test performance? The problem here is to disentangle causation from correlation. There is no doubt that such variables as resources of the home and parents' use of language are correlated with children's IQ scores, but such correlations may be mediated by genetic as well as (or instead of) environmental factors.

Behavior geneticists frame such issues in quantitative terms. Environmental factors certainly contribute to the overall variance of psychometric intelligence. But how much of that variance results from differences between families, as contrasted with the varying experiences of different children in the same family? Between-family differences create what is called "shared variance" or c2 (all children in a family share the same home and the same parents). Recent twin and adoption studies suggest that while the value of c2 (for IQ scores) is substantial in early childhood, it becomes quite small by late adolescence.

These findings suggest that differences in the life styles of families whatever their importance may be for many aspects of children's lives make little long-term difference for the skills measured by intelligence tests. We should note, however, that low-income and non-white families are poorly represented in existing adoption studies as well as in most twin samples. Thus it is not yet clear whether these surprisingly small values of (adolescent) c2 apply to the population as a whole. It re-mains possible that, across the full range of income and ethnicity, between-family differences have more lasting consequences for psychometric intelligence.

Biological Variables

Every individual has a biological as well as a social environment, one that begins in the womb and extends throughout life. Many aspects of that environment can affect intellectual development. We now know that a number of biological factors, including malnutrition, exposure to toxic substances, and various prenatal and perinatal stressors, result in lowered psychometric intelligence under at least some conditions.

Nutrition

There has been only one major study of the effects of prenatal malnutrition (i.e. malnutrition of the mother during pregnancy) on long-term intellectual development. Stein et al analyzed the test scores of Dutch 19-year-old males in relation to a wartime famine that had occurred in the winter of 1944-45, just before their birth. In this very large sample (made possible by a universal military induction requirement), exposure to the famine had no effect on adult intelligence.

In contrast. prolonged malnutrition during childhood does have long-term intellectual effects. These have not been easy to establish, in part because many other unfavorable socioeconomic conditions are often associated with chronic malnutrition. In one intervention study, however, pre-schoolers in two Guatemalan villages (where undernourishment is common) were given ad lib access to a protein dietary supplement for several years. A decade later, many of these children scored significantly higher on school related achievement tests than comparable controls. It is worth noting that the effects of poor nutrition on intelligence may well be indirect. Malnourished children are typically less responsive to adults, less motivated to learn, and less active in exploration than their more adequately nourished counterparts.

Although the degree of malnutrition prevalent in these villages rarely occurs in the United States, there may still be nutritional influences on intelligence. In studies of so-called "micro-nutrients," experimental groups of children have been given vitamin/mineral supplements while controls got placebos. in many of these studies, the experimental children showed test-score gains that significantly exceeded the controls. In a somewhat different design, Rush, Stein, Susser, & Brody gave dietary supplements of liquid protein to pregnant women who were thought to be at risk for delivering low birth-weight babies. At one year of age, the babies born to these mothers showed faster habituation to visual patterns than did control infants. Although these results are encouraging, there has been no long-term follow-up of such gains.

Lead

Certain toxins have well established negative effects on intelligence. Exposure to lead is one such factor. In one long-term study, the blood lead levels of children growing up near a lead smelting plant were substantially and negatively correlated with intelligence test scores throughout childhood. No "threshold dose" for the effect of lead appears in such studies. Although ambient lead levels in the United States have been reduced in recent years, there is reason to believe that some American children - especially those in inner cities - may still be at risk from this source.

Alcohol

Extensive prenatal exposure to alcohol (which occurs if the mother drinks heavily during pregnancy) can give rise to fetal alcohol syndrome which includes mental retardation as well as a range of physical symptoms. Smaller "doses" of prenatal alcohol may have negative effects on intelligence even when the full syndrome does not appear. Streissguth et al found that mothers who reported consuming more than 1.5 oz, of alcohol daily during pregnancy had children who scored some five points below controls at age four. Prenatal exposure to aspirin and antibiotics had similar negative effects in this study.

Perinatal Factors

Complications at delivery and other negative perinatal factors may have serious consequences for development. Nevertheless, because they occur only rarely, they contribute relatively little to the population variance of intelligence. Down's syndrome, a chromosomal abnormality that produces serious mental retardation, is also rare enough to have little impact on the overall distribution of test scores.

The correlation between birth weight and later intelligence deserves particular discussion. In some cases low birth weight simply reflects premature delivery; in others, the infant's size is below normal for its gestational age. Both factors apparently contribute to the tendency of low-birth-weight infants to have lower test scores in later childhood. These correlations are small, ranging from .05 to .13 in different groups. The effects of low birth weight are substantial only when it is very low indeed (less than 1500 gm). Premature babies born at these very low birth weights are behind controls on most developmental measures; they often have severe or permanent intellectual deficits.

Continuously Rising Test Scores

Perhaps the most striking of all environmental effects is the steady worldwide rise in intelligence test performance. Although many psychometricians had noted these gains, it was James Flynn who first described them systematically. His analysis shows that performance has been going up ever since testing began. The "Flynn Effect" is now very well documented, not only in the United States but in many other technologically advanced countries. The average gain is about three IQ points per decade; more than a full standard deviation since, say, 1940.

Although it is simplest to describe the gains as increases in population IQ, this is not exactly what happens. Most intelligence tests are "re-standardized" from time to time, in part to keep up with these very gains. As part of this process the mean score of the new standardization sample is typically set to 100 again, so the increase more or less disappears from view. In this context, the Flynn effect means that if twenty years have passed since the last time the test was standardized, people who now score 100 on the new version would probably average about 106 on the old one.

The sheer extent of these increases is remarkable, and the rate of gain may even be increasing. The scores of nineteen-year-olds in the Netherlands, for example, went up more than 8 points—over half a standard deviation-between 1972 and 1982. What's more, the largest gains appear on the types of tests that were specifically designed to be free of cultural influence. One of these is Raven's Progressive Matrices, an untimed non-verbal test that many psychometricians regard as a good measure of g.

These steady gains in intelligence test performance have not always been accompanied by corresponding gains in school achievement. Indeed, the relation between intelligence and achievement test scores can be complex. This is especially true for the Scholastic Aptitude Test (SAT), in part because the ability range of the students who take the SAT has broadened over time. That change explains some portion, but not all, of the prolonged decline in SAT scores that took place from the mid nineteen-sixties to the early eighties, even as IQ scores were continuing to rise.

Meanwhile, however, other more representative measures show that school achievement levels have held steady or in some cases actually increased. The National Assessment of Educational Progress (NAEP), for example, shows that the average reading and math achievement of American 13- and 17-year-olds improved somewhat from the early nineteen-seventies to 1990. An analysis of these data by ethnic group, reported in Section 5, shows that this small overall increase actually reflects very substantial gains by Blacks and Latinos combined with little or no gain by Whites.

The consistent IQ gains documented by Flynn seem much too large to result from simple increases in test sophistication. Their cause is presently unknown, but three interpretations deserve our consideration. Perhaps the most plausible of these is based on the striking cultural differences between successive generations. Daily life and occupational experience both seem more "complex" today than in the time of our parents and grandparents. The population is increasingly urbanized; television exposes us to more information and more perspectives on more topics than ever before; children stay in school longer; almost everyone seems to be encountering new forms of experience. These changes in the complexity of life may have produced corresponding changes in complexity of mind, and hence in certain psychometric abilities.

A different hypothesis attributes the gains to modern improvements in nutrition. Lynn points out that large nutritionally-based increases in height have occurred during the same period as the IQ gains: perhaps there have been increases in brain size as well. As we have seen, however, the effects of nutrition on intelligence are themselves not firmly established.

The third interpretation addresses the very definition of intelligence. Flynn himself believes that real intelligence-whatever it may be—cannot have increased as much as these data would suggest. Consider, for example, the number of individuals who have IQ scores of 140 or more. In 1952 only 0.38% of Dutch test takers had IQs over 140; in 1982, scored by the same norms, 9. 12% exceeded this figure! Judging by these criteria, the Netherlands should now be experiencing "...a cultural renaissance too great to be overlooked". So too should France, Norway, the United States, and many other countries. Because Flynn finds this conclusion implausibie or absurd, he argues that what has risen cannot be intelligence itself but only a minor sort of "abstract problem solving ability." The issue remains unresolved.

Individual Life Experiences

Although the environmental variables that produce large differences in intelligence are not yet well understood, genetic studies assure us that they exist. With a heritability well below 1.00, IQ must be subject to substantial environmental influences. Moreover, available heritability estimates apply only within the range of environments that are well-represented in the present population. We already know that some relatively rare conditions, like those reviewed earlier, have large negative effects on intelligence. Whether there are (now equally rare) conditions that have large positive effects is not known.

As we have seen, there is both a biological and a social environment. For any given child, the social factors include not only an overall cultural/ social/school setting and a particular family but also a unique "micro-environment" of experiences that are shared with no one else. The adoption studies reviewed in Section 3 show that family variables, such as differences in parenting style, in the resources of the home, etc., have smaller long-term effects than we once supposed. At least among people who share a given SES level and a given culture, it seems to be unique individual experience that makes the largest environmental contribution to adult IQ differences.

We do not yet know what the key features of those micro-environments may be. Are they biological? Social? Chronic? Acute? Is there something especially important in the earliest relations between the infant and its caretakers? Whatever the critical variables may be, do they interact with other aspects of family life? Of culture? At this point we cannot say, but these questions offer a fertile area for further research.

GROUP DIFFERENCES

Group means have no direct implications for individuals. What matters for the next person you meet (to the extent that test scores matter at all) is that person's own particular score, not the mean of some reference group to which he or she happens to belong. The commitment to evaluate people on their own individual merit is central to a democratic society. It also makes quantitative sense. The distributions of different groups inevitably overlap, with the range of scores within any one group always wider than the mean differences between any two groups. In the case of intelligence test scores, the variance attributable to individual differences far exceeds the variance related to group membership.

Because claims about ethnic differences have often been used to rationalize racial discrimination in the past, all such claims must be subjected to very careful scrutiny. Nevertheless, group differences continue to be the subject of intense interest and debate. There are many reasons for this interest: some are legal and political, some social and psychological. Among other things, facts about group differences may be relevant to the need for (and the effectiveness of) affirmative action programs. But while some recent discussions of intelligence and ethnic differences have made specific policy recommendations in this area, we will not do so here. Such recommendations are necessarily based on political as well as scientific considerations, and so fall outside the scope of this report.

Besides European-Americans ("Whites"), the ethnic groups to be considered are Chinese- and Japanese Americans, Hispanic Americans ("Latinos"), Native Americans ("Indians") and African-Americans ("Blacks"). These groups (we avoid the term "race") are defined and self-defined by social conventions based on ethnic origin as well as on observable physical characteristics such as skin color. None of them are internally homogeneous. Asian Americans, for example, may have roots in many different cultures: not only China and Japan but Korea, Laos, Vietnam, the Philippines, India, Pakistan. Hispanic Americans, who share a common linguistic tradition, actually differ along many cultural dimensions. In their own minds they may be less "Latinos" than Puerto Ricans, Mexican-Americans Cuban Americans, or representatives of other Latin cultures. "Native American" is an even more diverse category, including a great many culturally distinct tribes living in a wide range of environments.

Although males and females are not ethnic or cultural groups, possible sex differences in cognitive ability have also been the subject of widespread interest and discussion. For this reason, the evidence relevant to such differences is briefly reviewed in the next section.

Sex Differences

Most standard tests of intelligence have been constructed so that there are no overall score differences between females and males. Some recent studies do report sex differences in IQ, but the direction is variable and the effects are small. This overall equivalence does not imply equal performance on every individual ability. While some tasks show no sex differences, there are others where small differences appear and a few where they are large and consistent.

Spatial and quantitative Abilities

Large differences favoring males appear on visual-spatial tasks like mental rotation and spatio-temporal tasks like tracking a moving object through space. The sex difference on mental rotation tasks is substantial: a recent meta-analysis puts the effect size at d = 0.9. (Effect sizes are measured in standard deviation units. Here, the mean of the male distribution is nearly one standard deviation above that for females.) Males' achievement levels on movement-related and visual-spatial tests are relevant to their generally better performance in tasks that involve aiming and throwing.

Some quantitative abilities also show consistent differences. Females have a clear advantage on quantitative tasks in the early years of schoo but this reverses sometime before puberty; males then maintain their superior performance into old age. The math portion of the Scholastic Aptitude Test shows a substantial advantage for males ($d = 0.33$ to 0.50), with many more males scoring in the highest ranges. Males also score consistently higher on tests of proportional and mechanical reasoning.

Verbal Abilities

Some verbal tasks show substantial mean differences favoring females. These include synonym generation and verbal fluency (e.g., naming words that start with a given letter), with effect sizes ranging from $d = 0.5$ to 1.2. On average females score higher on college achievement tests in literature, English composition, and Spanish they also excel at reading and spelling Many more males than females are diagnosed with dyslexia and other reading disabilities, and there are many more male stutterers. Some memory tasks also show better performance by females, but the size (and perhaps even the direction) of the effect varies with the type of memory being assessed.

Causal Factors

There are both social and biological reasons for these differences. At the social level there are both subtle and overt differences between the experiences, expectations, and gender roles of females and males. Relevant environmental differences appear soon after birth. They range from the gender-differentiated toys that children regularly receive to the expectations of adult life with which they are presented, from gender-differentiated household and leisure activities to assumptions about differences in basic ability. Models that include many of these psychosocial variables have been successful in predicting academic achievement.

Many biological variables are also relevant. One focus of current research is on differences in the sizes or shapes of particular neural structures. Numerous sexually dimorphic brain structures have now been identified, and they may well have implications for cognition. There are, for example, sex related differences in the sizes of some portions of the corpus callosum; these differences are correlated with verbal fluency. Recent brain imaging studies have found what may be differences in the lateralization of language. Note that such differences in neural structure could result from differences in patterns of life experience as well as from genetically-driven mechanisms of brain development; moreover, brain development and experience may have bi-directional effects on each other. This research area is still in a largely exploratory phase.

Hormonal Influences

The importance of prenatal exposure to sex hormones is well established. Hormones influence not only the developing genitalia but also the brain and certain immune system structures Several studies have tested individuals who were exposed to abnormally high androgen levels in utero, due to a condition known as congenital adrenal hyperplasia(CAH). Adult CAH females score significantly higher than controls on tests of spatial ability; CAH girls play more with "boys' toys" and less with 'girls' toys" than controls.

Other experimental paradigms confirm the relevance of sex hormones for performance levels in certain skills. Christiansen and Knussman found testosterone levels in normal males to be correlated positively (about .20) with some measures of spatial ability and negatively (about -.20) with some measures of verbal ability. Older males given testosterone show improved performance on visual-spatial tests. Many similar findings have been reported, though the effects are often non-linear and complex. It is clear that any adequate model of sex differences in cognition will have to take both biological and psychological variables (and their interactions) into account.

INDIVIDUAL VS. GROUP IQ TESTING

There are two major types of intelligence test, those administered to individuals and thsoe administered to groups. The two main individual intelligence tests are the:

— Stanford-Binet Intelligence Test

— Wechsler tests, i.e. WISC for children and WAIS for adults These are individual intelligence tests which require one-on-one consultation with the child. The tests involve various verbal and non-verbal subtests which can be combined to give an overall IQ, but which also provide valuable separate subtest scores and measures based on the behavioural responses of the child to the test items. Some of the content of these tests is clearly culture-loaded, hence there is the:

— Kaufman Assessment Battery for Children - a more recent test which attempts to minimize cultural bias. The test also attempts to separate crystallised and fluid intelligence.

Group intelligence tests

Group-administered intelligence tests involve a series of different problems and are generally used in mass testing situations such as the military and schools. Examples of group tests are:

— Multidimensional Aptitude Battery

— The Cognitive Abilities test

— Scholastic Assessment Tests

There has been a trend towards the use of multiple choice items. Many of theses tests have separately timed sub-tests. A major distinction made between types of items is verbal and non-verbal. In recent years there has been a trend away from verbal and mathematical items towards non-verbal represented problems in pictures.

Part of the reason for shifting away from verbal-based tests, in particular, is the issue of culture-loading.

Advantages of group tests:

— can be administered to very large numbers simultaneously
— simplified examiner role
— scoring typically more objective
— large, representative samples often used leading to better established norms

Disadvantages of group tests:

— examiner has less opportunity to establish rapport, obtain cooperation, and maintain interest
— not readily detected if examinee tired, anxious, unwell
— evidence that emotionally disturbed children do better on individual than group tests
— examinee's responses more restricted
— normally an individual is tested on all items in a group test and may become boredom over easy items and frustrated or anxious over difficult items
— individual tests typically provide for the examiner to choose items based on the test takers prior responses - moving onto quite difficult items or back to easier items. So individual tests offer more flexibility.

KEY PLAYERS IN THE DEVELOPMENT OF INTELLIGENCE & TESTING

This is an overview of the 14 players in the modern history of intelligence testing – many of whom you may already be familiar with from their work on other aspects of psychology.

Francis Galton: The 1st Modern Attempt (late 1800s)

Intelligence tests are grounded in the work of Francis Galton in the late 19th century. Galton is considered to be the father of the study of individual differences [and, incidentally was the half-cousin of Charles Darwin]. For Galton, measurement of intelligence was to be as direct as possible a measure of underlying intelligence. Hence, Galton suggested reaction time as a feasible approach and pursued various sensori-motor measurements.

Interestingly, more contemporary "Galton-like" approaches are being pursued by psychologists such as Arthur Jensen and Mike Andersen who assert that they are assessing the integrity of the central nervous system - inherent capabilities (Intelligence A) - as opposed to manifestations of intelligence in everyday life (Intelligence B).

Alfred Binet: The origins of IQ Testing (early 1900's)

Alfred Binet is celebrated in history as the man who created the first 'intelligence test' in the form as we know them today. He is commonly known as the "father" of IQ testing. In 1904, Binet was commissioned by the French Ministry of Public Instruction to develop techniques for identifying primary grade children whose lack of success in normal classrooms suggested the need for some form of special education. In 1905 he produced the Binet-Simon scale [with Theodore Simon] - the first intelligence test. Binet took a pragmatic approach, choosing a series of 30 short tasks related to everyday problems of life. For e.g:

— attend to simple instructions
— name parts of the body
— compare lengths and weights
— counting coins,
— assessing which of several faces is 'prettier',
— naming objects in a picture,
— digit span (the number of digits a person can recall after being shown a long list),
— word definition, etc.
— filling in the missing words in sentences

Supposedly all these tasks involved basic processes of reasoning. The tests were arranged so as to be of increasing difficulty. Each level of tests matched a specific developmental level - i.e. all tests at a given level were capable of being solved by any normal child in that specific age-group.

This was a turning point in psychology: A new type of test had been produced in which the average level of performance was the criterion. In 1908 the test was revised and then again in 1911. This edition was the model for many future tests. The test results proved to be correlated with other criteria (e.g. results of school examinations, assessments of teachers, etc.)

Lewis Terman (1877-1956) of Stanford University in the US decided to use Binet's test. He found that the Paris-developed age norms didn't work very well for Californian school children. So he revised the test: adapted some items, added other items, established new age norms, and extended the upper age limit to "superior adults". This became the Stanford-Binet revision in 1916. In this revision the Intelligence quotient first appeared.

The Intelligence Quotient or IQ was a score meant to quantify intellectual functioning to allow comparison among individuals. To arrive at an IQ score, Terman relied on a formula expressing the relation between an individual's mental age and chronological age developed in 1912 in Germany by Wilhelm Stern: 1912 Wilhelm Stern proposed the following formula:

$$IQ = \frac{\text{mental age} \times 100}{\text{chronological age}}$$

Yerkes: Army Tests (WWI)

The US army at the beginning of WWI was faced with the problem of assessing the intelligence of great numbers of recruits in order to screen, classify, and assign them to suitable tasks. The Stanford-Binet test required a highly trained person for individual administration - thus it would prove time consuming and costly for large-scale use.

So, when the US entered WWI in 1917 a committee was appointed by the APA to consider ways that psychology might assist the conduct of the war. Head of this committee was Robert Yerkes. His brief was to develop group intelligence testing.

Robert Yerkes, a psychologist and army major, assembled a staff of 40 psychologists [including Terman] to develop a group intelligence test. This resulted in the Army Alpha and Army Beta tests. The Beta was a version of the Alpha specifically for use with non-English-speaking and illiterate persons. [Instructions to those taking the Beta were given by demonstration or pantomime, rather than orally or in writing.]

In the end, over a million people were tested, but not until late in the war. Thus the work actually had little effect on the war, but did a great deal to enhance the status of psychology. After the war, industry, business and education saw potential value of psychological testing. Note that the validity of the Beta test, in particular, has since been questioned rather damningly by Gould.

Charles Spearman: "g" (1920's)

Up to now, the approaches to intelligence had been very pragmatic - i.e. tests were developed for particular needs. However, another approach to understanding intelligence, involved analysing data that was already collected.

Charles Spearman analysed the relations among experimental intelligence tests using 'factor analysis'. He argued that, as a rule, people who do well on some intelligence tests also do well on a variety of intellectual tasks [vocabulary and mathematical and spatial abilities]. And if people did poorly on an intelligence test, then they also tended to do poorly on other intellectual tests. That is, he observed correlations among performance on a variety of intellectual tasks. Thus, he proposed, a 'two-factor' theory of intelligence:

— General Ability (g): which was required for performance of mental tests of all kinds; he called this a kind of 'mental energy' that underlies the specific factors

— Special Abilities: which were required for performance on just one kind of mental test.

Examples:

— Scores on a verbal comprehension test are largely determined by one's level of general intelligence but they are also affected by one's specific ability to perform verbal comprehension tasks.

— But the main thrust of Spearman's analysis was this idea of a general intellectual capacity. This formed a major theoretical platform for many subsequent approaches to intelligence.

— It might be also noted, however, that Spearman was perhaps excessively enthusiastic about g. For example, he advocated restricting voting rights to people whose g exceeded a certain level, and he was a eugenicist (eugenics comes from the Greek "eugenes" meaning well-born) - arguing that only people with a certain level of g should be allowed to have offspring. "g" was controversial then as now.

Weschler: Intelligence Scales for Adults and Children.

Another test designer was David Wechsler. Wechsler felt that the Binet scales were too verbally loaded for use with adults, so he designed an instrument with sub-tests to measure both verbal and nonverbal abilities, largely borrowing from many other tests, such as the US Army Alpha test. He adopted a mean score of 100, since the Stanford-Binet metric had become universally accepted. The original Weschsler-Bellevue test in 1939 proved quite successful in civilian and military applications.

In 1949, Wechsler produced the Wechsler Intelligence Scale for Children (WISC), which competed with the Stanford-Binet test. In 1955, he produced a revision of the adult scales named the Wechsler Adult Intelligence Scale (WAIS). And later he produced a scale which could be used with pre-primary children. These scales have all been revised, but still show a distinct resemblance to the original 1939 scale.

Thurstone: Primary Mental Abilities (1930's)

Another 'factor analyst', Thurstone (1938), accepted Spearman's hypothesis of a general factor. But he disputed its importance. He argued that g is in fact a second order factor or phenomenon - one which arises only because the primary or 'first-order' factors are related to one another. Thus, Thurstone identified 7 'primary mental abilities' which he judged to be more important. These were:

1. *Verbal Comprehension*: vocabulary, reading, comprehension, verbal analogies, etc.
2. *Word fluency*: the ability to quickly generate and manipulate a large number of words with specific characteristics, as in anagrams or rhyming tests

3. *Number*: the ability to quickly and accurately carry out mathematical operations
4. *Space*: spatial visualizations as well as ability to mentally transform spatial figures
5. *Associative Memory*: rote memory
6. *Perceptual Speed*: quickness in perceiving visual details, anomalies, similarities, etc.
7. *Reasoning*: skill in a variety of inductive, deductive, and arithmetic reasoning tasks

So, Thurstone's approach consituted the first multi-factor approach to intelligence. Thurstone's tests have largely dropped out of use because the hope that they would be able to more accurately predict academic or occupational performance than general intelligence was not fulfilled.

Nevertheless, the main argument and findings are important: that intelligence is better described and measured by considering distinct primary mental abilities, rather than a single factor g which does not provide specific information about specific intelligences.

Raymond Cattell: Fluid & Crystallised Intelligence (1960's)

Raymond Cattell (1963) [not to be confused with James McKeen Cattell, a contemporary of Galton's who was also significantly involved in early attempts at psychological measurement] suggested that there are two related but distinct components of g: fluid and crystallised intelligence.

— *Fluid*: ability to see relationships, as in analogies and letter and number series = primary reasoning ability

— *Crystallised*: acquired knowledge and skills = factual knowledge

Fluid intelligence decreases with age and crystallised intelligence increases with age. Thus mathematicians and scientists, who need fluid intelligence, produce their best work in thier 20s and 30s; whereas those in the field of history, philosophy and literature produce their best work in their 40s, 50s and beyond as they have accumulated more knowledge. Interestingly, poets, who depend more on fluid than crystallised intelligence, produce their best work earlier than prose authors: this has been observed in all cultures, languages and throughout history.

Guilford: many, many factors

Guilford (1967; 1988) parted company from the majority of factorial theorists by refusing to acknowledge the existence of any general factor at all. Instead, he proposed that intelligence comprises 180 elementary abilities. The 180 elementary abilities are made up of a combination of three dimensions which he calls:

— operations: what a person does (6-types)

— contents: the material on which operations are performed (5-types)

— products: the form in which the information is stored and processes (6-types).

Guilford proposed that each combination of a specific operation, a specific type of content and a specific type of product defines a unique type of intelligence. In later versions of his theory he proposed even more types of intelligence. Due largely to the practical implications of such a model, Guilford's theory has not significantly influenced psychological testing of intelligence.

Vernon & Carroll: Hierarchical Approaches (1960's - present)

Probably the most widely accepted factorial description of intelligence is a hierarchical one, e.g. Vernon and Carroll. Vernon accepted, in a sense, that both Spearman (single g factor) and Thurstone (multiple primary mental abilities) were right. Vernon suggested that intelligence can be described as comprising abilities at varying levels of generality:

— at the highest level of generality (i.e. top of the hierarchy) is g as defined by Spearman);
— at the next level are 'major group' factors, such as:
— verbal-educational ability [the kind of ability needed for successful performance in courses such as English, history, and social studies] and
— practical-mechanical ability [the kind of ability needed successful performance in courses such as draughtsmanship and car mechanics];
— at the next level are 'minor group' factors, which can obtained by subdividing the major group factors;
— and at the lowest (the bottom of the hierarchy) are specific factors again of the kind identified by Spearman.

So, Vernon inserted 2 further levels between Spearman's g and specific factors relevant to only one test. Carroll proposed the three-stratum model of cognitive ability. These hierarchical descriptions of intelligence may be viewed as filling in the gaps between the extreme approaches of Spearman and Thurstone.

Howard Gardner: Multiple intelligences

Howard Gardner supports Thurstone's notion that intelligence comes in different packages. The most widely cited version of Gardner's concept of intelligence is that there are seven different types of intelligence. Gardner has played around with this number and suggested a possible one or two more or even (in 1999) the possibility of a smaller number of intelligences. He argues that the seven intelligences are: verbal, mathematical, musical, spatial, kinaesthetic, interpersonal (social skills) and intrapersonal (self-understanding) functioning. He argues that these different intelligences are independent of one another.

Robert Sternberg (1970s to present)

Robert Sternberg together with his colleague Richard Wagner argues that there are three intelligences:

— Academic

— Practical

— Creative

NON-VERBAL REASONING TESTS

Group intelligence tests requiring recognition of similarities, analogies and patterns in unfamiliar designs, are referred to as non-verbal reasoning (NVR) tests. Like verbal reasoning tests, NVR tests are comprised of a variety of item types, including series completion, codes and analogies. However, unlike verbal reasoning tests, none of the question types requires learned knowledge for its solution. NVR tests are presented in multiple-choice format, which more recently have enabled some NVR tests to be machine scored via the use of an optically-read answer sheet.

In an educational context, these tests are typically used as an indication of a pupil's ability to understand and assimilate novel information independently of language skills. Scores on these tests can indicate a pupil's ability to learn new material in a wide range of school subjects based on their current levels of functioning. These tests have high reliability, typically in the region of 0.90 to 0.95, and good predictive validity, i.e. they are relatively good predictors of future academic attainment.

NVR tests have been widely used to measure general intellectual ability for many years and have been subject to continual development by theorists. Spearman proposed a 'two factor' theory of intelligence, whereby all test questions contained a general intelligence factor known as 'g' and another factor specific to each question, and it is this general intelligence factor 'g' which Spearman suggests represents reasoning ability.

Vernon developed a hierarchical model of intelligence, which stemmed from the earlier work by Spearman. Vernon proposed that the general intelligence factor 'g' could be divided into two group factors, a spatial-mechanical-practical factor and a verbal-educational factor, both of which were further divided into sub-factors. In comparison, Guildford adopted a model in which several equally important factors ran in parallel with each other, 'general reasoning' being identified as one of these factors.

Cattell however, defined NVR as a 'fluid-general intelligence', which involves the ability to reason with novel material, without the need to draw on learned knowledge. Cattell believed measures such as NVR tests could be considered 'culture fair' and thus provide a more appropriate measure of general intelligence, compared with verbal reasoning tests, for test takers not fluent in the language being used.

Studies comparing children with learning disabilities with their normally achieving peers indicate that, as a group, the former also experience more from social-emotional and behavioral difficulties. These difficulties have often been seen as secondary to the cognitive problems of the learning disability and have been attributed to the impact of negative experiences common to most children with LD, such as the frustration of repeated school failure. -However, research findings indicate that the central processing deficiencies underlying the cognitive, linguistic, and academic aspects of learning disorders may also underlie their social and emotional features.

The results of research suggest that children with LD tend to have difficulty in understanding those subtle cues inherent in nonverbal communication that play so important a role in social interaction. One critical aspect of nonverbal communication is the interpretation of facial expressions of emotion, and children with LD have been found to be less accurate than nondisabled children in making such interpretations. As Bandura (1986) has pointed out, the ability to read the signs of emotions in social interaction has important adaptive value in guiding actions toward others. Presumably, deficits in this area play a significant role in the social difficulties experienced by children with LD.

Three decades ago Johnson and Myklebust, on the basis of clinical observations, suggested the distinction between verbal and nonverbal learning disabilities, asserting that the latter may be more personally debilitating than the former, for they interfere with the ability to interpret the emotions of others. However, most studies of deficits in social perception and skills in children with LD have not focused on defining subgroups at particular risk for such difficulties.

In recent years, a rise in interest in differentiating the subtypes of learning disability has led to descriptions of a nonverbal, presumably righthemisphere disorder in children with LD as well as frankly neurologically impaired children characterized by a core set of symptoms consisting of emotional and interpersonal disturbance, poor visuospatial and nonverbal problem-solving ability, and low arithmetic achievement.

Of particular note in this context is the work of Rourke and his coinvestigators, who have studied the link between patterns of central processing abilities and disabilities and subtypes of both learning disabilities and socioemotional functioning. Their results indicate that children with impaired reading and spelling and significantly better arithmetic achievement tend to score poorly on measures of abilities thought to be subserved by the left hemisphere and satisfactorily on those subserved by the right. By way of contrast, children with nonverbal learning disabilities whose spelling and reading are above average and arithmetic is in the deficit range tend to perform adequately on measures of abilities i by the left hemisphere and poorly on those subserved by the right.

On the basis of data from a series of studies, Rourke has concluded that although socioemotional disturbance seems to be more common among individuals with LD than among their normally achieving peers, no single pattern of disturbance is characteristic, and many children with LD show no such difficulties. However, children suffering from the nonverbal learning disability pattern are at particular risk for serious psychopathology that tends to be progressive. These findings have led Rourke to underline the importance of taking adequate note of the heterogeneity of the learning disabled population in studies that attempt to clarify the relation between learning disabilities and socioemotional disturbance.

The present research studied the ability to interpret facial expressions of affect (one very important aspect of nonverbal social perception) in differentiated subgroups of children with LD and their nondisabled peers. Specifically, it compared the ability to identify six basic emotions from facial expressions among children with LD with nonverbal deficits (NVD), verbal deficits (VD), and both verbal and nonverbal deficits (BD), and nondisabled children. It was hypothesized that nondisabled children would have better interpretive ability than children with LD, but that children with LD with VD would do better than those with NVD or BD. It was also hypothesized that older children would be more accurate than younger children on this task.

Verbal and Nonverbal Functioning

The measures of verbal and nonverbal purpose learning and memory were the following:

1. The Rey Auditory Verbal Learning Test. A Hebrew version of this test of verbal learning and memory was used.
2. The Benton Visual Retention Test. This test of visual perception and memory consists of three parallel sets of 10 cards with geometric designs. Of the four possible BVRT procedures, participants were tested on Administration A, in which each design is exposed for 10 seconds and the student then draws it from memory, and Administration D, in which each design is exposed for 10 seconds and

the participant reproduces it from memory after a 15-second delay.

The administration and scoring for both of these tests was standard, as described by Lezak.

INTELLIGENT INTELLIGENCE TESTING

Psychologists are broadening the concept of intelligence and how to test it. Standardized intelligence testing, now almost 100 years old, has been called one of psychology's greatest successes. It is certainly one of the field's most persistent and widely used inventions.

Since Alfred Binet first used a standardized test to identify learning-impaired Parisian children in the early 1900s, it has become one of the primary tools for identifying children with mental retardation and learning disabilities. It has helped the U.S. military place its new recruits in positions that suit their skills and abilities. And, since the administration of the original Scholastic Aptitude Test (SAT)--adapted in 1926 from an intelligence test developed for the U.S. Army during World War I--it has spawned a variety of aptitude and achievement tests that shape the educational choices of millions of students each year.

But intelligence testing has also been accused of unfairly stratifying test-takers by race, gender, class and culture; of minimizing the importance of creativity, character and practical know-how; and of propagating the idea that people are born with an unchangeable endowment of intellectual potential that determines their success in life.

Since the 1970s, intelligence researchers have been trying to preserve the usefulness of intelligence tests while addressing those concerns. They have done so in a number of ways, including updating the Wechsler Intelligence Scale for Children (WISC) and the Stanford-Binet Intelligence Scale so they better reflect the abilities of test-takers from diverse cultural and linguistic backgrounds. They have developed new, more sophisticated ways of creating, administering and interpreting those tests. And they have produced new theories and tests that broaden the concept of intelligence beyond its traditional boundaries.

As a result, many of the biases identified by critics of intelligence testing have been reduced, and new tests are available that, unlike traditional intelligence tests, are based on modern theories of brain function, says Alan Kaufman, PhD, a clinical professor of psychology at the Yale School of Medicine.

For example, in the early 1980s, Kaufman and his wife, Nadeen Kaufman, EdD, a lecturer at the Yale School of Medicine, published the Kaufman Assessment Battery for Children (K-ABC), then one of the only alternatives to the WISC and the Stanford-Binet. Together with the Woodcock-Johnson Tests of Cognitive Ability, first published in the late 1970s, and later tests, such as the Differential Ability Scales and the Cognitive Assessment System (CAS), the K-ABC helped expand the field of intelligence testing beyond the traditional tests.

Nonetheless, says Kaufman, there remains a major gap between the theories and tests that have been developed in the past 20 years and the way intelligence tests are actually used. Narrowing that gap remains a major challenge for intelligence researchers as the field approaches its 100th anniversary.

Among intelligence tests for children, one test currently dominates the field: the WISC-III, the third revision of psychologist David Wechsler's classic 1949 test for children, which was modeled after Army intelligence tests developed during World War I. Since the 1970s, says Kaufman, "the field has advanced in terms of incorporating new, more sophisticated methods of interpretation, and it has very much advanced in terms of statistics and methodological sophistication in development and construction of tests. But the field of practice has lagged woefully behind."

Nonetheless, people are itching for change, says Jack Naglieri, PhD, a psychologist at George Mason University who has spent the past two decades developing the CAS in collaboration with University of Alberta psychologist J.P. Das, PhD. Practitioners want tests that can help them design interventions that will actually improve children's learning; that can distinguish between children with different conditions, such as a learning disability or attention deficit disorder; and that will accurately measure the abilities of children from different linguistic and cultural backgrounds.

Naglieri's own test, the CAS, is based on the theories of Soviet neuropsychologist A.R. Luria, as is Kaufman's K-ABC. Unlike traditional intelligence tests, says Naglieri, the CAS helps teachers choose interventions for children with learning problems, identifies children with learning disabilities and attention deficit disorder and fairly assesses children from diverse backgrounds. Now, he says, the challenge is to convince people to give up the traditional scales, such as the WISC, with which they are most comfortable.

According to Nadeen Kaufman, that might not be easy to do. She believes that the practice of intelligence testing is divided between those with a neuropsychological bent, who have little interest in the subtleties of new quantitative tests, and those with an educational bent, who are increasingly shifting their interest away from intelligence and toward achievement. Neither group, in her opinion, is eager to adopt new intelligence tests.

For Naglieri, however, it is clear that there is still a great demand for intelligence tests that can help teachers better instruct children with learning problems. The challenge is convincing people that tests such as the CAS—which do not correlate highly with traditional tests--still measure something worth knowing. In fact, Naglieri believes that they measure something even more worth knowing than what the traditional tests measure. "I think we're at a really good point in our profession, where change can occur," he says, "and I think that what it's going to take is good data."

Pushing the envelope

The Kaufmans and Naglieri have worked within the testing community to effect change; their main concern is with the way tests are used, not with the basic philosophy of testing. But other reformers have launched more fundamental criticisms, ranging from "Emotional Intelligence", by Daniel Goleman, PhD, which suggested that "EI" can matter more than IQ, to the multiple intelligences theory of Harvard University psychologist Howard Gardner, PhD, and the triarchic theory of successful intelligence of APA President Robert J. Sternberg, PhD, of Yale University. These very different theories have one thing in common: the assumption that traditional theories and tests fail to capture essential aspects of intelligence.

But would-be reformers face significant challenges in convincing the testing community that theories that sound great on paper—and may even work well in the laboratory--will fly in the classroom, says Nadeen Kaufman. "A lot of these scientists have not been able to operationalize their contributions in a meaningful way for practice," she explains. In the early 1980s, for example, Gardner attacked the idea that there was a single, immutable intelligence, instead suggesting that there were at least seven distinct intelligences: linguistic, logical-mathematical, musical, bodily-kinesthetic, spatial, interpersonal and intrapersonal. But that formulation has had little impact on testing, in part because the kinds of quantitative factor-analytic studies that might validate the theory in the eyes of the testing community have never been conducted.

Sternberg, in contrast, has taken a more direct approach to changing the practice of testing. His Sternberg Triarchic Abilities Test (STAT) is a battery of multiple-choice questions that tap into the three independent aspects of intelligence—analytic, practical and creative--proposed in his triarchic theory. Recently, Sternberg and his collaborators from around the United States completed the first phase of a College Board-sponsored Rainbow Project to put the triarchic theory into practice. The goal of the project was to enhance prediction of college success and increase equity among ethnic groups in college admissions. About 800 college students took the STAT along with performance-based measures of creativity and practical intelligence.

Sternberg and his collaborators found that triarchic measures predicted a significant portion of the variance in college grade point average (GPA), even after SAT scores and high school GPA had been accounted for. The test also produced smaller differences between ethnic groups than did the SAT. In the next phase of the project, the researchers will fine-tune the test and administer it to a much larger sample of students, with the ultimate goal of producing a test that could serve as a supplement to the SAT.

Questioning the test

Beyond the task of developing better theories and tests of intelligence lies a more fundamental question: Should we even be using intelligence tests in the first place?

In certain situations where intelligence tests are currently being used, the consensus answer appears to be "no." A recent report of the President's Commission on Excellence in Special Education (PCESE), for example, suggests that the use of intelligence tests to diagnose learning disabilities should be discontinued.

For decades, learning disabilities have been diagnosed using the "IQ-achievement discrepancy model," according to which children whose achievement scores are a standard deviation or more below their IQ scores are identified as learning disabled.

The problem with that model, says Patti Harrison, PhD, a professor of school psychology at the University of Alabama, is that the discrepancy doesn't tell you anything about what kind of intervention might help the child learn. Furthermore, the child's actual behavior in the classroom and at home is often a better indicator of a child's ability than an abstract intelligence test, so children might get educational services that are more appropriate to their needs if IQ tests were discouraged, she says.

Even staunch supporters of intelligence testing, such as Naglieri and the Kaufmans, believe that the IQ-achievement discrepancy model is flawed. But, unlike the PCESE, they don't see that as a reason for getting rid of intelligence tests altogether.

For them, the problem with the discrepancy model is that it is based on a fundamental misunderstanding of the Wechsler scores, which were never intended to be used to as a single, summed number. So the criticism of the discrepancy model is correct, says Alan Kaufman, but it misses the real issue: whether or not intelligence tests, when properly administered and interpreted, can be useful.

"The movement that's trying to get rid of IQ tests is failing to understand that these tests are valid in the hands of a competent practitioner who can go beyond the numbers--or at least use the numbers to understand what makes the person tick, to integrate those test scores with the kind of child you're looking at, and to blend those behaviors with the scores to make useful recommendations," he says.

Intelligence tests help psychologists make recommendations about the kind of teaching that will benefit a child most, according to Ron Palomares, PhD, assistant executive director in the APA Practice Directorate's Office of Policy and Advocacy in the Schools. Psychologists are taught to assess patterns of performance on intelligence tests and to obtain clinical observations of the child during the testing session. That, he says, removes the focus from a single IQ score and allows for an assessment of the child as a whole, which can then be used to develop individualized teaching strategies.

Critics of intelligence testing often fail to consider that most of the alternatives are even more prone to problems of fairness and validity than the measures that are currently used, says

APA President-elect Diane F. Halpern, PhD, of Claremont McKenna College.

"We will always need some way of making intelligent decisions about people," says Halpern. "We're not all the same; we have different skills and abilities. What's wrong is thinking of intelligence as a fixed, innate ability, instead of something that develops in a context."

WHAT DO IQ TESTS DO?

There are a number of tests available to psychologists that give measures of intelligence. Looking at the child's skills in a range of abilities and comparing their individual score with the average scores for their age group yields an intelligence quotient (IQ). In this way an examiner can grade a child's performance as average, below average or above average for their age group. However there has been much debate on the usefulness and relevance of these various tests.

While it has been proven that the traditional IQ tests give a good indication of future academic performance they have been criticized on a number of fronts. In recent years with the broadening of the definition of intelligence it has been pointed out that these tests only measure a limited range of abilities and do not measure a wide enough range of skills.

Another criticism of the traditional tests is that they can be influenced by cultural factors and may favor children from more advantaged backgrounds. New tests have been developed in recent years that try to address this issue.

Most professionals working with children would agree that there is a role for intelligence testing but stress that they need to be carried out by professionals who are trained on how to administer them and how to interpret the results. Intelligence testing has been found to be very useful in the following situations: -

— Predicting school performance
— Identifying the strengths and weakness of the child
— Identifying those children at risk of developmental delay and learning difficulties
— Helping to identify some neurological disorders
— Helping to plan an educational programme geared to the individual child
— Assessing the progress of a child after they have completed a special programme

Many psychologists who administer intelligence tests use this time to gain insights into the child's personality, self-image, attention span, perseverance and motivation as well as testing the child's level of intelligence. In the hands of a skilled clinician these tests can a very useful tool in giving an overall picture of a child's current skills and abilities.

NEW DEVELOPMENTS

There have been some exciting developments in recent years in the study of intelligence and new theories of intelligence stress the multifaceted nature of intelligence. These new views would seem to be leading the way to a new understanding of intelligence and the development of new ways of assessing intelligence. They have also caused psychologists to recognise that even though traditional testing has a useful role in testing the abilities of children they do tap a rather limited set of abilities. Future tests of intelligence will probably be broader in the range of abilities they assess and may help in predicting how a person will adjust to everyday life rather than just predicting their school career.

Testing practical intelligence is effective predictor of future success

ANN ARBOR—New research conducted among M.B.A. students at the University of Michigan Business School by renowned psychologist Robert Sternberg and collaborator Jennifer Hedlund provides further evidence that tests that assess students' practical abilities can be as valuable as standardized intelligence testing, like the Graduate Management Admissions Test (GMAT).

"The types of problems found on standardized intelligence or aptitude tests are quite different from the types of problems found in the real world," says Sternberg, a professor at Yale University and author of "Successful Intelligence." "Individuals who perform well on academic problems do not necessarily perform well on poorly defined practical problems. Thus, individuals who are successful by GMAT standards may not be successful by business standards."

In a study with two classes of incoming M.B.A. students at the U-M Business School in 1999 and 2000, Sternberg and Hedlund of Central Connecticut State University found that measures of managerial potential that assess practical abilities predict success in both academic and practical endeavors.

The researchers' framework for developing a better predictor of success was based on Sternberg's theory of successful intelligence, which proposes that success is an interactive function of analytic, creative and practical abilities. Case-based short-answer problems and situational judgment problems, in which answers are rated for quality rather than classified right or wrong as in standardized testing, were used in the study to measure successful intelligence (SI).

Sternberg and Hedlund found that the higher the scores on these two measures, the better the first-year and final grade point averages, and the higher the grade on an applied team-consulting project—a cornerstone of Michigan's M.B.A. first-year curriculum. They further found that students with higher SI scores participated in more academic clubs and held more leadership positions. GMAT scores also were found to predict grade point average in the M.B.A. program, but they did not necessarily predict grades on the applied project. Likewise, GMAT scores were unrelated to scores on the SI measures administered in the study. "The SI scores accounted for unique variance in both academic and practical performance beyond that accounted for by GMAT scores and undergraduate GPA," Sternberg says. "Although the amount of variance accounted for by the SI scores is modest, the results are quite promising given the preliminary nature of the measure.

The findings do suggest that both formats—case studies and situational judgment problems—are measuring unique abilities that are not tapped by existing methods." While the study shows that practical intelligence testing predicts successful performance and evaluates abilities distinct from those measured by the GMAT, it also found that this type of assessment displays less gender and racial disparity than do standardized tests. According to Sternberg and Hedlund, women scored significantly higher than men in both SI formats, while men scored significantly higher on the GMAT. African Americans scored only slightly lower on the practical intelligence measures, but substantially lower than whites on the GMAT.

"Our results confirm the findings that the GMAT disadvantages females and African Americans," Sternberg says. "Although the SI measures exhibit some disparities of their own, the results suggest that they do not exhibit the same pattern or degree of disparity found for the GMAT."

In all, the researchers say that their results, so far, are promising and that they plan further research and development on their new measures. Jeanne M. Wilt, assistant dean for admissions and career development at the U-M Business School, is excited about the possibilities offered by the use of SI measures.

"We are always looking for better ways to identify and develop leadership talent," she says. "This type of assessment not only has potential use as a complement to the GMAT in admissions decisions for M.B.A. programs, but it also can be used as a tool for teaching students practical problem-solving skills that can help them become more effective business leaders."

INDEX